Tax–benefit models are powerful tools for the analysis of the impact of policy reform, in regular use around the world in government and research organisations. This study focuses on one particular model, POLIMOD, and performs three tasks. It provides an illustration of the type of analysis that can be performed, and demonstrates the sensitivity of results to some of the key assumptions made; it steps inside POLIMOD and documents some of the inner layers of data manipulation and model construction that drive its outputs; and it provides a detailed assessment of the reliability of those outputs based on a validation against external sources.

The study offers those who use models like POLIMOD, or their outputs, an appreciation of the constraints and assumptions that shape the analysis they provide, and it provides those directly involved in the development of microsimulation models with a guide to methods.

University of Cambridge
Department of Applied Economics

Occasional paper 64

The arithmetic of tax and social security reform

DAE Occasional papers

Earlier titles in this series and in the DAE Papers in Industrial Relations and Labour series may be obtained from:
The Publications Secretary, Department of Applied Economics,
Sidgwick Avenue, Cambridge CB3 9DE

The arithmetic of tax and social security reform
A user's guide to microsimulation methods and analysis

GERRY REDMOND,
HOLLY SUTHERLAND
AND
MOIRA WILSON

CAMBRIDGE
UNIVERSITY PRESS

PUBLISHED BY THE PRESS SYNDICATE OF THE UNIVERSITY OF CAMBRIDGE
The Pitt Building, Trumpington Street, Cambridge CB2 1RP, United Kingdom

CAMBRIDGE UNIVERSITY PRESS
The Edinburgh Building, Cambridge CB2 2RU, United Kingdom
http://www.cup.cam.ac.uk
40 West 20th Street, New York, NY 10011-4211, USA   http://www.cup.org
10 Stamford Road, Oakleigh, Melbourne 3166, Australia

© Department of Applied Economics, University of Cambridge 1998

First published 1998

Printed in the United Kingdom at the University Press, Cambridge

Typeset in Times MT 10/12pt   [SE]

A catalogue record for this book is available from the British Library

ISBN 0 521 63224 2 hardback

Contents

Figures

Tables

Foreword

As Chairman of the Advisory Committee of the Microsimulation Unit, I very much welcome the publication of this Occasional Paper. As the subtitle indicates, the book is a user's guide to POLIMOD, the Unit's tax and benefit model. The results of such models are widely quoted in the media, and the findings of researchers are used by those pressing for reform of taxation and social security. The models have however remained relatively inaccessible to users. Their workings often appear mysterious and there is no way of judging the sensitivity of the conclusions to the assumptions made.

It is therefore extremely valuable to have readily available this account of the model construction, modelling assumptions, and the model outputs. The reader of a table of net gains and losses by income range can see what lies behind these results, and how different conclusions might be reached. An essential section of the book is that dealing with model validation. This aspect is often neglected, but is becoming increasingly important as more models are built and they may generate different results.

Anyone who doubts that there is progress in economic science should compare the sophistication of the calculations contained in this Occasional Paper with the very crude estimates in Number 18 (*Poverty in Britain and the Reform of Social Security*) which I wrote in 1969. At that time, I had no access to micro-data and had to rely on tabulations. For example, I based the income tax calculations on 25 income groups and 3 different family sizes, and even these required the high-powered computer used by the astronomers. We have come a long way in terms of the richness of analysis which is possible, and the present book will serve a most valuable function in making this more widely known.

Tony Atkinson

Acknowledgements

Much of the work reported in this book draws on research funded by the ESRC under grant number R000 233257. The financial support of the Department of Social Security and the Isaac Newton Trust is also acknowledged. The POLIMOD database used in this study was derived from 1991 Family Expenditure Survey microdata. These data are Crown Copyright. They have been made available by the Office for National Statistics (ONS) through The Data Archive and are used by permission. Neither the ONS nor The Data Archive bear any responsibility for the analysis or interpretation of the data reported here.

Many individuals have contributed to the construction of POLIMOD and to the analysis and evaluation reported here, and we are grateful to all of them. The support of Tony Atkinson, Frank Cowell and David Newbery has been invaluable. Technical and administrative assistance from Tim Cartledge, Howard Cobb, Diana Day, Patricia Edge, Margaret Guy and Karon Jerman has allowed us to concentrate on the areas we understand best. We are indebted to staff at the Department of Social Security Analytical Services Division who were most helpful in supplying unpublished tables and in checking their interpretation. Helpful comments and advice have been received from Malcolm Campbell, Grainne Collins, Martin Evans, Ruth Hancock, John Hills, Stephen Jenkins, Georgia Kaplanoglou and an anonymous referee as well as analysts at the Department of Social Security and the Office for National Statistics. We would like to thank Robyn Fowler, Don Gray and Jennie Nicol of the Social Policy Agency, Department of Social Welfare, New Zealand for allowing Moira the time to be involved in the final stages of preparation of the book. Finally, special thanks are due to Joanna Gomulka, whose inspiration and caution have guided us throughout.

Gerry Redmond, Holly Sutherland, Moira Wilson

March 1997

Part One

Tax–benefit models: methods and analysis

1 Introduction

This book is about the use of microsimulation models as tools for understanding the impact of tax and social security reform policy. Its aim is to demonstrate the power of such models, and to provide readers with an appreciation of microsimulation methods and analysis.

The study focuses on one particular microsimulation model, POLIMOD, and performs three tasks. It provides an illustration of the type of analysis that an arithmetic model like POLIMOD can perform, and demonstrates the sensitivity of results to some of the key assumptions that can be made in carrying out a microsimulation analysis. It steps inside POLIMOD and documents some of the inner layers of data manipulation and model construction that drive its outputs. And it provides a detailed assessment of the reliability of those outputs based on a validation against external sources. The intention is to provide those who use models like POLIMOD, or their outputs, with an appreciation of the constraints and assumptions that shape the analysis they provide. The study also offers those directly involved in the development of microsimulation models with a guide to the types of data and modelling problems that are often encountered, as well as a record of one specific approach to dealing with them.

POLIMOD takes information about a nationally representative population of households and *simulates* the impact of policy regimes on the incomes of that population. For each household in the database, information on income, expenditure and personal and family characteristics is used to perform the arithmetic necessary to calculate liability for personal taxes and entitlement to social security benefits under a given tax–benefit regime (or some other default policy). These are contrasted with parallel sets of calculations for an alternative regime. From these calculations, the distribution of changes in income resulting from the alternative policy regime can be established. From the government's point of view, the sum of these changes represents the impact of the alternative policy on revenue. Viewed from the perspective of households, it is the impact on the total tax burden, net of social security benefits. Throughout these calculations, no change in behaviour is modelled following a policy change. The estimates calculated are of the immediate, or 'morning after' effect of the change, before individuals, households and the economy adjust in response.

This seemingly straightforward procedure is known as 'static microsimulation'. It is *static* because it takes a single cross-sectional survey dataset and holds constant the demographic, economic and other descriptive characteristics of the sample. A dynamic simulation, in contrast, would alter characteristics through time, in response to changing conditions or to time itself. The procedure is known as *microsimulation* because it uses a *micro*data sample to *simulate* a population and to *simulate*, in fine or *micro* detail, the impact of policy changes. It involves a set of distinct processes which are brought together into the single consistent framework of a tax–benefit model. These processes include data cleaning and validation, imputation of missing data required for particular policy simulations, updating and re-weighting the data in order that they represent the desired population as closely as possible, applying detailed rule-modelling to simulate different policy regimes, and designing methods of presenting results.

The primary outputs of tax–benefit models are estimates of the revenue impact of a policy reform and of the distribution of associated income gains and losses across households. There are other policy tools that can provide partial or less robust estimates of this type. In order to estimate the revenue impact of a reform, for example, it may be possible to derive estimates from aggregates contained in the national accounts or from an income distribution for the target population. In order to examine the distributional effects of the change, one alternative approach is to calculate the effect on a set of hypothetical families.

These approaches can be helpful in the preliminary stages of policy design, and for some simple policy changes may be adequate. Compared to a microsimulation analysis based on representative microdata, however, they are limited in their ability to inform. The main limitation of other approaches to estimating revenue impacts is that it is impossible to take account of interactions between elements of the tax–benefit system and, depending on the method used, it may be difficult to draw conclusions about the distributional impact of the change. The main limitation of the hypothetical family approach to examining the distributional impact of a policy change is that it is often impractical to consider the full range of family and household circumstances that exist. Examining hypothetical family tables showing the impact of the tax and benefit system published by the UK Government, Atkinson and Sutherland (1983) found that only 4% of the real families appearing in household survey data were represented. While hypothetical families may be a useful tool for demonstrating the impact of tax and benefit policy, they cannot cover the whole population, and they rarely provide any guide as to the proportions of families who are affected in different ways.

Microsimulation models based on data that are representative of the population allow the revenue and distributional impacts to be estimated together, taking full account of the interactions of different policy components and taking full account of the range of possible circumstances in which families find themselves. The simultaneous generation of these estimates provides a powerful aid to policy design, prompting the designer to consider how expenditure aimed at achieving a particular distributional objective is to be paid for, or alternatively, how the impact of a measure aimed at raising a particular amount of revenue is distributed and how unintended losers might be compensated.

Most countries in Western Europe and many OECD countries have tax–benefit models. In the UK, there are several models all of which currently use the same data. Two are within government: one called IGOTM built for inter-departmental use and managed by the Office for National Statistics, the second built and maintained by the Department of Social Security (Department of Social Security, undated). Outside government there are several active models. One of the main modelling groups is the Institute for Fiscal Studies which has its own model, TAXBEN2 (Giles and McCrae, 1995). This is used to examine a wide range of research and policy questions. Another model, SPRUMOD, is based at the Social Policy Research Unit at the University of York (Williams, Hutton and Ditch, 1993). The other main non-government tax–benefit model is POLIMOD.

One of the features which distinguishes POLIMOD from other UK models is that it has been constructed with a commitment to making it accessible to a wide range of users in a variety of settings. Accessibility in this context has a number of dimensions. A convenient box with some buttons to push is not sufficient to ensure that a model is not misleading and will be used wisely. Genuine accessibility requires a clear structure which makes transparent the assumptions that have been made by the model builder and distinguishes those that must be chosen by the user (Hancock and Sutherland (eds), 1992). Related to this, the assumptions made by the model builder in the construction of the database and underlying the simulation process must be documented and explained so that model results may be interpreted correctly. A guide to the accuracy and reliability of the model results should also be provided so that their significance may be assessed. This can include information regarding the statistical reliability of model outputs (Pudney and Sutherland, 1994) or a comparison and validation of model results against other independent sources. The aim of this book is to provide all this information and to allow the reader inside what is often a 'black box': to explore the impact of assumptions made by the model user on model outputs; to understand how major elements of the tax–benefit system are simulated within POLIMOD; and to gain an appreciation of the relationship between model outputs and 'real world' data.

1.1 Outline of the book

All the chapters in each of the four parts of this book are designed to stand alone, allowing the reader to select those of interest. Extensive use is made of appendices and footnotes to contain information that readers with an appetite for technical or methodological detail may find useful.

Following this chapter, Chapter 2 provides an overview of POLIMOD, of what it can simulate, and of the choices that are available to the model user in carrying out analyses.

Part Two illustrates the way in which POLIMOD can be used to examine a policy question and demonstrates some of the dimensions in which assumptions made by the model user in conducting the analysis may alter the results he or she obtains. Chapter 3 presents an analysis of the impact of public policy changes in the UK since 1978/9 on the distribution of household incomes in 1996/7. Between 1978/9 and 1996/7 there were major reforms to local taxation, personal income tax and the system of means-tested benefits, as well as significant shifts in the rates of VAT, income tax and National Insurance contributions. The impact on the distribution of income of each change in each element of policy is relatively easy to predict – in direction, if not in size. However, it is not obvious in what direction the policy regime as a whole has been moving: was policy in 1996/7 more or less progressive in its impact than the 1978/9 regime would have been? To answer this question, we need to take account not only of each individual change but also of any interactions between the policy instruments.

In the course of this analysis particular assumptions are chosen from the enormous range available to the model user. Chapter 4 explores the sensitivity of our conclusions by examining the effects of some alternative assumptions on our results.

Part Three takes the reader inside POLIMOD, setting out the way in which data are used and the assumptions made in simulating elements of policy. Chapter 5 describes the treatment of indirect taxes in POLIMOD, focusing on assumptions about how prices and expenditure respond to tax changes. By their nature, household surveys on which models like POLIMOD are based cannot always provide the exact information that is required for policy simulations. There is a limit to the amount of information that such surveys can collect, and in some cases respondents are unable to provide information that is needed, or can provide it only for a less than ideal time period. The remaining chapters in Part Three set out the method by which these difficulties are worked around, making the best of the available data. Chapter 6 describes how an employee is imputed to be contracted-out of the State Earnings Related Pension Scheme and is hence paying reduced National Insurance contributions. Chapter 7 describes how liabilities for three different regimes of local taxes are estimated in POLIMOD. Finally, Chapter 8 explores a new method of disaggregating data on receipt of retirement pension and other non-means-tested benefits to extend the range of policy changes that can be simulated and to improve the precision with which some means-tested benefits are simulated.

To a great extent, the usefulness of POLIMOD depends on our ability to make household survey data replicate what happens in the 'real world', and to project from there the likely distributional effects of changes in policy. Part Four describes a comprehensive exercise which validates POLIMOD output against other sources, emphasising that each data source provides a different picture of the 'real world' from that of POLIMOD, and that account must be taken of inherent differences before a valid reconciliation can be carried out. Chapter 9 discusses methods of validation that are available and outlines the approaches to validation that are used in this study. It also provides a general assessment of the reasons why estimates produced by POLIMOD are bound to be different from estimates from other sources. Chapter 10 offers a validation of POLIMOD's income tax simulations against recorded income tax data in the Family Expenditure Survey and against the 'Ready Reckoner' tables produced by the UK Treasury. Chapter 11 sets out a detailed reconciliation of POLIMOD's estimates of aggregate income, taxes paid and benefits received and numbers receiving and paying each against official statistics, particularly national accounts data. Chapter 12 compares distributions produced by POLIMOD with available external data.

1.2 Prospects for further development

This study focuses on what POLIMOD and models like it do. Perhaps the most useful way of describing their present limitations and their prospects for further development is to explain what such models do *not* do. The main limitation of static tax–benefit models is their treatment of possible changes in individual behaviour or of consequential macroeconomic second-order effects. Changes in policy may have an effect on any individual economic-related activity such as working or saving, fertility or retirement. Modelling these effects is seen as necessary when a significant change in behaviour is expected, since it will need to be captured if the revenue effects of the policy change are to be accurate. Furthermore, if the *purpose* of the policy is to change behaviour – to make work or saving more attractive, for example – then a full evaluation of the change will need to estimate how many people do change what they do and the extent to which these changes are in the direction intended by the policy initiative.

The modelling of behavioural and second-order effects has not been incorporated on a routine basis into POLIMOD simulations, for the following reasons. First, modelling human behaviour is extraordinarily difficult. There are too many dimensions in which rationality may exist, too many interrelated factors involved for the task to be straightforward. Nor is it clear that the effort involved is justified by an improvement in reliability. Pudney and Sutherland (1996) show that incorporating a typical simulation of female labour supply can greatly increase the uncertainty with which some of POLIMOD's estimates are made.

Furthermore, the advantages of transparency should not be forgotten. The greater the choice of inputs in the form of estimates of behavioural effects, the larger the scope for manipulation of model results. Tests of alternative modelling assumptions presented in Chapter 4 show that there are already many ways in which static model results may be presented: econometric behavioural modelling provides another layer which potentially confuses debates about policy.

Finally, modelling the labour-supply response to policy changes within a model that only addresses the household sector raises the question of the supply of jobs and how this is affected, in the first place by the policy change and in the second place by the shift in labour supply. Similar problems arise in the detailed modelling of other household responses to policy changes. Modelling the full or equilibrium effect of any policy change requires a model of the whole economy. Typically, this is not something that retains the level of individual detail and variation that is offered by microsimulation models which depend on microdata.

However, a cautious approach to modelling complex higher order effects as a matter of routine should not be taken to suggest that experimentation should also be ruled out. The long-term agenda for the development of microsimulation models should include among its objectives: exploring methods to improve behavioural models and the reliability of estimates; making attempts to extend the scope of models; imposing a range of theoretical relationships as a way of exploring their implications; and closing the system in some, if not all, respects. The challenge is to achieve these innovations while at the same time maintaining that high regard for understanding the limitations and advantages of microdata on which this present study rests.

2   POLIMOD

2.1 Introduction

This chapter is intended to give a flavour of the possibilities offered by
POLIMOD. The introduction provides an overview of how the model
works, highlighting some points and directing the reader to later sections
of the chapter which discuss them in more depth. The distinction is drawn
between options from which the user may choose, and assumptions and
methods which, in standard runs of the model, are already built in.

There are two types of option over which the POLIMOD user has
control: changes to *policy parameters* and changes to *run options*. The
latter govern the methods used in the simulation as well as determining the
form of the output that is produced.

The range of policy options is described in section 2.2.
The range of run options is described in section 2.3.

Once the user has specified what they want POLIMOD to do, data on each
household in the Family Expenditure Survey (FES) database are read into
the model, in turn. The data are updated from the survey year to the date
corresponding to the sets of policy parameters (typically, the current year).
Net income is calculated twice for each household: once using parameters
describing the system before the policy change and once using the policy-
change parameters.

The updating strategy is discussed in section 2.4.

The difference in income as a result of the change in policy is weighted and
added up over all the households in the survey, to give an estimate of the
net national revenue effect of the change.

The output income measure is described in section 2.5.
The assumptions about incidence of taxes and benefits on household income
    and about behavioural response are explained in section 2.6.

The distributional effect of the aggregate change is calculated by counting the weighted numbers of cases gaining and losing and calculating the average gain or loss in each income group or quantile. The distribution of the change according to characteristics other than income may also be tabulated.

Options regarding the presentation of output are described under 'run options' in section 2.3.

2.2 Policy options

The central output from POLIMOD is a measure of household income made up of original income *plus* social security benefits *less* personal taxes and contributions. Section 2.5 provides more detail of this definition of income. In most POLIMOD simulations, the components of original income (earned income, income from capital, income from other households) remain unchanged. The main set of options offered by the model permits changes to parameters describing the elements of income that are simulated by the model.

Income tax, National Insurance contributions, VAT, excise duties, local tax, means-tested benefits and child benefit are all simulated using information on original income and household and personal characteristics in the survey database. National Insurance benefits and other non-means-tested benefits that depend on characteristics that are not observed in the database are not fully simulated: they may be inflated or reduced in value, but the basis of entitlement to the benefit cannot be changed (although it may be removed entirely).[1]

The user makes a policy change by altering a set of parameters which describe actual policy for each component of income. In some cases these parameters simply correspond to existing tax rates or benefit levels. In other cases they act as 'switches' between alternative structures: one can choose among three regimes of local tax, for example. Table 2.1 outlines the scope of possible policy changes that can be modelled. More detail on these changes is provided in Appendix 2.1.

One of the central elements of policy which POLIMOD addresses is income tax. Not only is it a key determinant of household incomes in itself, it also indirectly impinges on a number of other entitlements and liabilities in the UK tax–benefit system. Its importance to the model also arises from the interest that has been taken in direct tax reform over the post World War II period and the complex history of rates and structure that has resulted. POLIMOD aims to address all the major reforms to income tax that have taken place since 1978 and to be a flexible tool for

Table 2.1. *Changes simulated by* POLIMOD

POLIMOD simulates changes in:

- income tax
- National Insurance contributions for employees, employers and the self-employed
- means-tested and universal social security benefits
- VAT
- excise duties
- local taxes (domestic rates, community charge or council tax)
- some aspects of non-means-tested social security benefits

and the introduction of:

- basic income schemes
- the earnings top-up
- pension guarantee schemes
- policy directly affecting elements of original income, such as a minimum wage.

the analysis of new proposals as they arise. This results in the range of options for income tax being both large and complex: Appendix 2.2 provides a detailed explanation of the income tax policy options that are offered.

2.3 Run options

The user can make choices about the way the model runs and the nature of the output in the following respects, which are described in turn:

- unit of analysis
- grossing-up weights
- benefit take-up
- output.

Unit of analysis

There are three options regarding the choice of unit of analysis (or unit of tabulation):

- the household (all co-resident people, sharing some housekeeping)
- the family unit (adult single person or couple and any dependent children)
- the individual.

In the simulations described in Chapter 3 and Chapter 4, the household is used as the unit of tabulation: each person in a household is assumed to enjoy the same income or consumption level, and income change is assessed over the whole household. Many of the policy instruments we consider actually operate at the level of the individual (such as income tax since 1990) or the level of the narrower nuclear family unit (such as most means-tested benefits). There may therefore be individuals who gain and others who lose within the same household: our analysis captures the net effect. Although for many purposes this is adequate, in some cases we may wish to use the family or the individual as the unit of analysis. This is possible in POLIMOD, with a range of options regarding the allocation of collective resources (Sutherland, 1996). For simulations involving changes to indirect taxes, however, only analysis at the household level is feasible, since much of household expenditure is difficult to allocate to the consumption of individuals.

Grossing-up weights

Weights are provided which adjust the data to allow for differential response in the survey by family composition. Household weights have been derived so that consistent results are produced at each level of analysis (see Gomulka, 1994). An alternative of using uniform weights so that results are obtained which are scaled to the population level, without accounting for differential response, is available. A further option is to weight each case by unity.

Take-up of benefits

There is evidence, much of it based on analysis of the FES itself, that not all families apply for, or receive, the benefits to which they appear to be entitled.[2] It is important that we allow for this aspect of the means-tested benefits system so that our simulations represent the situation of low income families living without benefits. For this study we have assumed simple take-up rates of 62% for family credit (and family income supplement), 81% for income support (and supplementary benefit) and 91% for housing benefit and the benefits associated with local tax. Families are selected at random to take up benefits, regardless of the size of calculated entitlement or other characteristics. The same selections are made for each family each time benefit calculations are made.[3] This method of representing non-take-up is integrated into the model. However, the take-up rates are available as parameters for the model user to change: an assumption of full take-up is straightforward to implement, for example.

Output

As well as the aggregate effect on each element of the tax and benefit system and on each source of original income, distributional tables may be produced by one of two means. Firstly, the output microdata files may be read into a statistical or spreadsheet package. Or, secondly, POLIMOD's own set of tables which focus on the impact across the income distribution may be used.[4] These have their own set of options regarding equivalence scale, ranking and classifying variables, and categories of cases that may be analysed as subsets. A summary of the options is given in Table 2.2.

2.4 Updating

Typically, the year modelled by POLIMOD is the current year so that updating the database from the year of the data collection to the modelled year must take place. Different updating factors are used for each source of income and expenditure.

The Appendix following Chapter 12 documents the detail of the updating procedure. It is important to appreciate the general nature of the updating strategy. This rests, on the one hand, on a view about what is important to adjust, along with, on the other hand, the availability of suitable data with which to make suitable adjustments. Our procedure concentrates on adjusting the incomes and expenditures of households and individuals in the microdata. In effect, we 'pick up' our sample in the survey year, and 'parachute' it into the modelled year with most survey year demographic and economic characteristics intact, but with incomes and expenditures that reflect changes between the survey year and the policy year. In the case of earnings, some changes in distribution and in the differentials between men and women are captured, as well as aggregate effects. For other components of income and expenditure, adjustments are only made on an aggregate basis.

Structural shifts in the population's characteristics are extremely difficult to model in the absence of multi-dimensional data on the nature of these shifts. Two methods have been used in microsimulation modelling, each with drawbacks. First, observations may be re-weighted to account for changes in characteristics of the population. This 'static ageing' approach has the advantage of being relatively straightforward to carry out in principle, since it can be achieved in a similar way to grossing-up to adjust for differential non-response.[5] However, in practice it is not only difficult to obtain suitable control totals for the characteristics that have changed, it is also impossible to be sure that the sample has not been distorted with

Table 2.2. *POLIMOD output options*

- **Sub-groups of households** may be selected according to region, household composition or housing tenure, or all households may be included in the analysis.
- **Equivalence scales** may be selected independently for the *ranking* of households (or families) and the scaling of *changes* in income. In each case the choice is between:

   null scale (no equivalising)
   (number of people)^x – where x may be chosen by the user
   benefit relativity scale (single=1; couple=1.6; dependent child=0.4)
   OECD scale (single=1; other adult=0.7; child under 14=0.5)
   McClements scale (see Chapter 4, Appendix 4.1 for details).

   In each case, the scales are parameterised and the values may be changed by the user.
- **Weighting**: in ranking the households (or families), they may be given equal weights or may be weighted by the number of people in them.
- **The ranking measure** may be chosen from the following:

   net income (see section 2.5)
   gross income
   net income after housing costs
   expenditure (at household level only).

   The same choices (except expenditure) are available for the definition of **income change**.
- **Income groups** may be defined by income range (bands of the same width, groups of different sizes) or in terms of quantiles (bands of different widths, groups of the same size). Any number of groups may be chosen.

---

regard to characteristics for which there has been no control. In addition, limited sample size inhibits the number of controls that may feasibly be used in combination. The second method of adjusting for structural shifts in the population's characteristics involves ageing the sample 'dynamically'. Each year, the individuals in the sample become a year older; a proportion of them leave school, others marry, cohabit, divorce or have children. They may become unemployed, get promoted or retire. Probabilities of changing state are applied to each observation so that the sample evolves in an analogous way to the population over the period. Although attractive because it is in principle able to capture interdependencies between characteristics and changes in them, this approach is not only extremely laborious, it also faces problems regarding the availability of information about conditional probabilities in all the dimensions of interest.

In POLIMOD, the simple alternative method of holding all economic and demographic characteristics constant (while updating amounts of incomes and expenditures) is adopted on the basis of the explicit and transparent assumption that the size of structural shifts will be small. If small enough, the error introduced by ignoring them will be outweighed by the error arising from imperfections in more complex methods.

2.5 Income measure

The household income measure is the key output of the simulation which is used for the revenue change calculation and the definition of gainers and losers. It may in principle be defined in any way, within the limits set by FES data and given the fact that we simulate only immediate cash effects and do not take account of changes in welfare that are not reflected in cash changes. The standard definition, which is used throughout this study is *net disposable income after indirect tax* which is made up of:

original income (from earnings, self-employment, investments, occupa-
    tional and personal pensions, transfers such as student grants and
    maintenance)
plus   cash social security benefits
plus   basic income or other new benefit
less   income tax (net of tax reliefs at source)
less   employee and self-employed National Insurance contributions
less   council tax
less   VAT
less   excise duties.[6]

2.6 Incidence and behaviour assumptions

In POLIMOD in general, changes in the household post-tax income measure translate exactly into changes in government revenue: a loss to households corresponds to a gain to the Exchequer of the same amount. All changes to taxes and benefits that are simulated by POLIMOD are assumed to have their full impact on households without second-order effects. There are three exceptions.

First, changes to original income (such as the introduction of a minimum wage) are assumed to affect household income but to have no direct effect on government revenue. As well as the indirect effect of

increased taxes and decreased benefit entitlements following increases in
earnings, there would also in fact be an increase in the Exchequer cost of
public sector pay. This latter effect is not captured.

Second, employer National Insurance contributions are simulated by
POLIMOD and may be optionally included as part of Exchequer revenue.
However, it is not assumed that a change in contributions paid by employers has an effect on the income of the employee. It is implicitly assumed
that the incidence of these contributions falls elsewhere in the system.

Third, a change in indirect taxes, if reflected in changed prices, will affect
the retail price index (RPI) and hence the amount by which benefit levels
(and income tax thresholds) are indexed the following year. Benefit recipients are protected from increases in indirect taxes to the extent that the
RPI reflects the changes in prices that they face. It is possible to capture
these effects within POLIMOD by adjusting the parameters which set
benefit levels (or tax thresholds).

In general, however, no change in behaviour is modelled following a
change in policy. The 'first round' effects of the policy that are calculated
can be interpreted as the immediate effect of the change, before individual
behaviour has time to adjust. The general arguments for this approach are
presented in Chapter 1. One specific example, describing the approach to
modelling the incidence of indirect tax changes, is given in Chapter 5.
Patterns of spending might be expected to adjust more quickly than other
behaviour. However, we attempt no reconciliation of changed expenditure
with income (or vice versa). For example, a change in disposable income,
following a direct tax change, is generally assumed to have no impact on
household spending (or indirect taxes). This is not because we do not
think these relationships are important, but for two other reasons. First, in
the FES, data on incomes and expenditures are not collected in a consistent manner. Information on credit and saving is very limited. A reconciliation based on these data would be spurious. Second, as emphasised in
Chapter 1, we do not wish to impose a particular theoretical perspective
on a model that may be used for a wide range of purposes. Although the
'openness' we assume may be unsatisfactory in some contexts, it is at least
transparent, and provides benchmarks on which speculations about
further effects may be based.

Appendix 2.1 Policy parameters

CHILD BENEFIT

• rates for all children (aged under 16 or under 19 and in full time non-advanced
education)

- an additional amount for the first child
- differential rates by age range (0–4, 5–10, 11–15, 16–17 and 18).

INCOME TAX (see Appendix 2.2)

rates and thresholds:
- any number of bands

personal allowances:
- levels of all the main allowances
- marginal or fixed rate allowances/deductions
- age allowances (level, income limit, taper and qualifying ages)

child tax allowances:
- by child age group
- allowed against the income of the mother or the father

husband and wife:
- current structure or the pre-reform 1989 structure

tax reliefs:
- mortgage interest: either relief at source, at a fixed rate or the marginal rate; maximum loan
- life insurance premia (relief at source or at the marginal rate; maximum premia and maximum proportion of the total premium)
- pension contributions (relief may be fixed or at marginal rate)

tax base:
- any combination of components of income in the database plus any elements of the tax-benefit system simulated by POLIMOD
- tax child benefit as the income of the mother (or lone father) with or without transfer to any spouse and at various marginal rates
- rate for investment income within the standard rate band may be set separately; components of investment income may be taxed at the composite rate or under a separate investment income tax regime.

NATIONAL INSURANCE CONTRIBUTIONS

- Class 1 not-contracted-out rate, lower and upper earnings limits and the rate charged below the lower earnings limit
- Class 1 contracted-out reduction and married women's rate
- pre-1989 structure (two additional lower bands) or the pre-1985 structure as options for Class 1
- abolish Class 1 upper earnings limit with or without retaining the limit for contracting out
- employer contributions
- Class 2 lower earnings exemption
- rate of Class 2
- Class 4 the lower threshold and upper limit

- Class 4 rate
- each class may be deducted from the income tax base
- overall annual maximum NIC payment.

MEANS-TESTED BENEFITS

- *post-1988 reform benefits (1988/9 to 1996/7):*
  income support (including mortgage interest payments)
  housing benefit (rent allowances/rebates and rate rebates)
  family credit
  community charge benefit
  council tax benefit (including second adult rebate)
  earnings top-up
- *pre-1988 benefits (1978/9 to 1987/8):*
  supplementary benefit (including rent allowances and mortgage interest payments)
  housing benefit (rent allowances/rebates and rate rebates)
  family income supplement
  housing benefit supplement
- *for all the above benefits it is possible to model:*
  eligibility criteria
  definition and level of needs
  definition of resources
  imputation of tariff income from capital
  tapers
  non-dependent deductions (income support, council tax benefit, supplementary benefit and housing benefit).

LOCAL TAXES

- rates, community charge or council tax
- minimum age for liability
- local taxes at the level of local authority areas (each is made up of 6–7 local authorities)
- council tax band relativities

VALUE ADDED TAX & EXCISE DUTIES

- options for different rates of VAT on 50 categories of goods
- flat rate and *ad valorem* excise duties on motor cars, alcohol (5 types), tobacco (3 types), betting (2 types) and motor fuels (2 types)

Appendix 2.2 Options for income tax policy

In this appendix, the income tax policy options available to the user are explained. In particular, we focus on those changes analysed in Chapters 3 and 4 which have taken place since 1978.

Rate structure

Under the 1996/7 income tax regime there were three rates of income tax on three bands of taxable income. As taxable income rises above each threshold, the marginal rate on the next band up is charged on income above the threshold.

	Rate	Above taxable income of:
Reduced rate	20%	—
Standard rate[7]	24%	£3,900
Higher rate	40%	£25,500

For example, a taxable earned income of £27,000 would be liable for tax of

$$(£3,900 \times 0.20) + (£21,600 \times 0.24) + (£1,500 \times 0.40) = £6,564.$$

Any number of rate bands may be specified in POLIMOD. In 1978 there were eleven bands with the highest rate being 83% and the lowest 25%. Between 1988/9 and 1991/2 there were only two. In principle, some parts of the tax base may become taxable only when particular thresholds are crossed. This is not currently the case for any item of income. However, a recently discussed option was to tax child benefit only when taxable income from other sources crosses the 40% threshold. The simulated effects of this are discussed in Sutherland (1994).

There was until 1979/80, and has been since 1992/3, a tax band known as the 'reduced rate' band. The significance of this depends on the rest of the structure of income tax. In 1995/6 and 1996/7 it operated in a manner little different from any of the other tax bands. In 1978/9, on the other hand, although joint taxation of husband and wife was in operation, each partner was allowed their own reduced rate band of tax.

Another special term that has been applied to tax bands is the 'zero rate' band. This is a band of income on which no tax is paid and is equivalent in value to a single fixed rate personal allowance. It is possible in POLIMOD to specify a zero rate band instead of or in addition to a system of personal allowances which are allowed to vary in value according to the taxpayer's marginal rate.

Personal allowances

The annual personal allowances which are allowed against taxable income in the 1996/7 regime are set out below. The married couple's allowance (MCA) received by married couples, and the additional personal allowance (APA) received by non-married parents (both in addition to the single personal allowance) are set against income at the fixed rate of 15%. The single allowance and the higher allowances for older taxpayers are allowed at the marginal rate. The enhanced levels of age allowances are tapered away as taxable income rises above the threshold at a rate of 50%, so that in 1996/7, for example, a single taxpayer aged 74 had an allowance reduced to the level of the standard single allowance once his or her taxable income reached £17,490 per year ((£17,490 − £15,200) × 0.5 = £4,910 − £3,765). Prior to

1987/8, there was one rate of age allowance applying to taxpayers aged 65 or over. In 1987/8, a higher rate for people aged 80 or more was introduced, and in 1988/9 the age condition for this extra allowance was reduced to 75.

single personal allowance	£3,765
married couple's allowance	£1,790
additional personal allowance	£1,790
single age allowance (age 65–74)	£4,910
single age allowance (age 75+)	£5,090
married couple's age allowance (age 65–74)	£3,115
married couple's age allowance (age 75+)	£3,155
age allowance income limit	£15,200
age allowance taper	50%

The extra allowance received by married couples (the MCA) may be split between them in any proportion although it is allocated to the husband in the first instance. Since the MCA is allowable against income at a fixed rate only, this feature of the system can only change the distribution of tax between the couple, not alter their total joint tax. When operating at the family or household level, POLIMOD ignores this feature because the results are not affected.

As well as varying all the parameters set out above, it is also possible within POLIMOD to change the rate at which allowances are allowed against tax – their value in cash terms. They may be allowed at the marginal rate or at any fixed rate. In 1978, all personal allowances were set against tax at the tax unit's marginal rate. In principle it is possible to allow personal allowances against tax at marginal rates up to a certain limit (e.g. at rates up to but excluding the 40% rate).

1978/9 was the final year of the phasing out of child tax allowances. They were allowed against the earned income of the head of the tax unit at his (or her, in the case of single mothers) marginal rate and were of differential size depending on the age of the child. Since 1979, there has been no tax allowance for children (with the exception of the APA for single parents) and child benefit has acted as a fixed-value refundable tax credit to compensate for this. In POLIMOD, it is possible to re-instate child tax allowances, allowable against the income of the mother or the father in the case of couples, and at a fixed rate or the marginal rate of the taxpayer.

Some of the less common allowances are not simulated because of lack of data on which to base a calculation. For example, the blind person's allowance is not simulated.

Husband and wife

Since 1990, the incomes of husbands and wives have been separately taxed. The tax unit is the individual and the only factor distinguishing the taxation of single people and couples has been the higher allowance received by married couples. This allowance was not indexed for inflation between 1990/1 and 1996/7. It was raised in 1996/7, although the rate of 15% at which it was allowed was not altered. Before the reform of 1990, the tax unit was the married couple and unmarried couples were treated as two single people. The income of the wife was considered to belong to her husband, for tax purposes. An allowance, equal in size to the single allowance, was available to set against her earned income. Any unearned income of hers was always taxed with her husband's income, with no extra relief. The system of allowances was similar to the current structure, with the married man's allowance (MMA) pre-dating the married couples allowance. This, including the single person's allowance of a married man, could only be set against the income of the wife if she was the 'breadwinner', in other words if the husband did not earn enough to use all his allowances himself. (This is consistent with the notion that all income of the couple belonged to the husband.)

Under joint taxation, husbands and wives could elect to have their earnings taxed separately if they wished. This was only worthwhile for better-off couples where both partners were earning substantial amounts. In these cases the MMA was foregone but the earned income of the wife was taxed separately from that of her husband, meaning that more of their joint income was taxed at lower rates, and less at higher rates, than if it were taxed jointly.

One exception to joint taxation pre-1990 was that in 1978/9 there was a reduced rate band of tax which was allowed separately against the earnings of husbands and wives (but only one reduced rate band was allowed against joint investment income).

POLIMOD is able to simulate the pre-1990 structure and to vary all the main parameters that governed it.

Reliefs and allowances

POLIMOD simulates any existing tax relief and changes to the nature of this relief on mortgage interest, on life insurance premia, pension contributions and on Class 4 National Insurance contributions. It also automatically 'relieves' income that is not taxed at all by excluding it from the tax base.

Pension contributions

Occupational and private pension contributions currently attract full tax relief at the taxpayer's marginal rate. POLIMOD offers the option to limit relief to a fixed rate or to limit the relief to a proportion of the value of the contributions, as well as abolishing the relief altogether.

Class 4 National Insurance contributions (NICs)

Until 1996/7, half of Class 4 NICs were allowed against tax at the marginal rate. POLIMOD allows this proportion to be changed or offers the option of abolishing the relief entirely. The amounts of Class 4 NICs on which the relief calculations are based are themselves simulated using recorded information on self-employment income.

Mortgage interest tax relief

In 1996/7 mortgage tax relief was allowed on interest on up to a maximum amount owed of £30,000 at a fixed rate of 15%. This relief is deducted at source (by reducing repayments) and is thus given to non-taxpayers as well as to those with incomes above the tax threshold. POLIMOD treats tax reliefs as reductions in tax rather than reductions in payments. For non-taxpayers, mortgage tax relief appears as a negative amount of income tax. In parts of the net income simulation where mortgage interest net of tax relief, or income tax without the deduction of mortgage relief, are inputs into calculations (for example in the case of income support), these quantities are adjusted.

POLIMOD offers a wide range of options for the tax treatment of mortgage interest. The maximum amount of capital on which interest may be relieved may be changed (it has been fixed at £30,000 since 1983/4; before that it was £25,000); the rate at which relief is fixed may be altered (it was 25% from 1991/2, reduced to 20% in 1994/5 and 15% in 1995/6) or the relief may be allowed at the taxpayer's marginal rate (as was the case until 1991/2). Between 1983/4 and 1991/2, relief at higher rates of tax had to be claimed by completing a tax return (and was refunded through the following year's tax coding). Before 1983/4, all mortgage tax relief was granted in this way and none of it was deducted at source. Relief was given as a reduction in tax payment and was not available to non-taxpayers. This option is available in POLIMOD.

Life insurance premium relief

Since 1984, this relief has been in the process of being phased out by preventing new entrants to the scheme. Policies taken out before that time still attract tax relief on premia at a rate of 12.5% (up to a maximum of £1,500 per year). This relief is deducted at source (by reducing premia) and therefore benefits people with incomes below the income tax threshold. Between 1984 and 1988/9 the fixed rate was 15%. Relief on life insurance premia was not deducted at source until 1979/80. In 1978/9 relief had to be applied for; it was fixed at the basic rate (33%) and was applied to premia in full up to £10 per year and then to half of any remaining payments above that limit. Each of these structures of life insurance relief may be simulated in POLIMOD. As with mortgage tax relief, for non-taxpayers relief appears as negative amounts of tax. For others it is presented as a reduction in tax.

Tax base

The unified tax base includes all earnings and investment income, pensions, maintenance and statutory sick pay and statutory maternity pay. As well as the state retirement pension, the following social security benefits are taxed: unemployment benefit, widows' benefit, invalid care allowances and war pensions. Other social security payments are not taxed, and neither are student grants or student loans. Private and occupational pension contributions are fully deductible but NICs are not deducted from taxable income. The taxation of company cars and fuel for personal use is not included in the simulated tax base. However, it is possible to simulate changes to the tax base by including any proportion of each of the income components shown in Table 2.A2.1.

The elements of the tax base are defined at the individual level. Under joint taxation, the taxable income of each spouse is added together. Family- or household-level means-tested benefits are assumed not to be subject to income tax since they

Table 2.A2.1. *Income elements that may be aggregated (or deducted) to form the simulated tax base in* POLIMOD

Gross earnings	Occupational pension contributions
Luncheon vouchers	Self-supply goods + imputed under-
Self-employment income	reported amount
Gross investment income, banks	Gross investment income, building
Gross investment income, other	societies
Occupational pension (inc. SERPS)	Investment income, tax free
Student loan	Student grant
Income from trusts and covenants	Personal pension
Other income (currently non-taxable)	Other income (currently taxable)
Foster allowances	Income from childminding and
Income from relatives	babysitting
Unemployment benefit	Maintenance payments received
Maternity allowance	State pension (not including SERPS)
Statutory sick pay	Sickness benefit
Widows' benefits	Invalidity benefit
Invalid care allowance	Statutory maternity pay
Other benefits	Severe disability allowance
Attendance allowance	Industrial disablement pension
War pension	Training allowances
National Insurance contributions,	Mobility allowance
Class 1	Imputed under-reported investment
National Insurance contributions,	income
Class 4	National Insurance contributions,
Value of earnings in kind (free meals	Class 2
etc.)	Basic income

Note: See the Appendix at the end of this book for more precise definitions of these variables.

depend on after-tax income for their assessment. Child benefit may be added to the tax base either as the income of the mother or the father.

Since 1978, the main changes to the tax base have concerned investment income. Prior to April 1991, interest payments from building society accounts and high street bank accounts were taxed at source at a rate known as the 'composite rate'. Not only people who were income taxpayers but also those with incomes below the tax threshold were subject to the deduction, which was not refundable. The rate was set so that the aggregate amount collected from taxpayers and non-taxpayers would be the same as if the tax was levied at the individual tax unit's marginal rate.[8] Income taxed at the composite rate was included as taxable income in the calculation for higher rate tax. Taxation at the tax unit's marginal rate (zero for non-taxpayers) was introduced in 1991. Before 1982, only income from building society accounts was taxed at the composite rate and bank interest was taxed at the tax unit's marginal rate. POLIMOD permits the simulation of the composite rate, including any combination of income elements in the base for this treatment.

Until 1982, investment income was also taxed under an additional schedule, known as the investment income surcharge. A rate of 15% was applied on all investment income of the tax unit (with husband and wife taxed together as one unit) above an annual threshold. In 1978/9, the surcharge had a more complex structure with two rates and thresholds, and a higher set of thresholds for tax units where the head of household was aged over 65.

Notes

1 Chapter 8 explores one method of imputing sufficient information from reported receipt of these benefits to allow partial simulation of changes to benefit rules.
2 See Department of Social Security (1994a).
3 Chapter 11 considers the possible effects of these assumptions on aggregate simulated benefits.
4 These are used extensively in Chapters 3 and 4.
5 A simple example with limited objectives is provided in Chapter 4.
6 Lump sum incomes (such as redundancy pay) are not included in original income, nor are loans or their repayment. Private and occupational pension contributions, housing costs, child care costs, travel and other work costs are not deducted. Capital taxes are not deducted, nor are employer National Insurance contributions or other taxes on business.
7 From 1996/7, the standard rate charged on investment income within the standard rate band was discounted to 20%.
8 For example, it was 23.25% in 1988/9 when the standard rate – also the lowest rate – was 25%.

Part Two

Model outputs and modelling assumptions

3   The distributional effect of changes in UK policy since 1978

3.1 Introduction

The period between 1978 and 1996 was a time of substantial change in the personal tax and social security systems in the UK. Some changes took place as part of major structural reforms: to the taxation of husband and wife in 1990, to means-tested social security in 1988 (the Fowler Reforms) and to the complete system of local tax in 1989 and 1990 and again in 1993. Other changes were presented as flagship elements of government policy: the reduction in the standard rate of income tax was the prime example of the period. Less well-publicised changes, such as the reduction in the value of available mortgage interest tax relief, have also occurred. Taxes apart from income tax were increased (the main VAT rate was 17.5% in 1996/7 compared with 8% in 1978/9). Although there were no such dramatic movements in the overall value of benefits, there were significant changes: periods when the value of child benefit fell; a reduction in the coverage of some means-tested benefits accompanied by a widening of entitlement for others; and increased generosity in some benefits for the disabled.

It is not straightforward to predict what the overall effect of all these changes has been, either in aggregate, on groups in the population or at different points in the income distribution. Not only is each part of the system complex in itself, but also may interact with other parts of the system. For example, since the reforms of 1988, a change in income tax will affect entitlement to means-tested benefits. An assessment of the full effect needs to take account of such interactions.

We might also expect changes in tax and social security rules to have an impact on decisions people make about how they lead their lives, which in turn will affect their incomes. Working, saving, spending, benefit claiming and tax avoidance and evasion are among the activities that may be influenced. Furthermore, fiscal policy will have an impact on the economy

29

in ways that affect the availability of jobs, the level of demand and the rate of inflation, each of which will influence household incomes. Policy affecting personal incomes may also influence longer-term individual decisions regarding training, education, fertility and household formation or dissolution.

If we were to observe the role of tax payments and benefit receipt on household incomes in each of the two years we examine (for example, by analysing recorded data on household incomes from the two periods) we should not be able to identify the specific cause of any difference. We could not distinguish how much was attributable to a change in policy, how much was due to secondary effects resulting from changes in individual behaviour, or how much was as a result of consequential macroeconomic effects. Indeed, other independent macroeconomic changes and shifts in the economic, demographic and social environment as a whole would also have been important influences on household incomes.

Method

In this analysis we isolate the first round policy effects, in the sense of the *discretionary changes* to the rules governing personal taxes and social security benefits between 1978/9 and 1996/7. This is achieved by assuming a constant population with fixed levels of market income, expenditure unemployment, age distribution, occupational pension rights, family circumstance and so on.[1] We use the population represented by a single year of the Family Expenditure Survey (FES) and POLIMOD to simulate after-tax incomes under the two policy regimes. The 1991 FES is used for this exercise, adjusting the data to 1996/7 price and income levels.[2] We view 1978/9 policy from the perspective of 1996/7. The question we are seeking to answer is: 'What would be the impact of the 1978/9 tax and benefit system, if it were re-introduced in place of the 1996/7 system?'

In order to make this comparison, levels of benefit, tax allowances and thresholds, capital limits and exemptions that applied in 1978/9 are uprated to 1996/7 levels by the increase in prices over the period. This method bears a superficial resemblance to uprating as it has taken place in practice over much of the period we consider.[3] However, there are many elements of tax and benefit formulae – notably capital limits – that are not usually or regularly adjusted for inflation.

In this chapter, we decompose changes in household income into six elements: income tax, National Insurance contributions (NICs), local taxes, child benefit (including one parent benefit), means-tested benefits and indirect taxes.[4] We do not simulate changes to National Insurance benefits and disability benefits.[5] Section 3.2 compares the aggregate effect on

Table 3.1. *Average household taxes and benefits, 1996/7 and 1978/9 regimes (£s per week)*

Policy regime	Income tax	NICs	Local taxes	Indirect taxes	*Total taxes*	Child benefit	Means-tested benefits	*Total benefits*	Total taxes *less* benefits
1996/7	59.05	18.25	9.43	44.75	*131.48*	5.67	14.66	*20.33*	111.15
1978/9	83.42	12.57	8.24	32.56	*136.79*	4.07	14.53	*18.60*	118.19

household incomes of each of these six elements of the 1978/9 system with the effect of the 1996/7 tax-benefit regime. Section 3.3 examines the distributional impact of each element and decomposes the overall net change in household income under the two regimes into the six elements. Section 3.4 focuses on the gainers and losers from a hypothetical switch from the 1996/7 system to that of 1978/9. Section 3.5 concludes.

3.2 Average taxes and benefits

Simulation of the two regimes on the common population database shows that the aggregate effect on household incomes is similar in each case. Table 3.1 shows the average receipt of benefits is £20.33 under the 1996/7 regime compared with £18.60 under the 1978/9 regime (all in 1996/7 prices).[6] Average tax liability is £131.48 under the 1996/7 regime, and £136.79 under the 1978/9 regime. How these totals break down by type of tax and benefit is shown graphically in Figure 3.1. Shifts in the importance of each of the four main categories of tax that we consider are evident. Income tax makes up only 45% of total tax in 1996/7 but is 61% of the total in 1978/9. This major reduction is a reflection of cuts in the standard rate over the period (from 33% to 24%) and a substantial reduction in the number and level of higher rates: in 1978/9 there were nine higher rates, with the highest set at 83%, whereas in 1996/7 there was a single higher rate of 40%. Comparison of the value of personal allowances in 1996/7 with the 1978/9 values indexed by prices (see Appendix 3.1) shows that adult allowances too have become relatively more generous. The extra tax on investment income levied in 1978/9, the investment income surcharge, no longer existed in 1996/7. Set against these tax cuts are some increases: the abolition of child tax allowances and the substantial reduction in value of mortgage tax relief (the limit on the capital borrowed which attracts relief has more than halved in real terms). Other changes involve both gainers and losers. Examples include the reform of taxation of husband and wife

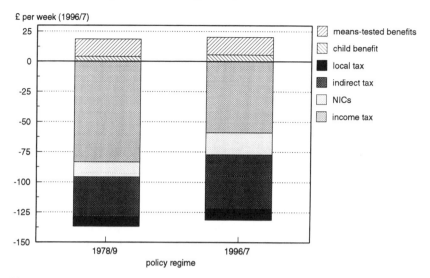

Figure 3.1 Tax liability and benefit receipt, 1978/9 and 1996/7 regimes

in 1990, the abolition of the composite rate of tax on building society interest and the introduction of the mortgage interest relief at source scheme (MIRAS).

Balancing the overall reduction in income tax are increases in all three of the other types of tax that we consider. The largest proportional increase is in NICs, which grew by 46%. This is mainly due to an increase in the not-contracted out rate which rose from 6.5% in 1978/9 to 10% in 1996/7.

An increase of 37% in the average amount of indirect tax paid by households between the two regimes is also mainly explained by a rate increase: the standard rate of VAT rose from 8% in 1978/9 to 17.5% in 1996/7. The coverage of VAT was also extended during the period, to include take-away food and domestic fuel (at a special rate of 8%). The standard rate of VAT has more than doubled since 1978/9, but the VAT charged on luxuries rose by a smaller amount – 5 percentage points – and increases in some excise duties were roughly balanced by decreases in others.

The average amount of local tax paid by households is also greater in 1996/7 than in 1978/9: £9.43 compared with £8.24. This increase is consistent with a general rise in the revenue raised through local taxation during the 1980s, and is not directly connected with structural changes in the local tax system. Moreover, the increase would have been considerably greater had central government not cut local taxes by £2.69 per adult per week in

1991 by greatly increasing the local government subsidy (which was financed by an increase in VAT from 15 to 17.5%).

Figure 3.1 indicates that benefits in 1996/7 are somewhat more generous than in 1978/9. The main difference is in child benefit and one parent benefit. The average household payment is 39% higher under the 1996/7 regime than under the 1978/9 regime. Although child benefit was frozen for several years in the late 1980s, Appendix 3.1 shows that the 1978/9 benefit, uprated according to inflation, is still less generous than the 1996/7 amount. Under the 1978/9 regime, universal child benefit was considerably lower, but residual child tax allowances were available for income tax payers. If we view child benefit as a credit against income tax which is refundable to non-taxpayer parents, then the average amount of income tax net of financial support for children falls from £79.35 in 1978/9, to £53.38 in 1996/7.

The average payment of means-tested benefit to households is very similar under the two regimes. This result is quite unlike what we should expect from an analysis of data collected in the two years that we compare. The growth of the cost of means-tested benefits has been substantial (see Department of Social Security, 1993a) and this contrast serves to remind us of the question that our analysis allows us to address. By holding the characteristics of our population constant we not only fix the numbers of unemployed, lone parents, long-term sick, low paid and pensioners who might qualify for means-tested benefits; we also hold constant National Insurance benefits and disability benefits at 1991 amounts (indexed to 1996/7). Thus in situations where levels of generosity or breadth of coverage of these benefits were in fact different in 1978/9 from those in 1996/7, this will have had implications for the relative size of means-tested benefit entitlements in the two years over and above any changes to the means-tested regimes. Our modelling does not capture this effect. The broadly similar levels of average payment shown in Figure 3.1 do not take account of any change in balance between means-tested and non-means-tested benefits (beyond those arising from changes to child benefit), only of changes within means-tested benefits themselves and in their relation to the taxes that we simulate.

3.3 Distributional effects

We should expect shifts in the composition of tax and changes in the structure of each tax or benefit to have re-distributive effects. These are investigated in two ways. First, we focus on the impact of each type of tax on households at different points in the 1996/7 income distribution under the two regimes. We then analyse the impact of a hypothetical return to the regime of 1978/9 on the distribution of household incomes, decomposing the proportional change in incomes according to the role played by each element of the system. In both sections, the effects on income are defined in terms of average changes within deciles of the 1996/7 income distribution. The definition of household net income we use is similar to that used in the Households Below Average Income (HBAI) analysis (Department of Social Security, 1995) with the major difference that in the present analysis we also deduct indirect taxes. There are other minor differences in income definition, but the further major departure is that this analysis *simulates* the elements of income that arc the subject of this study rather than using the information *recorded* in the FES data. Further differences from the HBAI methodology include the use of a different equivalence scale for ranking (here we use a simple scale of 1.0 for the first adult, 0.6 for other adults and 0.4 for dependent children) and the fact that we count each household once (rather than counting each individual within the household) in the formation of the decile groups. This latter choice is necessary in order to keep our accounting framework transparent: household gains are equivalent to Exchequer losses.

The distribution of tax burdens

In order to establish the impact of each tax on the distribution of household incomes we calculate the tax burden as the proportion of average gross income which is paid in tax by households in each net income decile.[7] The first three parts of Figure 3.2 show the tax burden by income decile for the three taxes that raise the most revenue: income tax, NICs and indirect taxes. The solid lines show the percentage of income paid as these taxes under the 1996/7 regime, the dashed lines show the percentage under the 1978/9 regime. The three graphs are not drawn to the same scale since the most dramatic point they make is in the differences in the shapes of the distributions. Income tax (Figure 3.2a) is most clearly progressive over the whole range of the distribution (both including and excluding child benefit). Owing to the upper limit on National Insurance contribution payments (Figure 3.2b), these show a clear inverted U-shape with the average proportion falling off sharply at high household incomes. Indirect taxes (Figure 3.2c) are regressive, with the high average tax rate of the bottom decile standing out in particular. This occurs because some households with low gross incomes have relatively high recorded expenditures.[8]

The burden of income tax is shown in two ways in Figure 3.2a: net of child benefit (darker lines) and excluding its effect (lighter lines). Treating child benefit as a tax credit results in the net burden becoming negative in the lower deciles where tax payments are exceeded by child benefit receipt. However, income tax burdens are lower across the whole income distribution under the 1996/7 regime than under the 1978/9 regime, whether child benefit is included or not. The progressivity of income tax net of child benefit is similar in both regimes except right at the top of the income distribution, where the slope of the line is steeper in 1978/9. The difference in progressivity is more marked when considering income tax alone: the changes since 1978/9 have reduced its progressivity. This is not at all surprising if one considers the dramatic drop in the standard and higher rates over the period. Incomes in the range affected by higher rates nearly all fall in the top decile of household incomes, and the reduction in the standard rate is likely to be of greater benefit to households in the middle to upper deciles. Not only have income tax burdens fallen, but the policy changes between 1978/9 and 1996/7 have reduced the progressivity of income tax throughout the distribution of household incomes.

Figure 3.2b shows that above the lowest decile group, the percentage of household income taken in NICs is clearly greater under the 1996/7 regime than under the 1978/9 regime. This differential increases with income level, but falls off at the top of the distribution. This is mainly because of the upper limit to contributions which has acted to limit their growth at the top of the distribution, in spite of substantial increases in contribution rates.

Figure 3.2c charts the increasing burdens of indirect tax since 1978/9 across the whole income distribution. The effect is somewhat larger at the bottom of the distribution, suggesting a small increase in the regressivity of indirect tax since the regime of 1978/9.

Figure 3.2d shows the aggregate effect for the three taxes and local tax together (net of child benefit). Disregarding the bottom decile, which is dominated by the indirect tax effect, we see that tax burdens under the 1996/7 regime rise fairly evenly from 29% in the second decile to 32% in the top decile. Under the 1978/9 regime the progression is steeper – rising from 25% to 41%. Tax burdens are lower under the earlier regime over the whole distribution, with the exception of the top two deciles.

Changes in household incomes

This subsection considers directly the question posed in the introduction: What would be the effect on household incomes in 1996/7 of a return to the policy regime of 1978/9? Table 3.2 shows the average change in weekly incomes following such a switch in policy for households in each decile of the income distribution. The change is analysed in two ways: the first indi-

(a) Income tax and child benefit as a percentage of gross household income

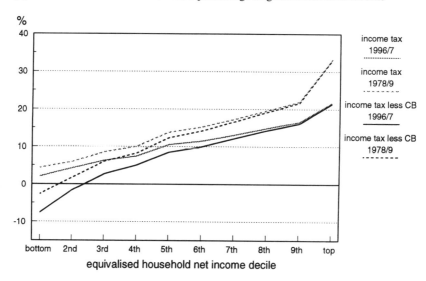

(b) National Insurance contributions as a percentage of gross household income

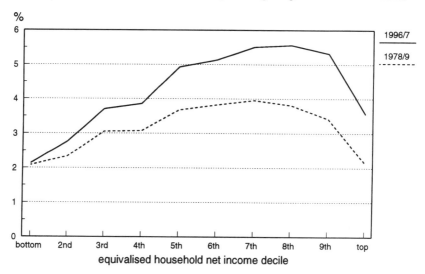

Figure 3.2   Tax burdens

(c) Indirect tax as a percentage of gross household income

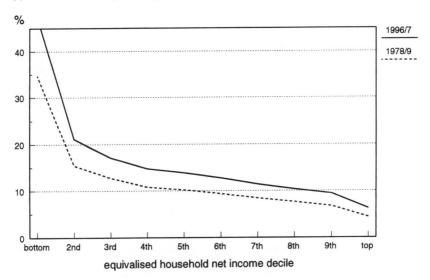

(d) Total tax as a percentage of gross household income

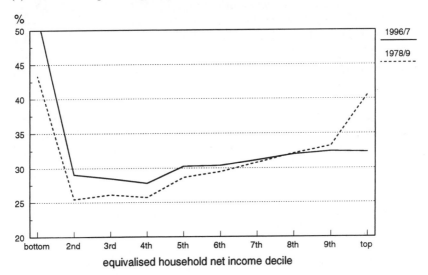

Table 3.2. *Switching from the 1996/7 to the 1978/9 policy regime: changes in household incomes*

Decile of household equivalised net income	Mean weekly equivalised net income	Cash net gain	Equivalised percentage gain
Bottom	£42.33	£8.63	14
2nd	£71.16	£3.21	3
3rd	£87.59	£3.12	2
4th	£102.97	£3.14	1
5th	£122.26	£4.42	2
6th	£145.54	£1.95	0
7th	£172.66	£1.37	0
8th	£209.36	−£1.19	0
9th	£262.12	−£5.19	−1
Top	£453.74	−£89.89	−12

cates how the average unequivalised cash effect (which may easily be translated into a revenue cost) shown in Figure 3.1 is distributed. Secondly, the *proportional* change in *equivalised* income is also shown.

The bottom decile of the 1996/7 distribution would on average be much better off under the 1978/9 policy regime: by 14% of their equivalised net incomes or over £8 in cash terms. In contrast, the top decile would be worse of by an average of almost £90 per week or 12% of their incomes on an equivalised basis. Apart from these two extremes, the net gain in incomes is small, and tends to decline as income rises. This overall picture illustrates the net effect of the regime switch. Within each decile some households gain and some lose. Section 3.4 explores this pattern of gain and loss across the distribution. In the remainder of this section we decompose the percentage change in incomes into different elements of the tax–benefit system.

Figure 3.3 plots the composition of the percentage income change shown in Table 3.2. Each bar has six segments: one for each of the elements of tax and social security. The part of the bar above the axis represents the changes that on average would benefit the households in the decile, following a switch to the 1978/9 policy regime. The elements in the bar below the axis represent changes that would reduce the incomes of the households in the decile. For example, we have seen that the bottom decile would be better off by 14% following a return to the 1978/9 regime. This is made up of an increase in means-tested benefits equivalent to 5% of

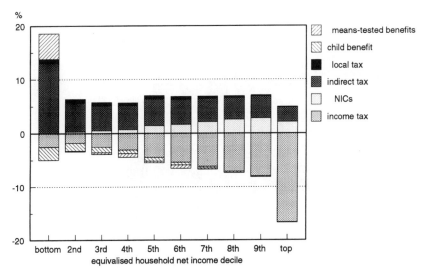

Figure 3.3   Percentage gains and losses from the 1978/9 regime

income, a reduction in local tax of 1%, and a reduction in indirect tax of 13%. These 'gains' are offset by an increase in income tax of 3% and a fall in child benefit, worth 2% of 1996/7 incomes. The average change in NICs is negligible in the bottom decile. In contrast, the top decile is worse off by 12% of its 1996/7 income level, on average. This is made up mainly of increased income tax of 17% of income and negligible reductions in means-tested benefits and child benefit. Offsetting these losses is a reduction in indirect tax of 3%, a reduction in NICs of 2% and a negligible reduction in local tax.

Although the overall impact of means-tested benefits is similar under the two regimes, Figure 3.3 shows that payments are distributed somewhat differently. The 1978/9 regime targets more effectively households in the bottom decile whereas households in the middle deciles benefit slightly more from the 1996/7 regime. This is explained by increased coverage and generosity of in-work benefits, particularly family credit, in 1996/7 combined with a steady reduction in effective coverage of social assistance over the period.[9] In addition, many of the families with children in the bottom decile, who would lose from a return to the child benefit regime of 1978/9, would be compensated by higher social assistance payments (supplementary benefit).[10] Lower child benefit in the earlier regime is of greater proportional significance to households in the lower income deciles: the effect is negligible at higher incomes. Figure 3.3 also shows that the impact of changes to NICs is particularly obvious in the top half of the distribu-

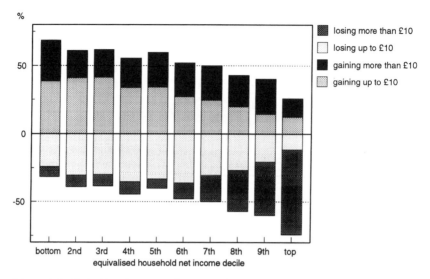

Figure 3.4   Switching from 1996/7 to 1978/9: households gaining and losing

tion, which is not surprising, since earnings are concentrated among better-off households.

Thus Figure 3.3 illustrates the relative importance of tax cuts to higher-income households and of increases in indirect tax and changes in means-tested benefits to the lowest decile. Although the net effect on household incomes in the middle of the distribution is small (see Table 3.2), Figure 3.3 shows that the substantial cuts in income tax have been roughly equally offset by increases in NICs and indirect taxes in 1996/7 compared with 1978/9. Within these middle-income groups, some households with particular compositions, incomes and expenditures will have done relatively well out of the shifts in importance of different taxes and benefits. Others will have done relatively badly. The next section considers the gainers and losers in each decile and examines how households with different characteristics are affected by the two regimes.

3.4 Gainers and losers

Figure 3.4 shows the proportion of households in each income group who would gain or lose from a switch to the 1978/9 policy regime. The upward-pointing bars above the axis show the proportion of gainers, with the darker portion showing the proportion of those gaining who would be better off by £10 a week or more (unequivalised). The downward-pointing bars show the losers. Nearly all households at all income levels would

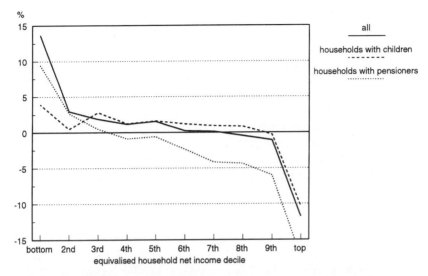

Figure 3.5   Switching from 1996/7 to 1978/9: net gain as a percentage of household income for households with children and pensioners

either gain or lose: very few are unaffected or break even. Households who would be better off under the 1978/9 regime slightly outnumber those better off under the 1996/7 regime (by a ratio of 1.07 : 1). Both gains and losses are observed over the whole distribution, with gainers from a return to 1978/9 predominating among lower income households, and losers from such a switch predominating at the top of the distribution. Large cash losses are most apparent in the top decile. Viewed in this way, Figure 3.4 suggests that the relative impact of the two regimes is as varied within an income group (horizontally) as it is across the income distribution (vertically).

In the remainder of this section we consider three groups in the population and examine the differential impact of the change in regime on each group relative to the rest of the population at the same income level. We consider two demographic groups of general interest: households with dependent children and households with people over pension age. We also focus on households with mortgages, the tax treatment of whom has changed dramatically over the period.[11]

Figure 3.5 plots the average percentage net equivalent gain in each decile from the switch to 1978/9 policy. The solid line is for all households (using data from the final column from Table 3.2). The dashed line shows the average gain for the households with children within the decile and the dotted line shows the same information for households with pensioners.

We compare the impact of the policy change on groups with different demographic characteristics in the same decile group. The proportions of households with children or pensioners in each decile may depart markedly from 10% – for example, 12.8% of households with children are in the bottom decile and 5.2% are in the top decile. By maintaining the same ranking of households we are able to assess the horizontal impact of the change in regime. In some cases the difference may be due to deliberate targeting of policy on children or on pensioners. In others it may be because households including these people are also likely to have attributes or characteristics which are directly affected by the policy changes: marital status, spending patterns, participation and age are all examples.

Households with children

Compared to all households, households with children in the 3rd to 8th income deciles would gain a small amount more (and in the top two deciles lose a small amount less) from a return to the regime of 1978/9. Differences in the bottom two deciles are more marked: whereas households in general would be much better off in 1978/9, households with children would be only slightly better off (by 4% in the bottom decile, compared with 14% overall, and by less than 1% in the second decile). This differential effect at the bottom of the income distribution is a reflection of efforts made during the 1980s to make means-tested benefits for families with children more generous. While households in the bottom decile in general would experience a 10% rise in benefit incomes under the 1978/9 regime, households with children would on average experience no increase at all. Higher up the distribution, the losses due to more generous child benefit in 1996/7 are nearly offset by the gain from child tax allowances under the 1978/9 regime. In addition, the fact that households with children would be on average slightly better off under the earlier regime is at least partly because a large proportion of them would also benefit from more generous relief on their mortgage interest.

Households with pensioners

With the exception of the second decile, households with pensioners would be worse off from a return to the regime of 1978/9, compared to households in general. This is particularly the case for pensioner households in the higher-income deciles. Under the 1978/9 regime, age-related income tax allowances are less generous than in 1996/7. It is also likely that many single pensioners would pay higher local taxes under the 1978/9 regime owing to the lack of discounts for such households in the system of domes-

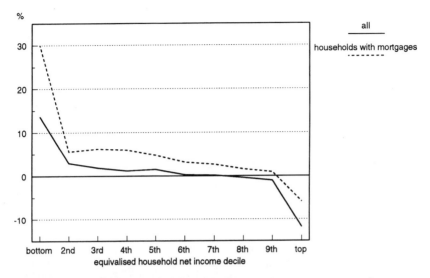

Figure 3.6   Switching form 1996/7 to 1978/9: net gain as a percentage of household income for households with mortgages

tic rates. Under the council tax in 1996/7, single adult households pay one quarter less than other households in equivalent dwellings.

At the other end of the income distribution, the increasing relative generosity of means-tested pensions and the introduction of local tax discounts for people living on their own over the period result in pensioner households in the lower deciles gaining less from a return to the 1978/9 regime compared to households in general.

Households with mortgages

Figure 3.6 compares the effect of the regime switch on all households with those who have mortgages. In each income group, households with mortgages would on average be better off than households overall from a switch to the regime of 1978/9. Given the restrictions in the tax treatment of mortgage interest, particularly the fall in the real value of the maximum allowable interest (see Appendix 3.1), this is not surprising. The effect is particularly strong in the bottom decile. This is associated with the fact that, under the 1978/9 regime, all mortgage interest costs were covered from the start of a supplementary benefit claim, whereas in 1996/7, only half total mortgage interest is included in the needs assessment for income support for the first 16 weeks of a claim. Although the means-tested benefits received by all households in the bottom decile is

10% higher under the 1978/9 regime, it is 41% higher for households with mortgages.

3.5 Conclusions

The 1978/9 tax–benefit regime would raise slightly more revenue for the government than the 1996/7 regime. It would particularly disadvantage households with high incomes, especially better-off pensioner households. Put another way, policy changes since 1978/9 have resulted in small average gains for households, but have benefited high income households in particular. This is not a surprising conclusion, given that income tax rates have fallen dramatically in the period. For many households with incomes below those in the top decile, the impact of reductions in income taxes has been substantially offset by cuts in the value of tax relief on mortgage interest and by increases in National Insurance contributions and indirect taxes. Households at the bottom of the income distribution have benefited least. They have gained little from reductions in income tax but suffered particularly from large increases in indirect taxes. Within this group, households with children fare less badly than those without (child benefit has become more generous) and households with mortgages have fared worse than those without. The fact that these two groups overlap to a large extent is an illustration of how the net impact of the changes on any one household results from the combination of many effects.

Appendix 3.1 Policy in 1978/9 and 1996/7

The differences in policy regarding income tax, child benefit, NICs and indirect taxes that are simulated are summarised in Table 3.A1.1. The 1978/9 value of an allowance or threshold is given, this value indexed by prices to the 1996/7 level and the actual 1996/7 value. Chapter 5 explains more about the modelling of indirect tax changes and an appendix to Chapter 2 documents some of the issues facing the modelling of income tax using the Family Expenditure Survey. The change in local tax is simulated using a method described in Chapter 7.

The system of means-tested benefits was reformed in 1988 in such a way as to make comparison of the old and new systems more difficult. The main differences between the two regimes are not so much in the levels of benefits but in the rules qualifying claimants for each benefit, in the treatment of special and additional needs and in the rights to which benefit receipt provided an automatic passport (such as free school meals). These differences are summarised in Table 3.A1.2. Some of the main rates of payment for supplementary benefit, housing benefit and family income supplement under the 1978/9 regime, and income support, housing benefit and family credit under the 1996/7 regime are shown in Table 3.A1.3. For a wider discussion of the impact of the reforms see Evans *et al.* (1994).

Table 3.A1.1. *Policy in 1978/9 and 1996/7 (£s per year unless otherwise indicated)*

Income tax	1978/9	1978/9 indexed	1996/7
Personal allowances			
Single (SPA)	985	3,106	3,765
Married couple's	—	—	1,790 @ 15%
Married man's (inc. SPA)	1,535	4,841	—
Additional (lone parent)	550	1,734	1,790 @ 15%
Age allowance			
Single (lower)	1,300	4,100	4,910
Single (higher)	1,300	4,100	5,090
Married couple's (lower)	—	—	3,115
Married couple's (higher)	—	—	3,155
Married man's (lower)	2,075	6,543	—
Married man's (higher)	2,075	6,543	—
Income limit	4,000	12,614	15,200
Taper	0.667	0.667	0.5
Child tax allowance			
age 0–10	100	315	0
age 11–15	135	315	0
age 16 plus	165	426	0
Taxation of husband and wife	joint	joint	separate
Rates and thresholds			
Reduced rate	25%	25%	20%
Standard rate	33%	33%	24%
Reduced rate threshold	750	2,365	3,900
Standard rate threshold	8,000	25,227	25,500
Number of higher rates	9	9	1
Range of higher rates	40–83%	40–83%	40%
Investment income surcharge			
Lower rate	10%	10%	—
threshold: age<65	1,700	5,361	—
threshold: age 65+	2,500	7,884	—
Higher rate	15%	15%	—
threshold: age<65	2,250	7,095	—
threshold: age 65+	3,000	9,460	—
Mortgage interest relief			
method	claimable	claimable	MIRAS @ 15%
capital limit	25,000	78,837	30,000

Table 3.A1.1 (*cont.*)

	1978/9	1978/9 indexed	1996/7
Child benefit (£s per week)			
per child	2.30	7.25	8.80
Addition for first child	0.00	0.00	2.00
One parent benefit	1.00	3.15	6.30
National insurance contributions (£s per week)	1978/9	1978/9 indexed	1996/7
Class 1			
Lower earnings limit (LEL)	17.50	55.19	61.00
Rate below LEL	6.5%	6.5%	2.0%
Upper earnings limit (UEL)	120.00	378.42	455.00
Not-contracted out (NCO) rate	6.5%	6.5%	10.0%
Contracting out reduction	2.5%	2.5%	1.8%
Married women's rate	2.0%	2.0%	3.85%
Class 2			
Lower earnings exemption	18.27	57.61	65.96
Flat rate	1.90	5.73	6.05
Class 4			
Lower earnings limit	39.46	124.44	131.92
Upper earnings limit	120.00	378.42	455.00
Rate	5.0%	5.0%	6.0%
Value added tax and excise duties	1978/9	1978/9 indexed	1996/7
Value added tax			
Housing, motoring, household goods/services, take-away and take-away and restaurant food, adult clothing, other goods and services, motor fuels	8%	8%	17.5%
Leisure goods, personal goods and services, alcohol and tobacco	12.5%	12.5%	17.5%
Domestic fuel	0%	0%	8%

Table 3.A1.1 (*cont.*)

	1978/9	1978/9 indexed	1996/7
Excise duty			
Vehicle excise duty (per car)	£0.96	£3.03	£2.70
Beer (per 100 litres)	£10.65	£33.58	£40.03
Cider (per 100 litres)	£5.32	£16.78	£23.78
Fortified wine (per 100 litres)	£97.11	£306.24	£187.24
Non-fortified wine (per 100 litres)	£71.49	£225.44	£140.44
Spirits (per litre pure alcohol)	£10.44	£32.92	£19.78
Petrol (per litre)	£0.066	£0.208	£0.343
Diesel (per litre)	£0.077	£0.243	£0.343
Cigars (per kilogramme)	£20.93	£66.00	£91.52
Pipe tobacco (per kilogramme)	£16.08	£50.71	£40.24
Cigarettes (per 1,000)	£9.00	£28.38	£62.52
Ad valorem *duties*			
Cigarettes	30%	30%	20%
Pools betting	40%	40%	37.5%
Other betting	7.5%	7.5%	7.75%
Ad valorem tax on insurance premia	0%	0%	2.5%

Table 3.A1.2. *Main changes to means-tested benefits, 1978/9–1996/7*

- Fowler Reforms of 1988 replaced family income supplement with family credit, supplementary benefit with income support and reformed housing benefit so that it was aligned with income support. The new benefits depended on after-tax incomes and the income tests and allowances are aligned to create a more integrated system.

- Family credit in 1996/7 was more generous than family income supplement (FIS) was in 1978/9. Although the taper became steeper, the rates of benefit were substantially higher for people with children who had very low in-work incomes. Under family credit, someone in the family must work 16 hours or more and higher rates of benefit are payable for those working at least 30 hours. To qualify for FIS a single parent had to work at least 24 hours, whereas the threshold for a couple was 30 hours. In 1978/9 there was no differentiation by age for children. In 1996/7 the rate for an 18-year old was almost 3 times that of a 5-year old.

- Income support is not generally payable to people aged under 18 and reduced rates are payable to those aged under 25. Supplementary benefit on the other

Table 3.A1.2.(*cont.*)

hand had no such restrictions. There was far more discretion within the supplementary benefit system, with additions available for special or sudden needs. Within income support these have been replaced by loans, on the one hand, and premia for identifiable groups such as the elderly, families with children and the disabled, on the other.

- Income from investments was included in the income tests for housing benefit and FIS under the 1978/9 system, but for supplementary benefit a tariff income for savings and investments (at a rather high implied rate of interest) above a certain limit was assumed. Since the Fowler Reforms, a uniform system of tariff incomes has been imposed for housing benefit, family credit and income support. Capital tests were also introduced with the Fowler Reforms (none existed in 1978/9), so that people with capital or assets over a given amount (homes are not included) are not entitled to claim means-tested benefits. These capital tests particularly affect claimants of income support and housing benefit who are over pension age.

- In 1978/9 housing benefit was payable only to those not receiving supplementary benefit. The calculation for payments of rent and rate rebates used 60% of the respective payments as the starting point. In addition, there was a cash maximum to the level of rent that was supported. Supplementary benefit claimants received all their housing costs and domestic rates as part of their benefit. Income support claimants are also entitled to receive 100% of their rent costs and council tax bills. However, under the supplementary benefit system in 1978/9, mortgage interest was supported in full from the start of the claim, while in 1996/7, only half was paid in the first 16 weeks, after which it was also supported in full.

Table 3.A1.3. *Means-tested benefit rates, 1978/9 and 1996/7*

Housing benefit (HB) and supplementary benefit (SB) income support (IS) (£s per week)	1978/9	1978/9 updated to 1996/7	1996/7
SB needs allowances			
single householder, long-term rate	17.90	52.97	—
single householder	14.50	42.91	—
single non-householder, long-term rate	14.35	42.46	—
single non-householder	11.60	34.33	—
couple, long-term rate	28.35	83.89	—
couple	23.55	69.69	—
single person aged 16–17, long-term rate	8.90	26.34	—

Table 3.A1.3 (*cont.*)

Housing benefit (HB) and supplementary benefit (SB) income support (IS) (£s per week)	1978/9	1978/9 updated to 1996/7	1996/7
single person aged 16–17	8.90	26.34	—
extra for each dependent child aged 0–4	4.10	12.13	—
extra for each dependent child aged 5–10	4.95	14.65	—
extra for each dependent child aged 11–12	6.10	18.05	—
extra for each dependent child aged 13–15	7.40	21.90	—
extra for each dependent child aged 16–17	8.90	26.34	—
extra for each dependent child aged 18	11.60	34.33	—
extra for non-householder family	1.45	4.29	—
HB needs allowance			
single person	25.25	74.72	—
couple	36.25	107.27	—
lone parent	36.25	107.27	—
extra for each dependent child	6.10	18.05	—
extra for pensioner or pensioner couple	0.00	0.00	—
extra one disabled person	2.60	7.69	—
extra for couple where both are disabled	4.10	12.13	—
IS and HB personal allowances			
single person aged 16–17 (housing benefit only)	—	—	37.90
single person aged 18–24	—	—	37.90
single person aged 25+	—	—	47.90
lone parent aged 18+	—	—	47.90
lone parent aged under 18	—	—	28.85
couple one/both aged 18+	—	—	75.20
dependent children aged under 11	—	—	16.45
dependent children aged 11–15	—	—	24.10
dependent children aged 16–17	—	—	28.85
dependent children aged 18	—	—	37.90
IS and HB premia			
family	—	—	10.55
lone parent (housing/council tax benefit)	—	—	11.50
lone parent (income support)	—	—	5.20
single pensioner aged less than 75	—	—	19.15
pensioner couple aged less than 75	—	—	28.90
single pensioner aged 75–79	—	—	21.30
pensioner couple aged 75–79	—	—	31.90
single pensioner aged 80+	—	—	25.90

Table 3.A1.3 (*cont.*)

Housing benefit (HB) and supplementary benefit (SB) income support (IS) (£s per week)	1978/9	1978/9 updated to 1996/7	1996/7
pensioner couple aged 80+	—	—	37.05
single person with disability	—	—	20.40
couple with disability	—	—	29.15
single person with severe disability	—	—	36.40
couple with severe disability (one qualifies)	—	—	36.40
couple with severe disability (both qualify)	—	—	72.80
disabled child	—	—	20.40
carer (for one person)	—	—	13.00
carer (for both in couple)	—	—	26.00

Family income supplement/family credit (£s per week)	1978/9	1978/9 updated to 1996/7	1996/7
FIS prescribed amounts:			
adult	39.80	117.77	—
child aged 0–10	4.00	11.84	—
child aged 11–15	4.00	11.84	—
child aged 16–18	4.00	11.84	—
Maximum FIS:			
adult	8.50	25.25	—
child aged 0–10	1.00	2.96	—
child aged 11–15	1.00	2.96	—
child aged 16–18	1.00	2.96	—
FC applicable amount	—	—	75.20
FC adult credit	—	—	46.45
FC child credit:			
age 0–10	—	—	11.75
age 11–15	—	—	19.45
age 16–17	—	—	24.15
age 18	—	—	33.80
FC premium for working 30 hours or more	—	—	10.30
Capital limit £	0	0	8,000
Taper	50%	50%	70%
Minimum hours of work per week	30/24[a]	30/24[a]	16

Note: [a] 30 hours for people in couples, 24 hours for single parents.
Sources: Department of Social Security, 1992b; *Employment Gazette*, various issues, Table 6.1.

Notes

1 Similar techniques have been used to look at the pure policy effect of changes in personal tax between 1985 and 1995 (Giles and Johnson, 1994), tax and benefit policy in 1978 and 1988 (Johnson and Webb, 1992), the 1988 social security reforms (Evans *et al.*, 1994) and at tax and benefit policy in several regimes since 1978/9 (Redmond and Sutherland, 1995). Note that in this exercise, we assume that all expenditure remains constant, although the amount of indirect taxes paid as part of that expenditure changes according to the regime modelled. Chapter 5 discusses this assumption, and others that can be made with POLIMOD regarding expenditure, in more detail.
2 The choice of 1991 to act as our base population is to some extent arbitrary. Had this exercise been carried out on data describing some previous or later population it would have produced different results. Chapter 4 considers this issue in greater depth. The process of updating from 1991 to 1996/7 is described in the Appendix at the end of the book.
3 Income tax thresholds and allowances, National Insurance contributions, excise duties, local taxes and non-means-tested benefits are uprated from 1978/9 to 1996/7 levels according to the growth in retail prices between September 1977 and September 1995: a factor of 315.35%. Means-tested benefits are uprated according to growth in the ROSSI index, which removes the effect of housing price changes, over the same period (295.91%). The uprating process used in this analysis does not include the rounding conventions that have operated in practice.
4 Chapters 5 to 7 explain how, respectively, indirect taxes, employee National Insurance contribution regimes and local taxes are simulated in POLIMOD. Income tax rates and allowances, NIC rates, benefit rates and indirect tax rates in 1978/9 and 1996/7 are explained in Appendix 3.1.
5 National Insurance benefits and disability benefits are held fixed at 1996/7 levels. This is because the information recorded in the FES is not sufficiently detailed for the modelling of contribution conditions or disability status. Chapter 8 explores the extent to which the information that is available in the FES may potentially be used to impute receipt of retirement pension.
6 Throughout this study, weekly household money amounts are quoted to the nearest penny. This should not be taken to suggest that the results are significant to this level of precision. Pudney and Sutherland (1994) discuss the issue of statistical reliability in tax–benefit models.
7 Gross income is defined as income, before the deduction of taxes or the addition of child benefit, one parent benefit or means-tested benefits.
8 In some cases a household may have no income apart from means-tested benefits, and gross income will be computed to be zero. To avoid division by zero, tax burdens are calculated by computing mean gross income in each decile and dividing this into mean tax for the decile.
9 Measures include the removal of 16 and 17 year-olds from entitlement and increased importance of capital tests.

10 Note that households are ranked using the 1996/7 system. Households in the bottom decile who would have had larger means-tested benefit entitlements under the 1978/9 system may not have been in the bottom decile under that system. The issue of how the households are ranked is considered more fully in Chapter 4.

11 The three groups are not mutually exclusive: a household may be included under all definitions or under none.

4 Adjusting the focus: the role of modelling assumptions

4.1 Introduction

The conclusions of Chapter 3 rest on many different assumptions: some built into POLIMOD and some chosen as options for the particular exercise. Clearly, the assumptions we make are likely to have an impact on our results. The aim of this chapter is to form some judgements about the sensitivity of model results to particular assumptions. We focus on four sets of assumptions regarding uprating, equivalence scales, ranking of households and grossing up. The first three of these assumptions can be changed routinely and easily by the POLIMOD user. Changing the fourth assumption involved some special programming for this exercise.

First, we examine the effect of uprating policy parameters from 1978/9 by the change in prices rather than some other index. In section 4.2 we consider two alternative uprating methods. The first makes the assumption that it is taxes as a proportion of incomes which would remain unchanged in a neutral situation, rather than the real value of the taxes (and benefits). We achieve this by uprating tax allowances and benefit levels by growth in incomes. The second alternative is to examine a revenue-neutral change, where both the 1996/7 and 1978/9 regimes have the same net revenue effect. This allows us to focus entirely on the changes in structure that have taken place, leaving aside changes in the overall level of taxation.

Second, in section 4.3 we examine the sensitivity of our results to the choice of equivalence scale. We also consider the effect of weighting each household by the number of people in it, as in the Households Below Average Income (HBAI) analysis (Department of Social Security, 1995) rather than counting each household once, as in Chapter 3.

Third, in Chapter 3 we assessed the distributional effects of the tax and benefit regimes according to their impact on the income distribution. It can be argued that expenditure is a more appropriate ranking variable if one wants to focus on household welfare. In section 4.4 we explore what difference this third choice makes to our conclusions about distribution.

Finally, in section 4.5 we explore what effect the choice of a particular population database has on our results, by re-weighting the household microdata to capture some of the main demographic and economic differences between the 1990s and 1978/9. Section 4.6 concludes.

It is worth noting that only the first assumption – the updating of 1978/9 policy – could result in a change in any individual household's income. The fourth sensitivity test, using re-weighting, could result in the aggregate, population-level effect being different, while the second and third assumptions merely change the emphasis of the same results presented Chapter 3.

4.2 Uprating

In order to assess the relative effects of policy regimes from two different years on the same household database, it is necessary to adjust some of the policy parameters in one or both of the policy years, in order to make them comparable. However, there is no single way in which to achieve this comparability. Price indexation, as assumed in Chapter 3, approximates to what is conventionally considered to be 'neutral': raising tax allowances and benefit levels in line with inflation (for example, see Johnson and Webb, 1992). Between 1978 and 1996, prices increased by 215% (or a factor of 3.15).[1]

However, if earnings or other incomes rise faster than prices, fiscal drag reduces the value of allowances and benefits relative to incomes as a whole. An alternative to price indexation is therefore to index by the growth in incomes. To test the effect of this alternative we uprate 1978/9 policy parameters by the growth in per capita GDP as a proxy for growth in incomes over the period. Between 1978 and 1996 this rose by 332%.[2]

The main focus of Chapter 3 is on the distributional effect of policy changes. For a package of changes that is not revenue-neutral it is somewhat problematic to evaluate the full distributional effect. We do not capture the effect of the revenue short-fall or excess in distributional terms. This drawback is avoided if we focus on the changes in *structure* that took place over the period 1978/9 to 1996/7 and calibrate the uprating factor to produce the same net revenue in both policy years. This is achieved if the amount of tax paid by the household sector, less the amount of benefits received, is the same under both 1996/7 and 1978/9 regimes. An uprating factor of 251% achieves this effect.

Table 4.1 provides some illustrations of 1978/9 policy parameters uprated by the three alternative indices.

Table 4.2 compares the overall impact of the 1978/9 tax–benefit regime on average taxes net of benefits paid by households under the three uprating assumptions. In comparison with price uprating, adjusting by income

Table 4.1. *Illustrative uprating of some key 1978/9 policy parameters to 1996/7*

	1978/9	Price uprating RPI (ROSSI)[a]	Income uprating per capita GDP	Revenue-neutral
Uprating factor	—	3.15 (2.96)	4.32	3.51
Child benefit (£s per week)	2.30	7.25	9.94	8.07
Income tax single personal allowance (£s per year)	985	3,106	4,255	3,457
Income tax 40% band threshold (£s per year)	8,000	25,227	34,560	28,080
NICs lower earnings limit (£s per week)	17.50	55.19	75.60	61.43
Mortgage interest relief capital limit (£s)	25,000	78,837	108,000	87,750
Single householder long-term supplementary benefit (£s per week)	17.90	52.98	77.33	62.83

Note: [a] The ROSSI index excludes the effect of housing and is used to uprate means-tested benefits under price uprating.

growth since 1978/9 raises less income tax, although still more than the 1996/7 system. This is to be expected, since tax allowances and thresholds are increased by more under income uprating, reducing the tax base. Furthermore, benefit levels are also increased by more, reflected in the substantially greater average benefit payments under income uprating. With price uprating, average child benefit is lower than in 1996/7 by 28%, whereas child benefit nearly reaches its 1996/7 level under income uprating. Means-tested benefits are at similar levels in the two policy regimes under price uprating but are inflated to 167% of their 1996/7 levels under income uprating. Other taxes are each slightly higher under income uprating. Overall, compared with the 1996/7 regime, the aggregate effect of the 1978/9 regime uprated by income growth is an average gain of almost £13 per household, compared with a £7 loss under the price uprating assumption.

Table 4.2 also shows that the impact on average taxes paid and benefits received by households, if we assume revenue neutral uprating, is somewhere between that of price and income uprating. However, the shift in

Table 4.2. *Average household taxes and benefits, 1996/7 and 1978/9 regimes* *(£s per week)*

Policy regime	Income tax	NICs	Local taxes	Indirect taxes	Child benefit	Means-tested benefits	Total taxes *less* benefits
1996/7	59.05	18.25	9.43	44.75	5.67	14.66	111.15
1978/9							
Price uprating	83.42	12.57	8.24	32.56	4.07	14.53	118.19
Income uprating	68.02	13.70	11.16	35.39	5.58	24.46	98.24
Revenue-neutral uprating	78.14	13.01	9.16	33.51	4.53	18.16	111.12

balance between the 1978/9 and 1996/7 regimes from income tax to NICs and to indirect tax, and the reduction in generosity of means-tested benefits observed under prices uprating in Chapter 3, remain evident.

Table 4.3 compares the distributional impact of a switch to the 1978/9 regime uprated by the three alternative methods. Compared with price uprating, the income uprating method makes the earlier regime look substantially more generous. This is particularly so for the bottom decile which on average is better off by 42% of 1996/7 incomes, compared with 14% under price uprating. This is not surprising, since we have seen that income uprating particularly inflates means-tested benefits. Focusing on the structural differences between the 1996/7 and 1978/9 systems, the final column of Table 4.3 shows that the effect of revenue-neutral uprating is again intermediate between those of price and income uprating.

Figures 4.1, 4.2 and 4.3 decompose the percentage income changes shown in Table 4.3 into the main elements of the tax–benefit system. Each is drawn to the same scale. The segments on each bar represent the contribution of each element of the system to the change in average incomes for each decile group. Segments below the axis indicate changes that reduce average incomes, and those above represent changes that increase them.[3] It shows that under the price uprating assumption, the reduction in indirect taxes contributes most towards the gains of the households in the bottom half of the distribution, while the increase in income taxes contributes most towards the losses occurring in the top half. Under the income uprating assumption, however, the contributions of indirect taxes and income tax to household gains and losses are actually reduced, while the contribution of means-tested benefits is increased enor-

Table 4.3. *Switching from the 1996/7 to the 1978/9 policy regime: comparison of uprating methods (percentage changes in household incomes)*

Decile of equivalent household income	Mean weekly equivalised net income	Percentage gain		
		Price uprating	Income uprating	Revenue-neutral uprating
Bottom	£42.33	14	42	25
2nd	£71.16	3	25	11
3rd	£87.59	2	18	8
4th	£102.97	1	14	6
5th	£122.26	2	9	4
6th	£145.54	0	6	2
7th	£172.66	0	4	1
8th	£209.36	0	3	1
9th	£262.12	−1	2	0
Top	£453.74	−12	−7	−10

mously (Figure 4.2). Households in the bottom decile receive about 35% more in means-tested benefits, while households in the second decile receive around 20% more. Increases in means-tested benefits continue noticeably to advantage households right up to the 7th decile. On the other hand, losses experienced as a result of increased income taxes are only noticeable in the top three deciles and, interestingly, the bottom decile. The picture shown in Figure 4.3, where revenue-neutral uprating is assumed, looks more like that in Figure 4.1, except that households in the bottom half of the distribution gain more as a result of increases in means-tested benefits. Average income tax payments are also slightly reduced in all decile groups.

Our conclusions about the distributional effect of policy changes over time are clearly dependent on the methods used to uprate policy parameters from the earlier year. Income tax and social security benefits are the parts of the system most sensitive to uprating assumptions. The greater the uprating factor, the more progressive the earlier system appears. Uprating of means-tested benefits will always have a considerable proportional impact on the incomes of those who receive them simply because they can constitute 100% of income, while this will never be the case with income taxes. Apart from the means-tested benefit effect, however, results depend on the specific income tax structure. The 1978/9 tax schedule contained many bands and was relatively progressive. The thresholds and personal allowances have been indexed by 117 percentage points more under

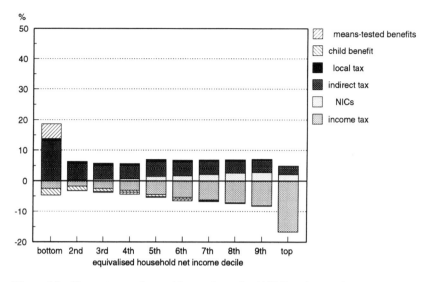

Figure 4.1   Percentage gains and losses from the 1978/9 regime: price uprating

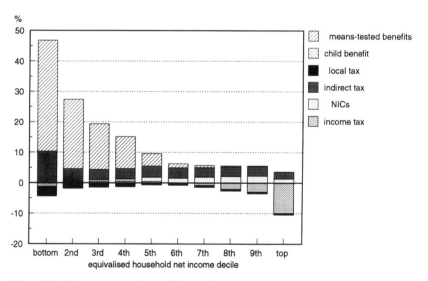

Figure 4.2   Percentage gains and losses from the 1978/9 regime: income uprating

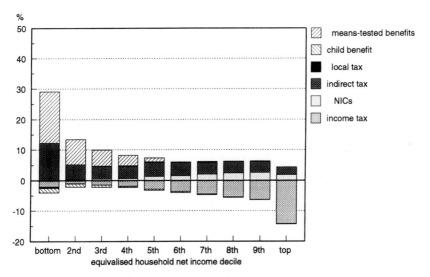

Figure 4.3 Percentage gains and losses from the 1978/9 regime: revenue-neutral uprating

income uprating than under price uprating. This has the effect of increasing post-tax incomes of lower income households by proportionately *more* than for high income households, in spite of the widening of the higher rate bands.

4.3 Adjusting for household size and composition

The analysis in Chapter 3 adjusts household incomes by an equivalence scale so that households are ranked by an income measure that takes relative household needs and economies of scale into account. The scale that is used (referred to here as the 'default' scale) is a simple one in which additional adults in the household are given a weight of 0.6 times that for a single person and each child is given a weight of 0.4 times the first adult. The analysis also counts each equivalised household income once, regardless of how many people live in the household. Here we consider the effect of some different assumptions.

First, we examine the effect of weighting each equivalised household income by the number of people in the household. Thus each *individual* has as much effect as every other individual on the income distribution (and hence small households have less weight than large ones). The assumption used in Chapter 3 is that each *household* is as important as

Table 4.4. *Switching from the 1996/7 to the 1978/9 policy regime: household and individual weighting (percentage changes in household incomes)*

Decile of household equivalised income	Households counted once	Individuals counted once
Bottom	14	10
2nd	3	2
3rd	2	2
4th	1	2
5th	2	2
6th	0	1
7th	0	1
8th	0	0
9th	−1	−1
Top	−12	−12

every other household: individuals in small households have higher weights than individuals in large households.[4]

Table 4.4 shows the effect on our standard distributional results of weighting each household by the number of people in it. Compared to the default scale where households are counted once, gains at the bottom of the income distribution are smaller, gains in the middle are slightly higher and losses at the top are slightly smaller. This suggests that it tends to be small households at the bottom of the income distribution who gain most from the switch to the 1978/9 regime – single person households in the bottom decile experience an average gain of 20%, while households with four or more persons experience gains of only 4% if households are ranked according to the 'default' scale. Larger households are also the biggest losers at the top of the distribution. Households with four or more persons in the top decile experience an average decrease in income of 15% as a result of the switch to 1978/9 policies, while single person households in the top decile see their incomes decline by 8%.

Second, we explore the effect of using other equivalence scales. The McClements (1977) scale assumes smaller economies of scale for second and subsequent adults and older children in the household (and hence gives a greater weight in the equivalence scale to these people). Younger and mid-age children are given a lower weight. Also considered are two extreme scales: the scale which treats each household as an equivalent unit and does not account for differences in composition (the 'null' scale) and a 'per capita' scale which assumes no economies of scale and weights each

Table 4.5. *Switching from the 1996/7 to the 1978/9 policy regime using different equivalence scales (percentage changes in incomes of households with children)*

Decile of household equivalised income	Equivalised percentage income gains			
	Default scale	McClements scale	'Null' scale	Per capita scale
Bottom	4	4	22	2
2nd	1	1	0	2
3rd	2	1	0	3
4th	3	2	0	2
5th	3	2	2	2
6th	1	2	2	1
7th	2	1	2	1
8th	1	1	2	1
9th	−1	−1	1	−5
Top	−12	−11	−7	−19

individual in the household by the same amount. Appendix 4.1 summarises the equivalence scales used and illustrates their effect by calculating the scales for some example households.[5]

In order to illustrate the effects of the different scales we focus on households with dependent children. Table 4.5 shows the average gain from switching to the 1978/9 policy regime for households with children. The decile ranges are those calculated for the population as a whole (as in Table 4.3): the figures provided are for the mean effect on households with children within those deciles. Table 4.6 shows the percentage of households with children in each decile of the all-household distribution using the four equivalence scales. There are more households with children in the lower deciles using the default scale compared with the McClements scale, reflecting the higher weight given to children on average in the default scale. However, under the 'null' scale which applies no adjustment to household income, the proportion of households with children in the bottom decile is very small: 4%. The large gains in income that these households experience as a result of the switch to 1978/9 policies arise from two particular policy elements that are very much related to household size, taxes on expenditure (larger households are likely to spend more) and means-tested benefits (nearly all means-tested benefits are calibrated according to the number and ages of children in the household).

On the other hand, under the per capita scale, where all household

Table 4.6. *Distribution of households with children within the overall 1996/7 income distribution using various equivalence scales*

Decile of household equivalised income	Percentage of households with children			
	Default scale	McClements scale	'Null' scale	Per capita scale
Bottom	13	12	4	21
2nd	12	11	4	17
3rd	11	11	9	12
4th	10	10	10	13
5th	13	12	11	9
6th	12	12	12	8
7th	9	10	14	8
8th	9	10	13	6
9th	7	6	11	4
Top	5	6	13	2
Total	100	100	100	100

members are weighted equally, the proportion of households with children in the bottom decile is very large (22%) and the proportion in the top decile is very small (2%). Gains in the bottom decile are on average relatively small. This is because many of these households pay income tax, which increases as a result of the switch to the 1978/9 regime and because their child benefits are lower.

Although the two extreme scales tell different stories about the relative impact of the two policy regimes on households with children, our main conclusions remain the same. A switch to 1978/9 policies results in gains at the bottom of the distribution, small gains in the middle and losses at the top. The two more central scales, our simple default scale and the McClements scale, give results that are similar but not identical to each other. This suggests that in the analysis of the distributional effects of policy change, results are not generally highly sensitive to the choice between commonly used scales, although the use of no equivalence scale or a per capita measure will result in a more extreme distributional effect. A sensible approach to the use of equivalence scales will always involve some sensitivity testing. However, it appears to be less important in the present analysis, which assumes a fixed population, than in one which compares different populations (across countries or over time, for example).

Income	Expenditure										Total
	bottom	2nd	3rd	4th	5th	6th	7th	8th	9th	top	
bottom	2.4	1.8	1.3	1.2	0.8	0.7	0.4	0.4	0.4	0.5	10.0
2nd	3.0	2.1	1.6	1.1	0.7	0.5	0.2	0.3	0.3	0.1	10.0
3rd	1.7	2.2	1.6	1.5	0.9	0.7	0.6	0.4	0.3	0.2	10.0
4th	1.3	1.4	1.7	1.5	1.2	1.1	0.7	0.6	0.4	0.2	10.0
5th	0.6	0.9	1.3	1.2	1.6	1.3	1.1	0.9	0.6	0.5	10.0
6th	0.3	0.5	0.8	1.3	1.3	1.5	1.6	1.3	0.9	0.6	10.0
7th	0.3	0.4	0.7	0.8	1.3	1.3	1.5	1.6	1.3	0.8	10.0
8th	0.2	0.3	0.4	0.6	1.1	1.2	1.7	1.5	1.7	1.4	10.0
9th	0.1	0.3	0.3	0.4	0.6	1.2	1.4	1.7	2.0	2.0	10.0
top	0.2	0.1	0.2	0.3	0.5	0.6	1.0	1.3	2.1	3.7	10.0
Total	10.0	10.0	10.0	10.0	10.0	10.0	10.0	10.0	10.0	10.0	100

Figure 4.4 Household income deciles by household expenditure deciles (%)

4.4 Ranking by expenditure

Goodman and Webb (1995) argue that most statistics about living standards in the UK have focused on the measurement of income. In this analysis, too, we have concentrated on measuring the impact of alternative policy regimes on the household income distribution. But as Goodman and Webb point out, income is not the only measure that could be used to capture the standard of living. How much a household spends on goods and services can also provide a measure of well-being, and therefore provides an alternative way of ranking households while analysing the impact of policy changes on their incomes.

Furthermore, Figure 3.2(c) in Chapter 3 shows that the bottom income decile contains households who have high VAT burdens because of their high levels of expenditure. This suggests that income may not be the most appropriate measure by which to rank households when analysing taxes on expenditure. The two alternative ranking measures, household income and household expenditure, are compared in Figure 4.4 which shows the distribution of income decile by expenditure decile. There is clearly a strong positive relationship between the two measures: half of all house-

Table 4.7. *Switching from the 1996/7 to the 1978/9 policy regime: ranking by expenditure (percentage changes in household incomes)*

Decile of household equivalised expenditure	Mean weekly equivalised income	Cash net income gain	Equivalised percentage income gain
Bottom	£90.56	−£3.08	−2
2nd	£101.30	−£1.85	−2
3rd	£112.97	−£0.96	−1
4th	£126.52	−£0.87	−1
5th	£158.77	−£12.62	−5
6th	£163.00	−£2.94	−1
7th	£185.86	−£3.89	−1
8th	£198.93	−£2.38	−1
9th	£228.88	−£7.07	−2
Top	£302.94	−£34.77	−7

holds are in identical or adjacent deciles under the two measures (shaded boxes on Figure 4.4). However, 15% of households with income in the top two deciles are in the bottom half of the expenditure distribution and 18% of the top two deciles of the expenditure distribution are in the bottom half in terms of incomes.

Table 4.7 shows average (equivalised) household incomes, in decile groups of (equivalised) household expenditure. This confirms that there is indeed a clear positive general relationship between household income and household expenditure: mean incomes rise in each decile all the way up the expenditure distribution. The third column shows the average net income gain as a result of the change in policy regime, and the fourth column shows the average percentage change in income in each decile of expenditure. This table can be compared with Table 3.2 in Chapter 3, which shows similar information for decile groups of the income distribution. The actual calculations for each household are the same as they are in Chapter 3: the households are simply arranged in a different order. Nonetheless, the two tables would lead us to make quite different conclusions about the relative impact of the regime that we model. Most notably, instead of a progression from gain to loss, moving up the deciles, *all* decile groups are worse off on average. The *number* of households gaining and losing is the same as when ranked by income (52% gain, and 48% lose), but the *distribution* of gainers and losers has changed. The size of the loss is largest in the top decile both in absolute terms and as a percentage of initial income.

Apart from this, there is no clear shape to this distribution of income change.

A notable feature of Table 4.7 is the bulge in the fifth decile, where average losses are £12.62 per week in cash terms (compared with £0.87 in the fourth decile and £2.94 in the sixth decile). This is explained by a small number of households with expenditure levels around the median on an equivalised basis but with very high incomes. These incomes, when subject to the 1978/9 income tax regime, attract high tax and result in large losses for the households concerned. This phenomenon is illustrated graphically in Figure 4.5(a) where income tax burdens under the two policy regimes are plotted across the distribution of household expenditure. The bulge is evident in the fifth decile under both regimes and is particularly prominent under the 1978/9 regime when tax rates on large incomes are substantially higher.

Figure 4.5(a) is similar to Figure 3.2(a) in Chapter 3, except for the ranking method used, and shows that income taxes (on their own and net of child benefit) are still largely progressive over the expenditure distribution, although not as progressive as they appear over the income distribution. Our general conclusions from Chapter 3 are generally unchanged: the 1978/9 system imposes higher taxes than the 1996/7 system at all income levels, both before and after child benefit is netted off, and the 1978/9 system is more progressive than the 1996/7 system.

Figure 4.5(b) charts the decreased burden of indirect tax across the expenditure distribution as a result of the switch from 1996/7 to the 1978/9 regime. As anticipated in Chapter 3, the distribution of indirect taxes by expenditure is very different from their distribution by income. While indirect taxes are very regressive when plotted on the income distribution (Figure 3.2(c) in Chapter 3) they appear neutral, or even mildly progressive if plotted on the expenditure distribution. Moreover, while indirect taxes, plotted on the income distribution, appear to be more regressive under the 1996/7 regime than those under the 1978/9 regime, the opposite is the case if they are plotted on the expenditure distribution.

Figure 4.5(c) shows the aggregate effect for income tax, indirect taxes, NICs and local taxes together (net of child benefit). In Chapter 3, we found that tax burdens were lower for all except the top two income deciles under the 1978/9 regime and that the progression of taxes across the income distribution was steeper under the 1978/9 regime than was the case under the 1996/7 regime (see Figure 3.2(d)). Plotting tax burdens across the expenditure distribution produces a different picture. First, in all expenditure deciles, tax burdens under the 1978/9 regime are the same or higher than under the 1996/7 regime. Second, while the 1978/9 regime

(a) Income tax and child benefit (CB) as a percentage of gross household income

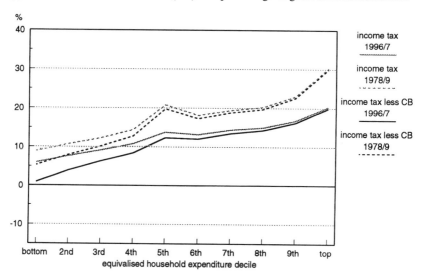

(b) Indirect tax as a percentage of gross household income

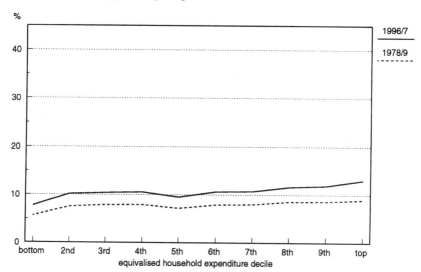

Figure 4.5   Tax burdens

(c) Total tax as a percentage of gross household income

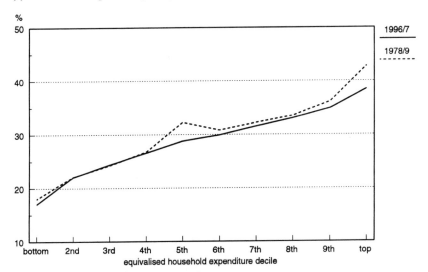

looks more progressive than the 1996/7 regime at the very top of the expenditure distribution, it looks less progressive at the very bottom.

Clearly, the choice of ranking measure has a major impact on distributional results. In particular, the distribution of a quantity dependent on income (such as income tax) across expenditure, and a quantity dependent on expenditure (such as indirect tax) across income will each present apparent anomalies. The choice of a single measure with which to rank households when considering a package that contains changes that are directly associated with both income and expenditure is indeed a problem. However, it is important to remember that neither measure used here is ideal: both are subject to measurement problems of their own (see Chapters 10, 11 and 12). Furthermore, neither measure adequately captures such aspects as saving, dis-saving, inter-household sharing, income packaging, household production or the consumption of goods in kind. Variations in each of these may be just as important as variations in the imperfect measures we use in determining differences in household well-being. The existence of off-diagonal cases in Figure 4.4 is simply confirmation of this, not evidence that one or other measure is superior. The development of improved concepts by which to rank households when evaluating public policy is a matter for further work.[6] However, the practical implementation of these concepts also requires that appropriate data are available to measure them.

Table 4.8. *Average household taxes and benefits, 1996/7 and 1978/9 regimes: variation in base population (£s per week)*

Policy regime	Income tax	NICs	Local taxes	Indirect taxes	Child benefit	Means-tested benefits	Total taxes *less* benefits
	Base population as in 1991						
1996/7	59.05	18.25	9.43	44.75	5.67	14.66	111.15
1978/9	83.42	12.57	8.24	32.56	4.07	14.53	118.19
	Base population re-weighted to 1978						
1996/7	59.28	19.80	9.54	47.25	6.95	15.17	113.77
1978/9	83.99	13.93	8.18	34.71	5.04	14.73	121.04

4.5 An alternative base population

Significant changes in the economic and demographic characteristics of the UK population have occurred since 1978. Some of these changes may have been influenced by policy developments themselves; others have certainly been independent of them. We have carried out simulations based on 1991 data re-weighted to reflect the 1991 distribution of households across different age and family groups, and updated to 1996/7 prices and incomes (see Appendix to the book). Here we test whether this choice of underlying population has any impact on our conclusions about the relative distributional effects of the two regimes. To do this we re-weight the 1991 household microdata to align them with aggregate indicators taken from the report of the 1978 Family Expenditure Survey (FES) (Department of Employment, 1979). The aim is to approximate to the 1978 household population, as represented by the FES of that year. The weights used to correct the 1991 survey for differential non-response are replaced by weights which take account of three characteristics: family composition, housing tenure and economic activity. The new weights are calculated simultaneously using the method described in Atkinson, Gomulka and Sutherland (1988) and Gomulka (1992).[7] In 1978 there were substantially more families with children, although fewer single parents. There were also fewer older elderly, fewer owner-occupiers and more tenants, particularly council tenants, as well as more male employees and fewer unemployed.

Table 4.8 shows that the synthetic '1978' population that we simulate would have raised slightly more income tax and NICs than the 1991 population under both policy regimes, not surprisingly since employment

Table 4.9. *Switching from the 1996/7 to the 1978/9 policy regime:*
alternative base populations (percentage changes in household incomes)

	Percentage gain	
Decile of household equivalised net income	1991 base population	1978 family composition housing tenure and employment
Bottom	14	9
2nd	3	2
3rd	2	2
4th	1	1
5th	2	1
6th	0	0
7th	0	0
8th	0	−1
9th	−1	−1
Top	−12	−11

was higher in the earlier year. Indirect taxes are higher as a result of higher employment and hence higher consumption. Child benefit is also higher, reflecting the larger numbers of families with children in 1978. The differences between amounts of total taxes collected less benefits paid under the two policy regimes are not large if we assume different population bases, although the level of taxes-less-benefits under both regimes is somewhat higher if the population base is re-weighted to 1978.

While the difference between total taxes-less-benefits under the two regimes is not greatly affected by the population base, the distributional effect of the switch in regime, shown in Table 4.9, is altered. The average percentage gain in the bottom decile is smaller by about a third and average gains are smaller (or losses larger) most of the way up the distribution. This is explained by the re-weighting causing some composition changes within the deciles: the bottom decile contains fewer lone parents, fewer low-income home owners and fewer elderly, for example.

This exercise can only approximate to the actual changes that took place to the household population in the 1980s and early 1990s. Indeed, the procedure we use to calculate the weights may be introducing distortions in the distributions of relevant characteristics that we cannot control, such as the number of earners in each household. However, it does suggest that the choice of population in a policy comparison exercise has an effect on results, but probably not a dramatic one. The shapes of the two alternative distributions of gain and loss in Table 4.9 remain very similar. At the same time, certain details may be sensitive to the choice of population base. Exercises focusing on groups that have changed in size, such as lone parents, low-income owner occupiers or dual-earner couples, would need to choose a population base that adequately represented the characteristics of these groups in the period of interest.

4.6 Conclusions

In considering the main areas where modelling assumptions can have an effect on the conclusions drawn about the relative impact of different policy regimes, two aspects stand out. The first is the way in which households are ranked in the distributional analysis. We have shown that this can have a significant effect on the composition of quantile groups, and hence on the patterns of gain and loss. The choice of concept used to rank households (income or expenditure, for example) needs to take account both of the specific application of the ranking – what is it that is of interest in relation to distribution – and of the limitations of the available measures used for ranking. Adjustments to the ranking measure, and the weights applied to the units for whom it is measured, have a noticeable impact on the analysis presented here, but not one that would cause us to change our conclusions in Chapter 3. They may be of greater importance in comparative studies where the characteristics of the population vary, as well as the policy regime they face.

The second important aspect is more specific to the type of analysis in Chapter 3: the need to uprate policy from a previous regime to make it comparable with the current regime. The choice of uprating factor affects the revenue and distributional estimates. Furthermore, it operates in a different way for each element of the tax–benefit system, depending on its structure. An analysis which compares the effect of uprating assumptions is able to illuminate the operation of fiscal drag and to highlight the importance of this to any assessment of the relative performance of different policy regimes.

Appendix 4.1 Summary of alternative equivalence scales

Table 4.A1.1. *Summary of alternative equivalence scales*

Household member	Default scale	McClements scale	'Null' scale	Per capita scale
Head of household	1.0	1.00	1.0	1.0
Spouse of head	0.6	0.64	0	1.0
Other second adult	0.6	0.75	0	1.0
Third adult	0.6	0.69	0	1.0
Subsequent adults	0.6	0.59	0	1.0
Dependant aged 0–1	0.4	0.15	0	1.0
Dependant aged 2–4	0.4	0.30	0	1.0
Dependant aged 5–7	0.4	0.34	0	1.0
Dependant aged 8–10	0.4	0.38	0	1.0
Dependant aged 11–12	0.4	0.41	0	1.0
Dependant aged 13–15	0.4	0.44	0	1.0
Dependant aged 16–18	0.4	0.59	0	1.0
Scales for some example households				
Single person	1.0	1.00	1.0	1.0
Couple with no children	1.6	1.64	1.0	2.0
Couple with two children aged 3 and 6	2.4	2.28	1.0	4.0
Couple with four children aged 3, 6, 9 and 12	3.2	3.07	1.0	6.0

Appendix 4.2 Family composition, housing tenure and employment activity in 1991 and 1978

Table 4.A2.1. *Family composition in 1991 and 1978*

Family composition	1991 number of families (000s)	1991 per cent of all families	1978 number of families (000s)	1978 per cent of all families	Ratio 1978 to 1991
Couple, 0 children	6,254	21.32	5,279	19.52	0.92
Couple, 1 child	2,228	7.60	2,325	8.59	1.13
Couple, 2 children	2,399	8.18	2,791	10.32	1.26
Couple, 3+ children	996	3.40	1,203	4.45	1.31
Pensioner couple aged 65–74	1,798	6.13	1,747	6.46	1.05
Pensioner couple aged 75+	845	2.88	521	1.93	0.67
Single male aged 0–29	3,646	12.43	3,165	11.70	0.94
Single male aged 30–54	1,573	5.36	1,339	4.95	0.92
Single male aged 55–64	437	1.49	419	1.55	1.04
Single female aged 0–19	744	2.54	1,162	4.30	1.69
Single female aged 20–39	1,709	5.83	1,228	4.54	0.78
Single female aged 40–59	933	3.18	930	3.44	1.08
Single male with children	118	0.40	97	0.36	0.90
Single female with children	1,205	4.11	733	2.71	0.66
Single male aged 65+	905	3.09	763	2.82	0.91
Single female aged 60–74	1,738	5.93	1,995	7.38	1.24
Single female aged 75+	1,806	6.16	1,354	5.01	0.81
Total families	29,332	100.00	27,051	100.00	1.00

Source: The family totals for 1991 listed in the above table are the same as those used by the DSS to gross up the FES for the series *Households Below Average Income* (see Department of Social Security, 1993b). Family totals for 1978 were also derived by the DSS, although not used in this series. The authors are grateful to Steven Webb of the University of Bath, who supplied the population estimates.

Table 4.A2.2. *Housing tenure in 1991 and 1978*

Tenure	1991 number of households (000s)	1991 per cent of all households	1978 number of households (000s)	1978 per cent of all households	Ratio 1978 to 1991
Local authority	5,011	21.44	6,581	33.44	1.56
Other rented	2,747	11.75	2,896	14.71	1.25
Owned with mortgage	9,927	42.48	6,025	30.61	0.72
Owned outright	5,686	24.33	4,180	21.24	0.87
Total households	23,371	100.00	19,682	100.00	1.00

Source: 1991 FES; housing tenure composition weights for 1978 are derived from Department of Employment (1979) Table 1.

Table 4.A2.3. *Economic activity in 1991 and 1978*

Economic activity	1991 number of persons (000s)	1991 per cent of all persons	1978 number of persons (000s)	1991 per cent of all persons	Ratio 1978 to 1991
Male employee at work	11,731	20.84	13,179	24.39	1.17
Female employee at work	10,615	18.86	9,710	17.97	0.95
Unemployed person	2,117	3.76	1,237	2.29	0.61
Other	31,817	56.53	29,916	55.36	0.98
Total persons	56,280	100.00	54,042	100.00	1.00

Source: 1991 FES; housing tenure composition weights for 1978 are derived from Department of Employment (1979) Table 2.

Notes

1 That is, growth in the All-Items Retail Prices Index was 215%. In accordance with official practice, means-tested benefits are uprated by the ROSSI index which excludes the effect of price changes related to housing. Over the period we consider the ROSSI index rose by 196% (Department of Social Security, 1996).

2 Source for per capita GDP growth: *Economic Trends*. Growth in per capita GDP is one of a range of measures that could be used as an indicator of the growth in incomes over the period considered, and is chosen because it is at the generous end of the scale of possibilities. For example, if we were to derive an index from growth in reported gross incomes in the Family Expenditure Survey between 1978 and 1996, it would increase by 281% (see Department of Employment, 1979 and Central Statistical Office, 1996).

3 Figure 4.1 is identical to Figure 3.3 in Chapter 3, except that it is drawn to a different scale.

4 The weights applied to each household to account for household size differences are distinct from the application of the equivalence scale. They are also distinct from any weights applied to each household to bring the sample up to population levels, or to adjust for differential non-response. It should be noted that weighting each household by the number of people in it does not depart from the assumption that household income is shared and each person within the household is assumed to benefit equally from aggregate household income.

5 Coulter, Cowell and Jenkins (1992) show that there is a systematic relationship between equivalence scale generosity and the extent of inequality and poverty: for a given income distribution, the extent of equivalent income inequality and poverty first falls, and then rises, as relativities are increased from their minimum level, where households are counted once to a theoretical maximum where all individuals are counted once.

6 Mercader-Prats (1995) considers a hybrid measure for use in the analysis of poverty.

7 Weights are calculated using software written by Joanna Gomulka of the London School of Economics. Appendix 4.2 shows the categories used and the numbers of units in the 1991 data in each category as derived from the 1978 FES (Department of Employment, 1979).

Part Three

Model construction: data and methods

5   Indirect taxes

5.1 Introduction

Indirect taxes affect the amount of income that is available for consumption, and therefore, the general level of welfare.[1] The loss that results from an increase in indirect taxes can best be understood in the context of a general tax–benefit model such as POLIMOD as additional tax paid, and can be added to the effect on household incomes of changes in direct taxes and cash benefits.

Sections 5.2 and 5.3 explain how liabilities for VAT and excise duties are calculated in POLIMOD under two extreme assumptions about the behaviour of individual consumers in response to changes in indirect taxes. The first assumption is that the quantity of a good purchased remains constant: households spend more if the tax goes up, and less if it decreases. The second assumption is that the amount households spend on the good in question remains constant: less is bought if the tax increases and more if it falls.[2] POLIMOD does not model cross-price elasticities: a change in the price or the expenditure on one good is assumed not to affect expenditure on other goods. This simple approach is adopted because it is transparent, and permits the modelling of changes at a highly disaggregate level. Some 50 expenditure variables are used (see the Appendix at the end of the book, section A.7). Section 5.4 draws out the implications of the two behavioural assumptions using numerical examples as illustrations, and section 5.5 explores a further option which assumes that any change in tax is absorbed by retailers. Section 5.6 concludes.

5.2 Calculation of VAT

Constant quantity

Under the constant quantity assumption, expenditure E on a given good will change if the taxes levied on that good change. Let us call expenditure under the 'old' policy regime E_b, and under the 'new' policy regime E_a. Given an 'old' VAT rate R_b, the 'old' amount of VAT V_b paid can be calculated as:

$$V_b = E_b R_b/(1+R_b)$$

That is, if expenditure E_b on a good is £11.00 including VAT, and the VAT rate R_b is 10% (or 0.1), then the amount of VAT paid V_b is

$$V_b = (11.00 \times 0.1)/(1+0.1) = 1.00$$

If, however, we propose a new VAT rate for the good, then we must calculate the new amount of VAT paid V_a, on the good

$$V_a = E_b R_a/(1+R_b)$$

where E_b is the old expenditure, R_b is the old VAT rate and R_a is the new VAT rate. Given $E_b = 11.00$, $R_b = 0.1$ and $R_a = 0.2$, V_a is:

$$V_a = (11.00 \times 0.2)/(1+0.1) = 2.00$$

We can also calculate new expenditure E_a, on the good:

$$E_a = V_a + E_b - V_b$$

Using the same example as above:

$$E_a = 2.00 + 11.00 - 1.00 = 12.00$$

That is, in order to maintain constant quantities purchased when VAT increases from 10% to 20%, expenditure on the good increases from £11.00 to £12.00.

Constant expenditure

Under the constant expenditure assumption, E will remain the same regardless of changes in VAT. VAT paid under the old regime V_b is calculated as:

$$V_b = ER_b/(1+R_b)$$

Using the same example as for constant quantity:

$$V_b = (11.00 \times 0.1)/(1+0.1) = 1.00$$

Under the new regime, VAT paid is calculated as:

$$V_a = ER_a/(1+R_a)$$
$$V_a = (11.00 \times 0.2)/(1+0.2) = 1.8333$$

5.3 Calculation of excise duties

There can be three elements of indirect tax on goods which attract excise duty: a flat rate or *specific* excise duty imposed on a quantity of the good (for example on a litre of petrol), an *ad valorem* excise duty imposed as a percentage of the retail price of a good, and VAT. In order to calculate the duty, we need to know retail prices per unit for goods that attract excise duties. When flat rate excise duties change, we have to make an assumption about how the retail price per unit of the product will be affected. In POLIMOD, we assume that prices change only to the extent that taxes increase.

Unit prices for goods that attract excise duties are obtained mostly from official sources, such as HM Customs and Excise (1996). It is worth noting, however, that prices for many goods that attract excise duties vary greatly from region to region, as well as from product to product. Moreover, with alcohol, the actual alcoholic strength of the product as well as its classification (beer, cider, fortified wine, non-fortified wine, sparkling wine, spirits) will affect the amount of duty imposed. Therefore, a can of beer with 8% alcohol content will attract twice as much duty as a can with 4% alcohol content. Data on alcohol expenditure in the FES tell us how much is spent on each class of alcohol, in both pubs and off-licences, but we do not know the alcoholic strength of the drink purchased. Therefore, to a very large extent, the excise duties we apply to expenditure on alcohol in POLIMOD are imputed. Table 5.1 gives typical retail prices and taxes for some goods where excise duties modelled in POLIMOD.

When calculating the effect of an increase in flat rate excise duties on the unit price of a good such as cigarettes, POLIMOD uses the following method:

$$P_a cigs = \frac{X_a + (P_b cigs - X_b - (R_b P_b cigs/1 + R_b) - (A_b P_b cigs))}{1/(1+R_a) - A_a}$$

Where $P_a cigs$ is the new unit price for cigarettes and $P_b cigs$ is the old unit price. X_a is the new flat rate excise duty and X_b is the old excise duty. A_a is the new *ad valorem* duty rate and A_b is the old rate. R_a is the new VAT rate and R_b the old rate. If $P_b cigs$ is £147.16 and the flat rate duty is increased from £62.52 to £68.77 (a 10% increase) while *ad valorem* rates and VAT remained constant, then the new unit price for cigarettes would be calculated as follows:

$$P_a cigs = \frac{68.77 + (147.16 - 62.52 - (0.175 \times 147.16/(1+0.175)) - (0.2 \times 147.16))}{1/(1+0.175) - 0.2}$$

$$= \frac{68.77 + 33.29}{0.8511 - 0.2} = \frac{102.06}{0.6511} = £156.75$$

Table 5.1. *Typical unit retail prices and taxes (as at October 1996) on some goods that attract excise duties*

Good	Quantity	Retail price (£s)	Flat rate excise duty (£s)	Ad valorem tax and excise duty (proportion of retail price)	VAT rate
Motor cars[a]	1	n/a	2.70	0.0	0.0
Beer (off-licence)[b]	100 litres	139.52	40.03	0.0	0.175
Cider (off-licence)	100 litres	170.07	23.78	0.0	0.175
Table wine (off-licence)	100 litres	407.35	140.44	0.0	0.175
Spirits (off-licence)[b]	2.5 litres	28.36	19.78	0.0	0.175
Cigarettes	1,000 cigs	147.16	62.52	0.20	0.175
Unleaded petrol	1 litre	0.58	0.3430	0.0	0.175
Diesel fuel	1 litre	0.58	0.3430	0.0	0.175
Betting on pools[c]	n/a	n/a	n/a	0.375	0.0
Other betting[c]	n/a	n/a	n/a	0.0775	0.0
Insurance premiums	n/a	n/a	n/a	0.025	0.0

Notes:

[a] Excise duty on motor cars, or vehicle excise duty, is more like a TV licence charge than an excise duty, in that it is not charged at point of purchase, but annually for each motor car a person owns. Therefore, a FES variable representing the number of motor cars owned in the household is used to derive weekly vehicle excise duty paid.

[b] Flat rate excise duty on beer assumes alcohol-by-volume content of 3.7%. Flat rate excise duty on spirits assumes alcohol-by-volume content of 40%.

[c] Excise duties are not charge per 'unit' of betting or insurance premium, so it is not necessary to calculate a unit price.

Source of prices: HM Customs and Excise (1996). Prices are uprated from January 1996 to October 1996 price levels using forecast inflation figures in HM Treasury (1995a), Table B1.

The new unit price of cigarettes after the increase in flat rate excise duty, $P_a cigs$, is £156.75. Note that £33.29 is the net unit cost of cigarettes, before the addition of taxes. It is assumed that this net unit cost remains constant. The implications of this assumption are discussed in Section 5.5.

Assuming constant quantity, we can work out quantity purchased Q as:

$$Q = E_b / P_b$$

where P_b is the old unit price before the policy change, and E_b is the old level of expenditure. Continuing the example of cigarettes quoted above, and assuming $E_b = £10.00$,

$$Q = 10.00/147.16$$
$$= 0.0680$$

That is, expenditure of £10.00 on cigarettes bought 0.0680 units of 1,000 cigarettes at price P_b.

Under the constant quantity assumption, new expenditure E_a is calculated as

$$E_a = Q P_a$$

where P_a is the new unit price. This translates into the following new level of expenditure on cigarettes (assuming taxes increase as a proportion of unit price):

$$E_a = 0.0680 \times 156.75$$
$$= 10.66$$

Flat rate excise duties raised Y_a are

$$Y_a = Q X_a$$
$$Y_a = 0.0680 \times 68.77$$
$$= 4.68$$

Ad valorem duties B_a are simply:

$$B_a = E_a A_a$$
$$B_a = 10.66 \times 0.2$$
$$= 2.13$$

Where there is no unit price for a good (as with betting), and no flat rate excise duty, new expenditure E_a is calculated as

$$E_a = E_b((A_a + R_a) - (A_b + R_b))$$

If expenditure on betting E_b is £5.00, and *ad valorem* excise duty on betting increases from $(A_b=)\,0.375$ to $(A_a=)\,0.4$, with VAT V_b and V_a remaining at 0,

$$E_a=5.00((1+0.4+0.0)-(0.375+0.0))$$
$$=5.125$$

Ad valorem excise duties are calculated in the same way as for cigarettes. Throughout VAT is calculated as outlined above in the section on VAT. Under the assumption of constant expenditure, excise duties are calculated in the same way, except E remains constant and the Q changes value. That is, Q_b is calculated as

$$Q_b=E_b/P_b$$

and Q_a is calculated as

$$Q_a=E_b/P_a$$

Therefore, if the unit price of a good rises as a result of an increase in tax, a smaller quantity of that good is purchased.

5.4 The implications of constant quantity and constant expenditure assumptions

The implications of assuming constant quantity or constant expenditure are different depending on whether the analyst is examining a change in flat-rate excise duties or percentage rate taxes such as VAT. This is principally because as a default POLIMOD makes the assumption that unit prices of goods change in response to tax changes, but that pre-tax prices remain constant. We consider the case of flat rate excise duties first.
    Assume:

Cost of cigarettes per 1,000:	£147.16
This includes:	
flat rate excise duty	£62.52
20% *ad valorem* excise duty	£29.43
17.5% VAT	£21.92
Therefore, total tax paid is	£113.87
Cost of cigarettes per 1,000 before tax is:	£33.29

Suppose flat rate excise duty increases from £62.52 to £68.77, a 10% increase. POLIMOD assumes that the unit price for cigarettes increases only to the extent that taxes increase, and that the price before tax remains constant. Therefore:

New cost of cigarettes per 1,000:	£156.75
This includes:	
flat rate excise duty	£68.77
20% *ad valorem* excise duty	£31.35
17.5% VAT	£23.35
Therefore, total tax paid is	£123.47
Cost of cigarettes per 1,000 before tax is:	£33.29

If a consumer purchased £5.55 worth of cigarettes before an increase in flat rate excise duties that consumer would, assuming constant expenditure, continue to purchase £5.55 worth of cigarettes after the policy change. POLIMOD would calculate the tax paid as:

	Before	After	Difference
Units of cigarettes purchased (£5.55/unit price)	0.0377	0.0354	−0.0023
Flat rate excise duty (units×excise duty)	£2.36	£2.43	£0.07
20% *ad valorem* excise duty (expenditure×0.2)	£1.11	£1.11	£0.00
17.5% VAT (expenditure×0.175/1.175)	£0.83	£0.83	£0.00
Therefore, total tax paid is	£4.30	£4.37	+£0.07

Assuming constant quantity, expenditure on cigarettes would increase from £5.55 to £5.91 (£156.75×0.0377), and the amount purchased would remain constant. POLIMOD would then calculate the tax paid as:

	Before	After	Difference
Units of cigarettes purchased (constant)	0.0377	0.0377	0.00
Flat rate excise duty (units×excise duty)	£2.36	£2.59	£0.23
20% *ad valorem* excise duty (expenditure×0.2)	£1.11	£1.18	£0.07
17.5% VAT (expenditure×0.175/1.175)	£0.83	£0.88	£0.05
Therefore, total tax paid is	£4.30	£4.65	+£0.35

There is a large difference between the two assumptions in terms of additional tax paid. Under the constant quantity assumption, the consumer would pay five times as much in extra tax as under the constant expenditure assumption.

The assumption is important when we are modelling tax changes on goods which attract flat rate or *ad valorem* excise duties. If we modelled a similar increase in VAT on another good, say take-away food, that does not attract excise duties, the choice of assumption would matter less. Under the constant quantity assumption:

	VAT @ 17.5%	VAT @ 25.36%	Difference
Pre-tax expenditure on take-away food	£4.72	£4.72	£0.00
VAT	£0.83	£1.20	£0.37
Total expenditure	£5.55	£5.92	£0.37

Under the constant expenditure assumption:

	VAT @ 17.5%	VAT @ 25.36%	Difference
Pre-tax expenditure on take-away food	£4.72	£4.43	−£0.29
VAT	£0.83	£1.12	£0.29
Total expenditure	£5.55	£5.55	£0.00

The amount of VAT paid under the constant quantity assumption is therefore 8 pence greater than under the constant expenditure assumption, a difference of 17%. Clearly, the assumption (of constant quantity or expenditure) made by the POLIMOD user is of some importance whenever indirect taxes are modelled, but in the case of flat rate excise duties, the difference in results from the two assumptions increases considerably.

5.5 An alternative assumption: constant retail prices

POLIMOD assumes that the full effect of an indirect tax increase is reflected in increased consumer prices. This is also the assumption made by the Treasury when it estimates the effect of tax increases on retail prices. If the *retail* price of the good affected by a tax increase were to remain constant, so that the tax increase was absorbed by producers and retailers, then households would experience no direct welfare loss, and there would be no difference between the assumptions of constant quantity and constant expenditure, although the amount of taxes households paid would change. If we make this assumption about the increase in flat rate excise duties on cigarettes discussed above:

	Before tax increase	After tax increase
Cost of cigarettes per 1,000:	£147.16	£147.16
This includes:		
flat rate excise duty	£62.52	£68.77
20% *ad valorem* excise duty	£29.43	£29.43
17.5% VAT	£21.92	£21.92
Therefore, total tax paid is	£113.87	£120.12
Cost of cigarettes per 1,000 before tax is:	£33.29	£27.04

A FES respondent's £5.55 expenditure on cigarettes would have the following revenue effects:

	Before	After	Difference
Units of cigarettes purchased (£5.55/unit price)	0.0377	0.0377	0.00
Flat rate excise duty (units×excise duty)	£2.36	£2.59	£0.23
20% *ad valorem* excise duty (expenditure×0.2)	£1.11	£1.11	£0.00
17.5% VAT (expenditure×0.175/1.175)	£0.83	£0.83	£0.00
Therefore, total tax paid is	£4.30	£4.53	+£0.23

As one might expect, this estimate lies between those that result from constant quantity and constant expenditure assumptions. With an increase in VAT on take-away food from 17.5% to 25.36%, however, the result would be the same as under the assumption of constant expenditure. The respondent's tax burden on £5.55 expenditure would be:

	VAT @17.5%	VAT @25.36%	Difference
Pre-tax expenditure on			
take-away food	£4.72	£4.43	−£0.29
VAT	£0.83	£1.12	£0.29
Total expenditure	£5.55	£5.55	£0.00

5.6 Conclusions

POLIMOD's approach of allowing for two alternative consumer reactions to changes in taxes on expenditure is simple and transparent, and sets parameters within which many households are likely to respond to the taxes. In many cases, the consumption pattern of households will change in response to indirect tax changes, although the magnitude and even direction of this response may be difficult to anticipate. For example, people may respond to an increase in taxes on cigarettes by increasing their expenditure on cigarettes, by maintaining their expenditure on cigarettes at a constant level, or by giving up cigarettes altogether. However, it seems reasonable to argue that most people are *likely* to respond to a change in indirect taxes, certainly in the short term, by choosing a level of consumption that lies between the two offered by POLIMOD. POLIMOD can also model the impact of indirect taxes under a third assumption that is again plausible in the short term, where consumer prices are kept constant. This has the effect of introducing distributional and revenue estimates that lie in between those produced under the other two assumptions where changes in excise duties are modelled.

Notes

1 Central Statistical Office (CSO) (1993) differentiates between *disposable income* and *post-tax income*, the former being gross income including benefits but less income taxes and employee National Insurance contributions, and the latter being minus indirect taxes. However, included in CSO's definition of indirect taxes are *intermediate taxes*, which indirectly affect the price of goods and services, such as employer's National Insurance contributions. POLIMOD does not model intermediate taxes.

2 Although the two assumptions are extreme, we recognise that they do not necessarily result in boundary estimates of the effects of indirect tax changes. There exist *combinations* of behaviour that would lead to more extreme results.

6 Employee National Insurance contributions

6.1 Introduction

Class 1 National Insurance contributions (NICs) are paid by employees on their gross earnings. Employers also contribute under a separate Class 1 schedule on behalf of their employees.[1] Class 2 and Class 4 contributions are paid by the self-employed, while Class 3 contributions are voluntary, and can be paid by anyone. POLIMOD does not model payment of Class 3 contributions because they are voluntary and therefore not part of tax *liabilities*. The modelling of Class 2 and Class 4 contributions for the self-employed is relatively straightforward, in that liability depends almost solely on earned income.[2] In the case of employees, however modelling is more problematic because three distinct regimes exist under which employees can pay contributions, and the Family Expenditure Survey (FES) does not collect data on the types of contributions that are made.

The regimes are: Not Contracted Out (NCO), Contracted Out (CO) and Reduced Rate (RR). To some extent, employees can choose the regime under which they wish to pay. NCO contributions are at the highest rates, and pay for membership of the State Earnings Related Pension Scheme (SERPS). CO contributions are at lower rates than NCO contributions, as the employee has 'contracted out' of SERPS and is paying separate contributions to an occupational or private pension scheme (otherwise, the employee is not allowed to contract out). RR contributions are lower still, but are only available to married women or widows who elected not to participate in the contribution scheme before 11 May 1977 and have remained in the labour force since then. FES data tell us the amount of contributions paid by employees in a particular week, but not the regime that applies to them. This information must be imputed if we are to model NICs. In principle, it can be imputed using information on the amount of contributions paid, and on gross earnings reported in the FES data. In practice the process is not so straightforward. This is partly because the structure of contributions, which is described in Section 6.2 is relatively complex, and partly because the earnings data, described in Section 6.3 do not necessarily 'match' the data on NIC payment. Section 6.4 explores several methods of imputing the contribution regime and Section 6.5 compares the results with external evidence. Section 6.6 concludes.

6.2 Class 1 NIC rates

All employees in the UK aged between 16 and pension age and earning more than the Lower Earnings Limit (LEL) are liable for Class 1 contributions. In calendar year 1991 (the year of the POLIMOD database) there were a total of four different *marginal* rates at which Class 1 contributions could be deducted:

9%   the rate between the LEL and Upper Earnings Limit (UEL) for those who are NCO

7%   the rate between LEL and UEL for those who are CO

3.85%   RR, up to UEL where earnings are equal to or greater than LEL

0%   (i) the rate between £0 and LEL where earnings are less than LEL
        (ii) the rate for earners aged under 16 or over pensionable age
        (iii) the marginal rate for those earning above the UEL.

There was also one basic rate for the deduction of contributions:

2%   the rate between £0 and LEL for NCO and CO employees, where earnings are greater than, or equal to, LEL

In principle, the regime for each employee can be imputed according to the amount of NICs, relative to gross weekly earnings, that they report paying in the FES.[3] For the purposes of this exercise, earnings are defined as being from primary employment only. Earnings (and contributions) from subsidiary employment are ignored. Employees aged under 16 and those over pension age are excluded, as these groups are not liable to NICs.

6.3 Earnings

In POLIMOD, only FES respondents who report receiving earnings last week or last month (*A250*=1) are counted as employees. This corresponds with liability for Class 1 NICs, which is based on current earnings.[4] Earnings can be defined in two ways:

(i)   last gross pay (*P003*) if paid in last pay period;
(ii) normal gross pay (*B315*) if paid in last pay period.

Table 6.1. *Employee National Insurance contribution earnings brackets*

	Weekly earnings criteria	
Earnings bracket	1991, 1st quarter	1991, 2nd to 4th quarter
Below LEL	Less than £46	Less than £52
Between LEL and UEL	£46 to £350	£52 to £390
Above UEL	More than £350	More than £390

Source: 1991 FES: own calculations.

Reported NICs (*B306*) always refer to earnings in the last pay period. Therefore, since this is the crucial variable in our imputation of National Insurance contribution regimes, *P003* is used as the gross earnings variable in this exercise.[5] Table 6.1 shows NIC employee earnings brackets for 1991. The calculation of contributions under the three regimes for an employee with gross earnings of £210 (between the LEL and the UEL) who was interviewed after the first quarter in 1991 is as follows:

NCO
$(52.00 \times 0.02) + (210.00 - 52.00) \times 0.09 = £15.26$
CO
$(52.00 \times 0.02) + (210.00 - 52.00) \times 0.07 = £12.10$
RR
$210.00 \times 0.0385 = £8.09.$

The next section shows how calculated contributions are matched with reported contributions to produce an imputed contributions regime.

6.4 Imputing NIC regimes

Table 6.2 shows that there were 6,593 FES respondents in the 1991 survey with a wage last week/month. All respondents in this subgroup have a positive value for *P003* (gross earnings). Of these, 186 are either aged less than 16 or above pension age, leaving 6,407 who are potential members of an NIC regime. However, not all of these have a value for *B306* (NICs deducted from earnings). For the 692 observations with earnings below the LEL, this is expected, since an employee with earnings below this level is not liable to NICs. However, there are 107 observations where gross earnings are greater than LEL, and no contributions are recorded.[6] There are also some cases where gross earnings are less than the LEL and contributions are reported.

Table 6.2. *FES 1991: number of employees with recorded earnings and National Insurance contributions information*

Total FES sample	17,089
Employees with wage last week/month (*A250*=1)	6,593
Employees with wage last week/month and aged less than 16 or over pension age	186
Employees with wage last week/month and of working age of which:	6,407
Gross wage below LEL	692
Gross wage above LEL	5,715
of which:	
Gross wage above LEL and no contributions	107
Employees with gross wage above LEL and contributions	5,608

Source: 1991 FES: own calculations.

Since POLIMOD simulates liability rather than actual payment of taxes, discrepancies may sometimes arise. In the two cases described above, the discrepancies are obvious, in that contributions are reported where they are not expected, or no contributions are reported where they are expected. Less obvious discrepancies between reported contributions and estimated liabilities arise where the amounts reported and calculated are quite close, but not the same. For example, as we have seen, an employee with £210 in gross weekly earnings after the first quarter of 1991 is liable for a contribution of £15.26 under the NCO regime, and £12.10 under the CO regime. If this respondent reports paying £12.11 in contributions, we may feel justified in allocating them to the CO regime. We may be less sure if they report paying £14.08. A set of rules are required which can be used to determine membership of contributions regimes. For those respondents who cannot be satisfactorily allocated a regime under these rules, we must explore other ways of imputing the contributions regime to which they belong.

The task of simulating contribution regime membership is therefore divided into three parts. In Round 1 we simulate membership for those respondents who are employees and whose earnings fall below the LEL. In Round 2, we simulate membership for employees who report earnings above the LEL and who report contributions which are within an acceptable margin of error of one of the amounts calculated for each regime. In Round 3 we examine ways of simulating membership for those whose earnings are above the LEL, but who do not report NICs, or whose reported contributions fall outside the margins of error applied in Round 2.

Round 1: respondents with earnings below the LEL

There are 692 respondents who report earnings below the LEL. Of these, 35 report paying contributions. For the purposes of imputing regimes, these contributions are ignored, and POLIMOD assigns all respondents in this category to the NCO regime. Therefore, if the abolition or reduction of the LEL were to be simulated using POLIMOD, respondents who become liable for contributions as a result would be liable under the NCO regime. Similarly, if a minimum wage were simulated, employees brought above the LEL would pay contributions according to the NCO regime.

Round 2: respondents with earnings above the LEL who report NICs

There are 5,608 respondents in this category. The level of contribution is initially used on its own to determine contribution regime membership for this group. That is, the regime that produces the contribution amount arithmetically closest to the recorded value of *B306* is chosen, if that amount is within both 10 pence and 5% of the recorded weekly figure. This margin of error is arbitrary, but is sufficiently narrow to ensure that we can be reasonably confident in the estimation procedure.

An additional constraint applies to membership of the RR regime. The option to opt out of full contributions was abolished in 1977, but women who remained married or who were widowed were allowed to continue to opt out so long as their earnings were never below the LEL or Class 2 limit for more than 2 years at a time.[7] Therefore, if a 1991 FES respondent is female, married or widowed, aged 35 or over,[8] earning more than the LEL and her reported contribution is closest to the RR contribution calculated from her gross earnings, then POLIMOD assumes that she is liable for RR contributions. This assumption is not wholly satisfactory. The FES does not contain data on whether respondents were married or widowed in 1977, or whether they were continuously in the labour market until 1991.

At this stage, no attempt is made to constrain membership of the CO regime to respondents who report payments into an occupational or private pension scheme. This is not done because some employees, for example some public servants, do not themselves pay contributions, even though they are still contracted out of SERPS. (Their employer pays them.) In addition, it is possible that some employees who are NCO also

Table 6.3. *Difference between calculated and recorded National Insurance contribution amounts, by nearest National Insurance contributions regime*

	NCO nearest	CO nearest	RR nearest	Total	Total (%)
Absolute difference					
£0.00–0.10	1,859	2,046	155	4,060	72.4
£0.10–0.25	70	122	9	201	3.6
£0.25–0.50	249	204	16	469	8.4
£0.50–1.00	108	146	7	261	4.7
£1.00–2.00	103	159	7	269	4.8
£2.00–5.00	85	151	4	240	4.3
More than £5.00	66	41	1	108	1.9
Total	2,540	2,869	199	5,608	100.0
Percentage difference					
0–5%	2,137	2,413	155	4,714	84.1
5–10%	169	215	9	396	7.1
10–15%	85	93	16	187	3.3
15–20%	34	29	7	64	1.1
20–25%	22	22	7	45	0.8
25–50%	72	39	4	118	2.1
More than 50%	21	58	1	84	1.5
Total	2,540	2,869	199	5,608	100.0
Combined difference					
Within 10 pence and 5%	1,857	2,045	155	4,057	72.3
Not within 10 pence and 5%	683	824	44	1,551	27.7
Total	2,540	2,869	199	5,608	100.0

Source: 1991 FES: own calculations.

pay contributions to private pensions. Therefore, respondents are allocated to the CO or NCO regimes at this stage purely on the basis of proximity between calculated and reported contributions.

As Table 6.3 shows, 72.4% of those employees whose earnings are above the LEL, and who report NICs, report amounts which are within £0.10 of contributions calculated by POLIMOD for one of the three regimes. Over eight in ten (84.1%) report contributions which are within 5% of one of the contribution amounts calculated by POLIMOD. This picture is much the same for all three regimes, suggesting a high degree of accuracy in our primary imputation of regimes. Overall, if we restrict our primary imputation to those observations whose reported contribution amounts fall within both 10 pence *and* 5% of one of the amounts calculated by POLIMOD, then 4,057 observations (72.3%) are allocated to a regime at Round 1.

However, there are 1,551 observations (27.7% of the total with contributions) where calculated NICs are more than 10 pence or 5% adrift of reported NICs. There may be several explanations as to why this is so. For example, it is possible that in some of these cases gross earnings or contributions are imputed at the coding stage by CSO (see ESRC Data Archive, 1992, pp. B24–9), or that some part of earnings reported by the respondent is undeclared for tax purposes. The FES data allow us to investigate two possibilities – that pay may be affected by additions on which contributions are not paid, and that a payslip was not consulted. Firstly, Table 6.4 shows that the inclusion of extra payments in earnings does not appear to affect the relative proximity of reported to simulated contributions. Indeed, respondents whose reported contributions are within 10 pence or 5% of calculated contributions for one of the three regimes are slightly more likely to report a factor that affects their earnings than respondents whose reported contributions fall outside this limit.

Secondly, Table 6.5 shows that where a payslip was examined in the course of the interview, respondents were not much more likely than average to report contributions that were close to one of the calculated regime amounts. But it is also clear from Table 6.5 that of the minority of respondents (6%) who did not consult payslips, two in three (67%) reported contributions that were not close to any of the calculated regime amounts. This might suggest that respondents who do not consult payslips are also more likely report contributions inaccurately.

However, both Table 6.4 and Table 6.5 suggest that there is little information available in the FES as to why over a quarter of respondents in our sample have contributions that do not correspond closely with calculated amounts for one of the regimes. Indeed, it is worth noting that some of these cases report contributions that are greater than the ceiling for Class 1 contributions, the maximum weekly amount any employee should have to pay (£28.28 in Quarter 1 of 1991, £31.46 in Quarters 2 to 4). For the purpose of this exercise we will assume that the reported contribution of those 1,551 observations in the 'Not within 10 pence and 5%' categories in Table 6.3 is problematic and therefore some method other than level of reported contribution alone must be used to impute Class 1 regime membership. In addition, we must also allocate 107 observations who do not report any contributions, but who report earnings that are above the LEL, to a regime.

Table 6.4. *FES employees whose last pay is affected by special circumstances (%)*

Reported contributions within 10 pence and 5% of a calculated regime?	Last pay affected by					Total
	holiday or back pay	shift loading	irregular overtime or bonus	tax deductions and other reasons	no additions/ deductions	
Yes	78.5	78.8	80.0	75.3	71.2	72.3
No	21.5	21.2	20.0	24.7	28.8	27.7
Number of cases	205	179	390	393	4,441	5,608

Source:1991 FES:own calculations.

Table 6.5. *FES employees who consulted a payslip (%)*

Reported contributions within 10 pence and 5% of a calculated regime?	Consulted payslip		
	yes	no	total
Yes	74.8	33.0	72.3
No	25.2	67.0	27.7
Number of cases	5,278	330	5,608

Source: 1991 FES: own calculations.

Round 3: respondents with earnings above the LEL whose contributions are more than 10 pence or 5 % adrift of the nearest calculated regime

There is no immediately obvious way of allocating these 1,658 'problematic' observations to a Class 1 contributions regime. In this section, therefore, we attempt three allocation methods. The most successful method is the one which allocates cases to contributions regimes in such a way as to produce grossed-up totals that are closest to aggregate data. The three methods are: arithmetic matching, characteristics matching, and logistic regression.

Method 1: arithmetic matching

This is the simplest of the three approaches. Each observation is allocated to a regime on the basis of which calculated regime figure comes closest to the reported contributions figure. For those observations which report contributions, the results are shown in Table 6.3: 2,540 respondents have contributions that are arithmetically closest to the NCO regime, 2,869 are closest to the CO regime and 199 are closest to the RR regime. We allocate the remaining 107 respondents who do not report contributions as follows: if they report paying superannuation contributions, then they are allocated to the CO regime. Otherwise, they are allocated to the NCO regime. Final totals for each regime are shown in the first part of Table 6.6.

Method 2: characteristics matching

With this method, all observations that do not satisfy the criteria at Round 2 are allocated to the NCO regime unless they report paying superannuation contributions ($B318>0$), in which case they are allocated to the CO regime. No extra cases are allocated to the RR regime. Final results for each regime using this method are on the second part of Table 6.6.

Table 6.6. *Estimating National Insurance contributions regimes by arithmetic and characteristics matching*

Difference between estimated and reported NICs	NCO	CO	RR	Total	Total (%)
Method 1: Arithmetic matching					
Less than 10 pence or 5%	1,857	2,045	155	4,057	71.0
More than 10 pence or 5%	683	824	44	1,551	27.1
Reported NIC missing	98	9	0	107	1.9
Total	2,638	2,878	199	5,715	100.0
Method 2: Characteristics matching					
Less than 10 pence or 5%	1,857	2,045	155	4,057	71.0
More than 10 pence or 5%, or reported NIC missing	1,005	653	0	1,658	29.0
Total	2,862	2,698	155	5,715	100.0

Source: 1991 FES: own calculations.

Method 3: logistic regression

This approach is more complex than the other two, and involves investigation of respondents' observed characteristics that may be associated with membership of a regime. These characteristics include sex (*A004*), age (*A005*), marital status (*A006*), superannuation contributions (*B318*), gross earnings (*P003*), partner's gross earnings (*P003*) and the size of the establishment where the respondent works (*SIZEEST*). As Table 6.7 shows, all these variables vary within contributions regime for the 4,057 observations allocated at Round 2. Therefore, with the independent variables that are summarised in Table 6.7, we attempt a two stage logistic regression on these respondents whose earnings are above the LEL and who have been allocated a regime at Round 2.

At stage one, we regress the independents on *$NCOCO* which has a value of 1 if the nearest Round 2 contribution regime is NCO, and a value of 0 if the nearest regime is CO. The 155 respondents whose nearest Round 2 regime is RR are excluded from this stage. We use a logistic regression model which takes the form:

$$p(\$NCOCO=1)=\frac{e^z}{1+e^z}$$

where z equals $(\beta_0+\beta_1 X_1+\ldots+\beta_n X_n)$. $X_1 \ldots X_n$ are the independent ratio level variable *$LOGP003* (the natural log of gross earnings), and the dummy variables

Table 6.7. *Characteristics of respondents allocated to a regime at Round 1 by nearest National Insurance contributions regime*

	NCO nearest	CO nearest	RR nearest	Total	Total (%)
Sex					
male	959	1,306	0	2,265	55.8
female	898	739	155	1,792	44.2
Marital status:					
single/widowed/divorced	588	495	7	1,090	26.9
married	1,099	1,427	148	2,674	65.9
cohabiting	170	123	0	293	7.2
Age					
16–24	477	190	0	667	16.4
25–34	560	604	0	1,164	28.7
35–44	394	618	17	1,029	25.4
45–64	426	633	138	1,197	29.5
Size of enterprise where respondent is employed in main job					
less than 25 employees	736	332	54	1122	27.7
25–1,000 employees	996	1,282	83	2,361	58.2
over 1,000 employees	125	431	18	574	14.2
Respondent pays superannuation contributions on main earnings					
no	1,717	267	71	2,055	50.7
yes	140	1,778	84	2,002	49.4
Average earnings	£212.03	£324.51	£178.88	£267.46	
Average earnings of partner	£94.57	£99.75	£165.58	£99.89	
Total	1,857	2,045	155	4,057	100.0

Source: 1991 FES: own calculations.

$MALE$ (sex is male)
$AGE1624$ (respondent's age is less than 24)
$AGE2534$ (age is between 25 and 34)
$AGE3544$ (age is between 35 and 44)
$MARRIED$ (respondent is married)
$COHABIT$ (cohabiting)
$SINGLE$ (single)

Table 6.8. *Logistic regression statistics for predicting CO/NCO status of respondents (model predicts probability of NCO status)*

Dependent variable:	NCO=1: 1,857 observations	NCO=0: 2,045 observations			
	Parameter estimates				
Independent variables	Bi	Probability	Standard error	Wald chi-sq	Pr >chi-sq
INTERCEPT	7.6101		0.5469	193.6575	0.0001
$SUPERANN	−4.2381	0.01	0.1169	1,314.8578	0.0001
$LOGP003	−0.9818	0.27	0.1061	85.5552	0.0001
$SE2	−0.7853	0.31	0.1301	36.4484	0.0001
$SE3	−1.4128	0.19	0.1872	56.9532	0.0001
$AGE2534	−0.2698	0.43	0.1301	4.3027	0.0381
$AGE3544	−0.4383	0.39	0.1383	10.0471	0.0015
$MALE	0.6115	0.65	0.1274	23.0553	0.0001
Percentage of concordant pairs:		93.5%	Gamma:	0.873	
Percentage of discordant pairs:		6.4%	Somers' D:	0.871	
Percentage of tied pairs:		0.2%			
Goodness of fit (Hosmer/Lemeshow): 13.152 with 8df (pr=0.1067)					

Source: 1991 FES: own calculations.

$SUPERANN (respondent pays pension contributions)
$PWAGE1 (partner has employee earnings)
$SE2 (25 to 999 workers in the establishment)
$SE3 (1,000 or more workers in the establishment).

$AGE4564, *$OTHER* and *$SE1* are the omitted variables. Of the variables
that are included, the standard errors of *$AGE1624*, *$PWAGE1*,
$MARRIED, *$SINGLE* and *$COHABIT* are high, and they do not
achieve the 0.05 significance level criterion which we have set for retention
in the model. This suggests that their coefficients are not significantly
different from the intercept β_0. Therefore, the independent variables in the
final model are *$SUPERANN*, *$LOGP003*, *$SE2*, *$SE3*, *$AGE2534*,
$AGE3544 and *$MALE*. The regression statistics for these variables are
shown in Table 6.8.

Overall, Table 6.8 shows that the model fits well, with 94% of observations producing predicted CO/NCO regimes that are consistent with
those calculated at Round 2. The Hosmer/Lemeshow test suggests that
the fit is statistically significant. Of the independent variables, the most
important is the intercept, which suggests that respondents aged 45 and
over who work in small firms with fewer than 25 employees are particularly likely to be NCO. *$SUPERANN* is also important – the probability
statistics show that if *$SUPERANN* changes from 0 to 1, the probability
of a respondent being NCO (*$NCOCO*=1) is reduced to 0.01. Put
another way, if *$SUPERANN* changes from 0 to 1, the probability of a
respondent being CO (*$NCOCO*=0) increases to 0.99, controlling for all
other factors.[9]

This model is eminently plausible, in that it predicts not only that
respondents with superannuation contributions are very likely to be CO,
but also that older workers, and workers who work in small firms are likely
to be NCO. Although there is little hard evidence to support this model, it
seems sensible to suggest that older workers may be NCO because the
growth in private and occupational pensions has been relatively recent. In
addition, it is plausible to suggest that small firms are less likely to have an
occupational pension scheme to which workers can contribute.

We apply similar models to predict RR/NCO and RR/CO status (an
RR/not RR model does not fit the data so well), where *$NCORR*=1 repre-
sents a predicted NCO regime, and *$CORR*=1 represents a predicted CO
regime, the alternatives in both cases being a predicted RR regime. These
models are restricted to respondents who fulfil criteria for being in the RR
regime (within the limitations of FES data), that is, they are female,
married or widowed, and aged over 35. The following variables are entered
in the models:

Table 6.9. *Logistic regression statistics for predicting RR status of respondents*

MODEL 1: *$NCORR*=1 where Round 2 regime is NCO; *$NCORR*=0 where Round 2 regime is RR

Dependent variable: NCO=0: 155 observations   NCO=1: 281 observations

Independent variables	Parameter estimates					
	Bi	Probability	Standard error	Wald chi-sq	Pr >chi-sq
INTERCEPT	38.0914		4.2678	79.6620	0.0001
$SUPERANN	1.8212	0.86	0.1169	40.8015	0.0001
$LOGAGE	−10.0456	0.00	0.1061	82.0907	0.0001
Percentage of concordant pairs:	84.6%	Gamma:	0.717		
Percentage of discordant pairs:	13.9%	Somers' D:	0.707		
Percentage of tied pairs:	1.5%				
Goodness of fit (Hosmer/Lemeshow): 7.7895 with 8df (pr=0.4543)					

MODEL 2: *$CORR*=1 where Round 2 regime is NCO; *$CORR*=0 where Round 2 regime is RR

Dependent variable: CO=0: 155 observations   CO=1: 323 observations

Independent variables	Parameter estimates					
	Bi	Probability	Standard error	Wald chi-sq	Pr > chi-sq
INTERCEPT	36.5495		4.7640	58.8597	0.0001
$SUPERANN	−2.6823	0.06	0.3233	68.8513	0.0001
$LOGAGE	−9.1159	0.00	1.2251	55.3646	0.0001
$PENS1	1.3598	0.80	0.6081	5.0003	0.0253
Percentage of concordant pairs:	87.0%	Gamma:	0.768		
Percentage of discordant pairs:	11.4%	Somers' D:	0.756		
Percentage of tied pairs:	1.5%				
Goodness of fit (Hosmer/Lemeshow): 12.79 with 8df (pr=0.1193)					

Source: 1991 FES: own calculations.

$SUPERANN

$LOGGROSS (the log of the total gross original incomes of the respondent and her partner)

$LOGAGE (the log of the respondent's age)

$SE2

$SE3

$PENS1 (dummy variable to indicate if respondent receives a pension)

$PENS2 (dummy variable to indicate if respondent's partner receives a pension)

$EARN2 (dummy variable to indicate if the respondent's partner has earnings).

The results for both models are shown in Table 6.9. In both models, the variable *$LOGAGE* is the most important variable in predicting regime membership, and suggests that older women are considerably more likely to be RR. This finding is borne out by DSS statistics which are reproduced in Table 6.13, and which show that over 60% of women who are RR are aged over 50. The models' fit is good, although not as good as that of the *$NCOCO* model: 85% of the *$NCORR* model pairs, and 87% of the *$CORR* model pairs are concordant with the regimes allocated at Round 2.

In applying the parameter estimates of the three models *$NCOCO*, *$NCORR* and *$CORR*, we use the formula outlined at the start of this section on those observations that are not allocated a regime at Round 2. The criteria we use are:

(i)   if p($NCOCO$=1)$\geq$0.5 then regime is NCO
(ii) if p($NCOCO$=1)$<$0.5 then regime is CO

All unallocated observations are therefore first allocated to either the NCO or CO regimes. Those respondents who fulfil the criteria for RR membership are further allocated as follows:

(iii) if p($NCORR$=1)$<$0.5 and 0.2$<$p($NCOCO$=1)$<$0.5 then regime is RR
(iv)   if p($CORR$=1)$<$0.5 and 0.5$<$p($NCOCO$=1)$<$0.8 then regime is RR

That is, respondents are only assigned RR membership if their probability of their being CO or NCO is less than 0.8. We are therefore introducing bias into our model and reducing the possibility of membership of the RR regime. We justify this with the argument that the *$NCOCO* model (Model 1) produces a better fit than the *$NCORR* model (Model 2) or the *$CORR* model (Model 3), and therefore more weight should be given to

Table 6.10. *Estimating National Insurance contributions regimes by logistic regression*

Difference between estimated and reported NICs	NCO	CO	RR	Total	Total (%)
Allocated at Round 2	1,857	2,045	155	4,057	71.0
Fulfil criteria:					
(i)	1,002			1,002	17.5
(ii)		656		656	11.5
(iii)	(−3)		3		
(iv)		(−7)	7		
Total	2,856	2,694	165	5,715	100.0

Source: FES: own calculations.

the results it produces. Final results are shown in Table 6.10. Almost half the respondents (2,856) are allocated to the NCO regime, 2,694 are allocated to the CO regime, and 165 are allocated to the RR regime.

6.5 Validation of results

Final numbers of weighted observations (that is, grossed-up to be representative of the UK as a whole) placed in each contributions regime using the three methods outlined in Section 6.4 are shown in Table 6.11. Aggregate Department of Social Security statistics for the numbers of contributors in each regime are also shown. These are taken from a 1% sample survey of all National Insurance numbers ending in a specified number that is carried out in April of every year. Comparisons are difficult, for two principal reasons. Firstly, the surveys use different sampling methods, and secondly, they have different sampling frames. If a person in the Department of Social Security sample made *any* contribution during the previous year, they are included as a contributor to the appropriate regime(s). But a person in the FES sample is only counted as a contributor if they were an employee *at the time of interview*. For this reason, there are observations with 'mixed' contributions in the DSS sample, but not in the FES sample.[10] Secondly, the sampling frames of the two surveys are different. The FES is a sample of *households*, and excludes people who live outside households, while the DSS sample on the other hand, is a sample of *administrative records*, and therefore includes both household and non-household members who are 'in the system'. These differences would lead

Table 6.11. *1991 FES employees: estimated National Insurance contributions regimes*

Millions of contributors	FES employee respondents			
	Method 1 Arithmetic matching	Method 2 Characteristics matching	Method 3 Logistic matching	DSS sample
(Below lower earnings limit)	(2.270)	(2.270)	(2.270)	
NCO	9.027	9.799	9.779	12.056
CO	9.643	9.017	9.003	8.102
Mixed CO/NCO				1.191
RR	0.680	0.534	0.567	0.642
Mixed NCO/RR				0.032
Totals	19.350	19.350	19.350	22.023

Source: 1991 FES: own calculations.

us to suggest that FES estimates of NCO membership are likely to be lower than DSS estimates.

The Department of Social Security sample shows twelve million contributors to the NCO regime. None of the three estimates based on the grossed-up FES sample is higher than 9.8 million.[11] This big difference between DSS and FES sample-based estimates may perhaps be explained by two sampling differences outlined above. Firstly, since FES data are a snapshot, and Department of Social Security figures for 1991 refer to anyone paying NICs at one of the three rates at any stage during the year,[12] it seems reasonable to suggest that many of those who in the FES report earnings below the LEL (A grossed-up total of 2.27 million employees) may have paid contributions at some stage in the previous year, and that those contributions were likely to be NCO, since CO contributions are associated with better-paid work, as Table 6.7 shows. Secondly, it is possible that people who do not live in households (who are therefore excluded from the FES sample but included in the DSS sample), including people who live in institutions and students in halls of residence, are more likely to contribute to NCO regimes than other regimes.

Of the three methods used to estimate NCO regime membership in the FES sample, Methods 2 and 3 produce very similar results, with each estimating total membership of 9.8 million employees, compared with an estimate of 9 million if we use Method 1.

Table 6.12. *1991 FES employees: estimated National Insurance contributions regimes by sex (%)*

	FES employee respondents			
	Method 1 Arithmetic matching	Method 2 Characteristics matching	Method 3 Logistic matching	DSS sample
Male				
NCO	44.0	47.9	47.8	51.0
CO	56.0	52.1	52.2	43.7
Mixed CO/NCO				5.3
Total (millions)	11.24	11.24	11.24	12.12
Female				
NCO	50.3	54.4	54.3	59.3
CO	41.3	39.0	38.7	28.3
Mixed CO/NCO				5.5
RR	8.4	6.6	7.0	6.5
Mixed NCO/RR				0.3
Total (millions)	8.11	8.11	8.11	9.91

Source: 1991 FES: own calculations. DSS, 1993b, Table H101, DSS, 1994a, Table H102. DSS figures for calendar year 1991 are calculated from fiscal year data.

In contrast to NCO, we would expect that CO employees (including, for example, most public servants) are more likely to remain in stable employment. Therefore, it is reasonable to expect that there would be fewer differences between the FES and DSS samples. This is indeed the case: in the FES samples estimated membership ranges between 9 million and 9.6 million contributors, compared with 8.1 million in the DSS sample. There are two possible explanations for these differences: firstly, if those DSS respondents who have both CO and NCO contributions are added to the CO totals, then the new total (9.3 million) is within the range of FES estimates. It is possible that a majority of DSS respondents with mixed contributions followed the CO regime for most of the year. Secondly, for the sampling method and sampling frame reasons outlined above, it is possible that those factors which cause the number of NCO employees to be under-stated in the FES are the same factors which cause the number of CO employees to be over-stated when compared with the DSS sample. It is therefore important to bear in mind that the samples are measuring slightly different phenomena.

Comparing Method 1, Method 2 and Method 3 with the DSS total, however, it is clear that Method 1 compares least well for both NCO and CO, and that there is very little difference between Methods 2 and 3. The similarity between Methods 2 and 3 is perhaps not surprising, given that in both cases membership of the CO regime is driven by *$SUPERANN*, explicitly in the case of Method 2 and through a logistic regression equation in the case of Method 3. The more sophisticated approach in Method 3, however, would tend to confirm the validity of the simpler approach in Method 2, where *$SUPERANN* is the only independent variable which explains membership of the CO regime. Method 1 offers the closest estimate, in comparison with the DSS, of membership of the RR regime, with Method 3 the next closest.

Table 6.12 shows the percentages of men and women who are assigned to the three regimes under the three methods compared with DSS figures, and Table 6.13 shows an age distribution. Table 6.12 also shows that Methods 2 and 3 produce results that are closer to those of the DSS than Method 1. However, all three methods particularly overestimate the proportion of women who follow the CO regime when compared with the DSS figures. The age distribution in Table 6.13 is interesting mainly because of the similarity of the three estimates and the DSS estimate.

6.6. Conclusions

Two principal conclusions can be drawn from this exercise. Firstly, it is clearly possible to estimate most FES respondents' Class 1 NIC regime by simply comparing their reported NIC payments with imputed amounts for each regime calculated from gross earnings, and allowing for a relatively tight margin of error. In the exercise described in this book, almost three quarters of respondents who are liable to Class 1 NICs were allocated a regime using this method. This would suggest that in most cases, respondents' Class 1 NICs are reliably reported.

Imputing a regime for the remaining quarter of respondents who are liable for Class 1 contributions is more problematic. Perhaps the most important conclusion that can be reached regarding these cases is that the three different methods attempted in this exercise produce broadly similar results: this gives us some confidence in our estimates.

The second conclusion that we can draw is that it is difficult to validate our findings. The robustness in the results produced by the FES data leads us to suggest that some of the differences that exist between DSS and FES samples are principally a function of the different sampling techniques used by DSS with their 1% samples, and in the FES. The two samples may be measuring different aspects of the same phenomenon.

Table 6.13. *Estimates of membership of National Insurance contributions regimes by age (%)*

	16–19	20–24	25–29	30–34	35–39	40–44	45–49	50–54	55–59	60–64	Total
NCO regime											
Method 1	8.9	18.7	16.1	12.6	10.2	9.8	9.0	7.0	4.9	2.8	9.027
Method 2	8.7	19.0	16.2	12.7	10.4	9.6	9.4	7.0	4.6	2.5	9.799
Method 3	8.7	19.0	16.2	12.7	10.3	9.6	9.4	7.0	4.6	2.5	9.779
DSS estimate	9.7	19.3	15.6	11.8	9.9	10.1	8.6	6.5	5.1	3.4	12.057
CO regime											
Method 1	2.0	10.0	15.9	14.3	14.1	13.6	13.0	9.5	5.7	2.0	9.643
Method 2	1.5	8.8	15.5	14.2	14.3	14.2	13.0	10.0	6.3	2.3	9.017
Method 3	1.5	8.8	15.5	14.2	14.4	14.2	13.0	9.9	6.3	2.3	9.003
DSS estimate	1.4	8.7	14.1	14.1	13.4	14.3	13.0	9.6	7.4	4.1	8.102
RR regime											
Method 1	0.0	0.0	0.0	0.0	3.7	11.9	24.5	32.3	27.6	0.0	0.680
Method 2	0.0	0.0	0.0	0.0	1.2	9.7	26.0	33.6	29.5	0.0	0.534
Method 3	0.0	0.0	0.0	0.0	1.1	9.7	25.7	33.9	29.6	0.0	0.567
DSS estimate	0.0	0.0	0.0	0.0	1.3	9.0	22.2	30.1	31.6	5.8	0.642

Sources: 1991 FES: own calculations. DSS estimates – DSS, 1993b, H.102 and DSS, 1994a, H.103.

Appendix 6.1 Variables

1991 FES variables

A004	sex
A005	age
A006	marital status
A250	last pay was last week/month
SIZEEST	size of establishment where respondent works
OCCUP91	respondent's occupation
P003	last gross pay
B306	National Insurance contributions deducted from last pay
B318	Superannuation contributions deducted from last pay
WKSWEMP	Number of weeks paid work in the last year
PAYAFFC	Pay affected by special circumstances
GROSSPAY	Gross pay from payslip

Variables derived for this analysis

1. Independent variables

$SUPERANN	IF ($B318>0$) THEN *$SUPERANN*$=1$
	OTHERWISE *$SUPERANN*$=0$
$MALE	IF ($A004=1$) THEN *$MALE*$=1$
	OTHERWISE *$MALE*$=0$
$AGE1624	IF (($A005>15$) AND ($A005<25$)) THEN *$AGE1624*$=1$
	OTHERWISE *$AGE1624*$=0$
$AGE2534	IF (($A005>24$) AND ($A005<35$)) THEN *$AGE2534*$=1$
	OTHERWISE *$AGE2534*$=0$
$AGE3544	IF (($A005>34$) AND ($A005<45$)) THEN *$AGE3544*$=1$
	OTHERWISE *$AGE3544*$=0$
$AGE4564	IF (($A005>44$) AND ($A005<65$)) THEN *$AGE4564*$=1$
	OTHERWISE *$AGE4564*$=0$
$LOGAGE	*$LOGAGE*$=\ln(A005)$
$MARRIED	IF ($A006=1$ OR 2) THEN *$MARRIED*$=1$
	OTHERWISE *$MARRIED*$=0$
$COHABIT	IF ($A006=3$) THEN *$COHABIT*$=1$
	OTHERWISE *$COHABIT*$=0$
$SINGLE	IF ($A006=4$) THEN *$SINGLE*$=1$
	OTHERWISE *$SINGLE*$=0$
$OTHER	IF ($A006>4$) THEN *$OTHER*$=1$
	OTHERWISE *$OTHER*$=0$
$SE1	IF ($SIZEEST=1$ OR 2) THEN *$SE1*$=1$
	OTHERWISE *$SE1*$=0$
$SE2	IF ($SIZEEST=3$ OR 4) THEN *$SE2*$=1$
	OTHERWISE *$SE2*$=0$

$SE3   IF ($SIZEEST$=5) THEN $SE3$=1
                OTHERWISE $SE3$=0
$LOGP003 $LOGP003$=ln($P003$)
$PWAGE   IF (partner's $P003$>0) THEN $PWAGE$=1
                OTHERWISE $PWAGE$=0
                [partner occurs where $A006$=1 or 3]
$EARN2   IF (partner's ($GWAGE+GWAGENT+LV+SEINC+SEINCNT$)
                >0) THEN $EARN2$=1
                OTHERWISE $EARN2$=0
                [partner occurs where $A006$=1 or 3]
                [for derivation of $GWAGE$, $GWAGENT$, LV, $SEINC$ and
                $SEINCNT$ see Appendix, Section A.5]
$PENS2   IF (partner's ($PEN+PPEN+OPEN$)>0) THEN $PENS2$=1
                OTHERWISE $PENS2$=0
                [partner occurs where $A006$=1 or 3]
                [for derivation of PEN, $PPEN$ and $OPEN$, see Appendix,
                Section A.5]
$UELASTYR   IF ($WKSWEMP$<52) THEN $UELASTYR$=1
                OTHERWISE $UELASTYR$=0
$LOGGROSS $LOGGROSS$=ln($GWAGE+GWAGENT+LV+SEINC+$
                $SEINCNT+PEN+PPEN+OPEN$)
                [partner occurs where $A006$=1 or 3]
                [for derivation of $GWAGE$, $GWAGENT$, LV, $SEINC$,
                $SEINCNT$, PEN, $PPEN$ and $OPEN$ see Appendix, Section
                A.5]

2. Dependent variables

$NCOCO   IF ($NCOCO$=1) THEN National Insurance regime is NCO
                IF ($NCOCO$=0) THEN National Insurance regime is CO
$NCORR   IF ($NCORR$=1) THEN National Insurance regime is NCO
                IF ($NCORR$=0) THEN National Insurance regime is RR
$CORR   IF ($CORR$=1) THEN National Insurance regime is CO
                IF ($CORR$=0) THEN National Insurance regime is RR

Notes

1 Employers' contributions have no direct or immediate distributional impact on personal incomes, but they have a *revenue* impact, which can offset the revenue impact of changes in taxes and benefits that do directly affect households. POLIMOD models the revenue impact to the government of changes in employer contributions, but assumes that these have no direct impact on household incomes.

2 Certain married women are exempted from Class 2 contributions; see Booth, 1991, p. 126.

3 Unlike income tax, NIC liabilities are weekly and non-cumulative; that is,

liability is calculated separately on each week's earnings rather than cumulatively over the year. There is, however, an annual maximum payment.

4 This chapter necessarily frequently refers to FES variables. These are italicised in the text (eg., as in *B303*, *B306*) and are explained fully in the Appendix to this chapter.

5 It is worth noting that in some cases where the FES respondent did not give full information on gross earnings and deductions from them, *P003* is itself imputed.

6 According to FES documentation, NICs and tax are imputed where this information is missing and net or gross earnings are reported but this is not done for the 107 cases with missing contributions data (see ESRC Data Archive, 1992, pp. B24–9).

7 See Booth (1991), pp. 372–5.

8 This suggests that the respondent would have been aged at least 21 in 1977. Social Security Statistics show that no one who made contributions under the RR regime in 1990–1 or 1991–2 was aged less than 35 (Department of Social Security, 1993b and 1994, Table H102).

9 If our model were to predict membership of the CO regime where $NCOCO=1$ represents CO membership, then the parameter estimates Bi in Table 6.8 would be identical, but their signs would be reversed. Thus, Bi for *$SUPERANN* would be 4.2381, and the probability associated with this would be 0.99.

10 There is one way in which FES respondent employees could be paying contributions under two different regimes at the time of interview: if they are employed in a subsidiary job, they may pay Class 1 contributions on earnings from this job under a different regime than for their main job. In this exercise, however, we are only concerned with modelling the contributions regime for employees' main jobs.

11 FES data are grossed up according to family composition weights. The method is described in the Appendix to the book.

12 For a discussion of sampling frames and methods in the surveys see DSS Department of Social Security (1995a) and Central Statistical Office (1992).

7 Local taxes

7.1 Introduction

Local taxes in the UK are levied by local authorities according to rules set by central government. Although central government sets out the basic parameters, local authorities are free to determine the scale of local tax within these parameters. Since 1989, there have been two major changes in British legislation governing local taxation. In the analyses in Chapters 3 and 4 domestic rates are simulated for 1978/9 and the council tax for 1996/7. Between 1989 (1990 in England and Wales) and 1992/3, the community charge was the prevailing local tax. POLIMOD can simulate each of these regimes.

Sensitive modelling of local taxation requires highly disaggregated data. Ideally, we require information for respondent households that is identical to that used by local authorities to calculate their liability for local taxes. Not all this information is available from the 1991 Family Expenditure Survey (FES). In particular, two vital elements are missing. Firstly, for reasons of respondent anonymity, there are no data in the public access dataset which identify the local authority area in which the respondent household lives. These data are necessary for calculating taxes under any locally determined tax regime. Secondly, there are no data on the value of dwellings, necessary for modelling liability to council taxes, the current system of local taxation in England, Scotland and Wales.

This chapter examines how this information deficit can be overcome, and describes some methods by which the distributional effects of the three recent local tax policy regimes can be simulated using the FES. Section 7.2 examines the way in which local areas within the FES are defined for the purposes of determining a household's liability to local taxes. Section 7.3 looks at how domestic rates bills can be calculated using FES. Section 7.4 describes how community charge amounts can be imputed for FES respondents. Section 7.5 examines some issues in the estimation of house values, and describes how POLIMOD models council tax.[1] Section 7.6 concludes.

7.2 Defining local authority areas

The most accurate way to model local taxes would be to apply the appropriate level of taxation for the policy year we are modelling to the local authority in which the FES household resides. For example, if we know that a FES household lives in the City of Cambridge, then we can calculate its liability to community charge in 1991/2 by multiplying the 1991/2 community charge imposed by Cambridge City Council by the number of liable adults living in the household. Information on community charges and other local taxes in any given year is available for all local authorities from CIPFA.[2]

However, for reasons of respondent anonymity, local authority data for individual households in FES are not publicly available. The most detailed area information available in the public access FES is the Local Authority (LA) Group in which the respondent household resides. LA Groups in the 1991 FES were derived by Central Statistical Office (CSO) for the Department of Social Security on the basis of region and level of community charge levied in 1991/2.[3] In the 1991 FES, each LA Group covers between two and seven LA areas within one of the 11 British regions that charge similar levels of community charge (Northern Ireland has not been included in any of the local taxation reforms imposed on the rest of the UK in recent years). Although smaller than standard regions, these local authority groups are still very large. While there were about 500 local authority areas in Britain in 1994/5, each determining its own levels of local tax, there are only 78 local authority groups in the FES data.[4] Therefore, for any one household in the FES sample, it is possible that the estimated 'average' local tax may bear little relation to the actual local tax liability of that household. For example, the Greater London region is split into five LA groups. In one of these LA groups, community charge ranges from £180 to £250, while the average calculated for the LA group is £215.55. It is not possible to validate calculated local tax liabilities for individual households using the information available to us in the FES. However, we should expect to be able to validate *average* and *aggregate* local tax liabilities calculated in the course of this exercise against external sources.

Once LA groups have been defined, it is possible to apply an imputed rate of local taxation based on some measure of the average local tax rate in the LA group to all households in that group. Methods for doing this are explored with regard to domestic rates, community charge and council tax in sections 7.3, 7.4 and 7.5, respectively.

7.3 Domestic rates

The domestic rates system of local taxation was in place until April 1989 in Scotland, April 1990 in England and Wales, and is still in place in Northern Ireland. Therefore, the 1991 FES has no information on rates paid by households surveyed, except in Northern Ireland. However, the 1991 FES does provide data on rateable values for each dwelling in the survey. With imputed rate poundages we can calculate each household's liability to domestic rates. In this exercise, we examine two ways of imputing this liability.

Method 1: using external data to estimate rate poundages

Using data from the CIPFA Statistical Information Service for 1989, we estimate average rate poundages for each LA Group in 1989/90 in England and Wales, and 1988/9 in Scotland. We do this by dividing the estimated total domestic rates revenue (the product of total rateable values RV_i and rate poundages RP_i for each LA, i, in a group of n LAs) by the total domestic rateable value, RV_i, for all the local authorities in the LA Group, to produce an average rate poundage, RP_g, for each group:

$$RP_g = \frac{\sum_{i=1}^{n} RP_i(RV_i)}{\sum_{i=1}^{n} RV_i}$$

Using this method we estimate rate poundages that, if applied to CIPFA data on aggregate rateable values in each local authority area, produce an amount of rates revenue that equals the total estimated by CIPFA for the year 1989/90 (or 1988/9 in Scotland). Table 7.1 shows how rate poundages are imputed for one LA group in the North of England. These estimated rate poundages for each FES household are then adjusted from 1989/90 to another year so that their distributional impact can be compared with that of other local taxation schemes, or examined in the context of current policy.

Chapters 3 and 4 use the following method of adjustment to estimate the distributional impact of domestic rates (as part of the wider tax–benefit regime) in 1978/9. Firstly, the 1989/90 (1988/9 if Scotland) rate poundages are deflated according to the growth recorded in average house-

Table 7.1. *The calculation of average rate poundages in a local authority group*

Local authority area	Total domestic rateable value 1988/9	Rate poundage 1988/9	Estimated rates revenue 1988/9
Sedgfield	£4,636,000	3.4120	£15,818,032
Gateshead	£11,583,000	3.2693	£37,868,302
South Tyneside	£9,149,000	3.2260	£29,514,674
Copeland	£3,403,000	3.1000	£9,433,300
Total	£28,771,000		£92,634,308

Average domestic rates poundage for this group: 92,634,308 / 28,771,000=3.26

Source: CIPFA Statistical Information Service (1990b).

hold rates charges in England, Scotland and Wales to the modelled year. For example, since average household rates quadrupled in England between 1978/9 and 1989/90, rate poundages at 1978/9 prices are estimated to be about a quarter of their 1989/90 levels. These adjusted rate poundages are then uniformly uprated according to changes in prices (Chapter 3) or changes in incomes (section 4.2 of Chapter 4) from the policy year in question to 1996/7, so that they can be compared with each other. These factors are reproduced in Table 7.2. This shows that English local authority group rate poundages in 1989/90 are multiplied by 0.2542 to arrive at an estimate of rate poundages in 1978/9. In order to make this figure comparable with local taxes in 1996/7, these estimates are then multiplied by 'standard' uprating factors: 3.154 for price uprating (Chapter 3) or 4.294 (incomes uprating in Chapter 4).

It is worth highlighting a potential shortcoming associated with this approach. Validation of our estimates of rate poundages is problematic, given that our FES sample was surveyed in 1991, our rates data are taken from 1989/90 (or 1988/89 for Scotland) and our policy regime is updated to 1996/7. Any simulations produced using the method described above may be related more to local taxes in 1989/90 (or indeed in 1991) than to the policy year of interest. In 1989, for example, the average rateable value in England and Wales was £201. In 1978, it was £192 (see Board of Inland Revenue, 1979 and 1989). This increase in average rateable values is most likely due to the construction of some new homes and demolition of other, older homes between 1978 and 1989. The current method does not take account of the impact of changes in the composition of housing, nor of changes in the regional distribution of local taxes.

Table 7.2. *Uprating factors for rates 1978/9 to 1996/7*

	Backdating from 1989/90 (1988/9 in Scotland)			Uprating to 1996/7	
	England	Wales	Scotland	prices	incomes
1978/9 regime	0.2542	0.3530	0.2545	3.154	4.294

Sources: Derived from CIPFA, 1979 and CIPFA, 1990a. Average rate payment per domestic hereditament, Table 2 (1979) and page A3 (1990a).

Method 2: using FES data to estimate rate poundages

Kent (1994) proposes an alternative method of estimating rate poundages from the 1991 FES in a way that directly uses information present in the FES for each household. This involves calculating the average community charge bill faced by households in each LA group in 1991 (using FES data), and dividing this by the average rateable value, to produce an average rate poundage for the LA group. CC_j is the amount of community charge faced by the jth person in household i, which contains p people who are liable to community charge. There are n households in the LA group, and RV_i is the rateable value for the dwelling in which the ith household lives.

$$RP_g = \frac{\sum_{i=1}^{n}\sum_{j=1}^{p} CC_j}{\sum_{i=1}^{n} RV_i}$$

Rate poundage multiplied by actual rateable value in 1991 provides an estimate of the domestic rates each household would be liable for if rates were to replace the community charge in 1991. The basic assumption of this method is that the amount of revenue collected in local tax remains constant regardless of system of local taxation modelled. This method is useful if we wish to model the impact of a change in the system of local taxation in isolation from other tax–benefit changes, and particularly where we wish the impact of the change to be revenue-neutral, overall and within LA groups. Therefore, this method addresses the question: 'What would be the distributional impact of a switch to domestic rates, given that the amount of revenue raised by each local authority remained constant?' With some adjustments, it would be possible to use this method to model a change in local taxation, maintaining overall revenue-neutrality, but introducing redistribution between local authority areas and regions.

Table 7.3. *Average rate poundages in the GB regions using Methods 1 and 2*

Region	Updating to 1996/7	
	Method 1	Method 2
North	2.64	3.82
Yorks	2.61	3.21
North West	2.94	3.32
East Midlands	2.95	3.05
West Midlands	2.63	2.77
East Anglia	2.04	2.63
London	1.80	1.71
South East	2.05	2.14
South West	2.82	2.97
Wales	3.62	1.91
Scotland	0.95	0.78
Average	2.46	2.57

Table 7.3 shows average rate poundages in the eleven regions of Great Britain, imputed using Methods 1 and 2. Method 1 (backdated to 1978/9 and then updated to 1996/7) produces an average rate of £2.46 and Method 2 (based on community charge levels after April 1991, updated to 1996/7) produces an average rate of £2.57. The differences resulting from the two methods are large in some regions, particularly the North, Yorkshire & Humberside, East Anglia and Wales. On the other hand, differences are small in London, the South East and the West Midlands. Where rate poundages are larger under Method 2 than under Method 1, it suggests that the community charge raises more revenue than the 1978/9 system of rates. In other regions (particularly in Wales), rate poundages are smaller under Method 2 than under Method 1, suggesting that the community charge system raises less than the rates system did. Either way, it is clear that Methods 1 and 2, with their different assumptions, can produce very different results.

7.4 The community charge

The community charge was levied in Scotland between 1989/90 and 1992/3, and in England and Wales between 1990/1 and 1992/3. Unlike rates, the community charge was levied on all individuals aged over 18 who live in private households, and not on dwellings. The 1991 FES data include imputed community charge amounts for all liable respondents

Table 7.4. *The calculation of average community charge in a local authority group*

Local authority area	Total number of community charge payers 1992/3	Annual community charge 1992/3	Total community charge 1992/3
Sedgfield	67,352	£266.02	£17,916,979
Gateshead	147,732	£272.00	£40,183,104
South Tyneside	116,972	£283.00	£33,103,076
Copeland	54,756	£277.69	£15,205,194
Total	386,812		£106,408,353
Average community charge per person for this group: £106,408,353/386,812=£275.09			

Source: CIPFA Statistical Information Service (1993) *Community Charge Demands and Precepts, 1992–3.*

both before and after April 1991. Moreover, as has already been noted, the LA Groups to which 1991 FES households are attached are derived in accordance with community charge levels in 1991. Using POLIMOD, Redmond and Sutherland (1995) simulate the impact of re-introducing 1992/3 levels of community charge in the policy year 1994/5 by imputing the community charge in 1992/3 for each LA group using original CIPFA data.[5] The imputed charge is uprated to 1994/5 levels by using the same updating factors as are used in the case of rates. Community charge CC_g for each LA group is imputed according to the following formula, where average community charge is weighted by the number of payers in each local authority area in the LA Group:

$$CC_g = \left(\sum_{i=1}^{m} CC_i n_i \right) \Big/ m$$

CC_i is the community charge for local authority i, there being n chargepayers in local authority i, and m local authorities in each LA Group g. Table 7.4 shows how the average community charge is estimated for one local authority group.

7.5 Council tax

Council tax bands

Council tax is set according to market value as determined by a government survey that placed all dwellings into one of eight valuation bands on

Table 7.5. *Council tax valuation bands in England, Scotland and Wales*

Valuation band	Range of values		
	England	Scotland	Wales
A	up to £40,000	up to £27,000	up to £30,000
B	£40,001–£52,000	£27,001–£35,000	£30,001–£39,000
C	£52,001–£68,000	£35,001–£45,000	£39,001–£51,000
D	£68,001–£88,000	£45,001–£58,000	£51,001–£66,000
E	£88,001–£120,000	£58,001–£80,000	£66,001–£90,000
F	£120,001–£160,000	£80,001–£106,000	£90,001–£120,000
G	£160,001–£320,000	£106,001–£212,000	£120,001–£240,000
H	over £320,000	over £212,000	over £240,000

Source: Ward, 1993, pp. 37–8.

1 April 1991. England, Wales and Scotland each have their own valuation bands, outlined in Table 7.5. The difference in banding between England, Scotland and Wales reflects the fact that house values in England are on average higher than in the other two countries. However, there is no recognition in the council tax scheme of other regional differences, for example between London and the rest of England.

Market value of dwellings

Market values of dwellings of households surveyed in the 1991 FES have to be imputed since the FES does not contain this information. Hills (1991) and Davies and Rajah (1992) elaborate methodologies for estimating the market values of houses in the FES by regressing coefficients derived from the 1988 Building Society Mortgages Survey (BSMS) on FES data. In his analysis, Hills imputes house values for households in the 1982 FES, while Davies and Rajah impute house values for the 1988 FES. Both analyses are similar in many respects, and highlight two problems in particular: firstly, the BSMS is a survey of houses for which mortgages have been taken out, rather than a survey of house values. Both argue that houses in the BSMS sample are likely to have lower average values than in the UK as a whole. Secondly, both choose 1988 as their BSMS survey year because this is the last year in the survey for which rateable values of houses are reported for a substantial number of observations (about half the total sample).[6] But they point out that house prices were very unstable during this year and they attempt to make some allowance for this in their estimations. Both studies use Ordinary Least Squares (OLS) regressions of logged house price on stock characteristics that are common to the FES and the BSMS, and then apply the resulting coefficients associated with the BSMS characteristics to the FES data. Their regression equations are variations on the following form:

$$\ln(purchase\ price) = constant + \ln(rateable\ value) + \ln(number\ of\ rooms) + region\ dummies + dwelling\ type\ dummies + construction\ date\ dummies + garage\ dummy + time\ of\ purchase\ dummies$$

The method used in this analysis follows Hills and Davies and Rajah, but our model is more restricted: we are not able to include dummy variables representing dwelling type or date of construction because they are not present in the 1991 FES. The other characteristics variables – number of rooms, presence of garage and rateable value – are examined in Table 7.6.

The 1988 BSMS sample is compared with distributions from the 1991 FES, classified by tenure type. The top half of the table refers to England and Wales, and the bottom half refers to Scotland. All the FES sub-samples display different characteristics from the BSMS samples – this is even true for the FES 'owned with mortgage' subsamples. For example, over 27% of dwellings in this FES group in England and Wales have seven or more rooms, compared with about 12% of the BSMS sample. On the other hand, mean rateable values in the England and Wales FES samples (although not in the Scotland samples) are considerably lower than in the BSMS sample, in spite of the larger room sizes in the FES samples. The mean rateable value for all England and Wales FES households is £197.31. This compares well with the average rateable value for all dwellings in the UK population in 1989 of £201 (Board of Inland Revenue, 1989, p. 108), and poorly with a mean rateable value of £290.21 in the BSMS. This suggests that dwellings for which mortgages were being sought in 1988 are not representative of houses in general in England and Wales. Furthermore, the relationship between number of rooms and rateable value appears to be very different in the two surveys. This may reduce our ability to impute from one survey to the other.

The differences associated with tenure type within the FES, however, make intuitive sense. Dwellings that are privately owned, with or without a mortgage, are larger than rented dwellings, they are more likely to have garages and their average rateable values are higher. The large proportion of privately rented dwellings with just one room may reflect the fact that the FES includes in its sample households in shared accommodation – for example, separate households sharing a house, each having their own bedroom. This type of housing is unlikely to reach the market in the form in which FES respondents inhabit it, and is therefore almost non-existent

Table 7.6. *Characteristics of 1988 BSMS and 1991 FES compared (% except where otherwise indicated)*

	BSMS 1988	FES 1991				
		local authority tenants	private tenants	owned with mortgage	fully owned	all house-holds
England and Wales						
Number of rooms						
1	0.5	0.8	16.4	0.3	0.0	1.8
2	1.6	2.9	3.5	0.8	0.3	1.4
3	7.4	21.3	11.1	3.2	2.6	7.7
4	23.1	29.5	18.0	13.3	18.2	18.5
5	32.2	28.8	20.9	29.1	27.8	27.9
6	23.5	13.7	15.1	26.3	27.5	22.8
7	7.5	2.4	8.2	13.2	11.4	9.9
8 or more	4.2	0.6	6.8	13.9	12.4	9.9
Garage in dwelling?						
No	43.4	92.4	76.1	45.3	39.6	57.1
Yes	56.6	7.6	23.9	54.7	60.4	42.9
Mean rateable values (£s)	290.21	161.63	168.27	213.22	211.46	197.31
Scotland						
Number of rooms						
1	0.2	0.3	15.7	0.0	0.0	1.3
2	3.3	1.7	5.8	1.6	2.4	2.1
3	15.7	20.5	8.8	10.3	3.2	13.2
4	29.3	46.9	21.7	25.7	30.3	35.2
5	30.2	25.0	8.2	27.5	21.0	23.8
6	13.3	5.6	12.7	12.7	18.4	10.8
7	4.6	0.0	14.9	10.9	15.4	7.4
8 or more	3.4	0.0	12.4	11.4	9.3	6.3
Garage in dwelling?						
No	32.6	96.0	70.4	55.5	36.9	70.3
Yes	67.4	4.1	29.6	45.5	63.1	29.7
Mean rateable values (£s)	722.03	545.23	561.98	714.70	761.70	640.71

Source: BSMS 1988 and FES 1991 (own calculations); FES is grossed-up to be representative of UK population. See Appendix to this book for grossing-up method.

in the BSMS sample. Similarly, local-authority-owned dwellings are unlikely to have garages, and their rateable values are lowest of all.

It is important to stress that the extent to which we can use BSMS data to predict the market value of rented or non-mortgaged dwellings in the FES is uncertain, for the simple reason that the market value of a dwelling can only really be determined when it is put up for sale. Therefore, in using

Table 7.7. *House price regression, using BSMS 1988 (quarter 1):*
parameter estimates for England and Wales, and Scotland

		England and Wales	Scotland
Adjusted R^2		0.5486	0.2746
Variable		Parameter estimates	
INTERCEP	y intercept	7.6703	9.2276
LOGRAT	ln (rateable value)	0.3418	−0.0120
LOGROOM	ln (no. of rooms in dwelling)	0.3437	0.5869
GAR	garage dummy	0.3066	0.3831
YOR	Yorks & Humberside dummy	0.1171	
EMI	East Midlands dummy	0.2365	
EAN	East Anglia dummy	0.5291	
GLO	Greater London dummy	0.9176	
SEA	South East (except London) dummy	0.8099	
SWE	South West dummy	0.6558	
WMI	West Midlands dummy	0.1379	
NWE	North West dummy	0.0820	
WAL	Wales dummy	0.1480	
MONTH1	First month in year dummy	−0.0414	−0.2148
MONTH2	Second month in year dummy	−0.0603	−0.1406
MONTH3	Third month in year dummy		−0.0950
MONTH4	Fourth month in year dummy		−0.0120
MONTH5	Fifth month in year dummy		0.1046

the BSMS, we are assuming that market prices for dwellings in the rented sector, for example, would be agreed on much the same basis as prices for private dwellings. Moreover, the extent to which these imputed (or even actual) market values match council tax bandings is another issue, which is explored further below.

The following model is used to predict dwelling values in the 1991 FES from the 1988 BSMS using the variables summarised in Table 7.6.

$$\ln(purchase\ price) = constant + \ln(rateable\ value) + \ln(number\ of$$
$$rooms) + region\ dummies + garage$$
$$dummy + month\ of\ sale\ dummy^7$$

The regression is restricted to the first quarter of 1988 in England and Wales, and the first two quarters in Scotland, in order to control for house price volatility during that year (this is the approach taken by Hills, 1991). In common with Hills (1991) and Davies and Rajah (1992), two separate

Table 7.8. *House prices by region in 1991: FES (imputed) and BSMS (£s)*

Region	BSMS 1988 (updated 1991)	FES 1991 (households with mortgage)	FES/BSMS
Northern England	47,118	42,009	0.89
Yorks & Humberside	50,311	50,255	1.00
North West	51,163	51,658	1.01
East Midlands	50,311	49,618	0.99
West Midlands	55,216	52,534	0.95
East Anglia	48,774	48,345	0.99
Greater London	70,413	71,047	1.01
South East	66,823	70,439	1.05
South West	58,845	64,472	1.10
Wales	45,703	38,075	0.83
Scotland	39,475	41,519	1.05

models are estimated, one for England and Wales, and one for Scotland. Table 7.7 summarises the results and shows that the model is less able to explain prices in Scotland than in England and Wales (the Scottish adjusted R^2 is about half the value for England and Wales). Table 7.7 shows the contribution of each independent variable to the adjusted R^2. This demonstrates the importance of rateable values in England and Wales in predicting purchase price in the BSMS. This is less the case in Scotland, where the resulting R^2 is considerably lower. The *GAR* dummy is of some importance in all the regressions. Regional dummies are also important in the case of England and Wales, and there is a clear difference between the Southern regions, which have large parameter estimates, and the rest (in the example in Table 7.7, *NOR* (North of England) is the omitted region dummy).

The parameter estimates in Table 7.7 are used to impute the value of dwellings in the FES. We eliminate parameter estimates for month of purchase from our calculations, since this has no relevance in the FES. Rather, we assume that we are calculating purchase prices or market values for March 1988 in England and Wales, and for June 1988 in Scotland (these are the omitted 'month of purchase' variables in our two equations). These market values are then updated to April 1991 prices using the Halifax Price Index. Table 7.8 compares the imputed 1991 FES house values for households with mortgages with those in the 1988 BSMS. Both sets of figures are adjusted to April 1991 prices. In general, average regional imputed house values for households with a mortgage in 1991 FES compare quite well

Table 7.9. *Percentage of dwellings in council tax bands: GB population, 1988 BSMS and 1991 FES*

Council tax band	England			Wales			Scotland		
	Pop.	BSMS	FES	Pop.	BSMS	FES	Pop.	BSMS	FES
A	26	53	31	20	69	45	26	61	16
B	19	15	21	26	16	24	26	13	46
C	22	15	25	20	8	20	16	9	12
D	15	10	15	15	5	10	11	29	14
E	9	5	6	12	3	1	11	6	11
F	5	2	1	4	0	0	6	2	0
G	4	1	0	3	0	0	4	0	0
H	1	0	0	0	0	0	0	0	0

Sources: BSMS, 1988: own calculations; FES, 1991: own calculations; CIPFA Statistical Information Service, 1993. BSMS house values are adjusted by month of sampling and region to April 1991 levels.

with regional 1988 BSMS prices, updated to 1991. The averages that make the worst comparison are for North of England and Wales.

Table 7.9 shows the distribution of dwellings in the 1991 population across council tax bands. This is compared with the distribution of dwellings in the 1988 BSMS sample and the imputed 1991 FES sample. The table indicates that 1988 BSMS purchase prices, adjusted to April 1991 levels, are low compared with those in Great Britain as a whole if we accept council tax banding as being a true reflection of the market value of dwellings. Given that local authority rented accommodation is likely to be of lower value than purchased accommodation, and that accommodation which is owned with a mortgage is likely to be of lower value than fully owned accommodation, we should expect the BSMS sample to be under-represented in the lower bands, over-represented in the middle and under-represented at the top. Table 7.9 shows that the BSMS sample is overly concentrated in the bottom band and almost totally absent from the top bands. It is also apparent, and not surprising, that low-value dwellings are over-represented in the imputed FES sample and that high-value dwellings are remarkable by their absence. This is likely to be a reflection of the under-representation of high-value dwellings in the BSMS, and of very wealthy households in FES. It may also be the result of several unobserved factors, such as the methodology used in assessing dwellings for council tax banding.

It is important to emphasise that the methodology employed in this

Table 7.10. *Allocation of dwellings to council tax bands: the effect of calibration (%)*

Effect of calibration	England	Wales	Scotland	All
One band lower	0	0	9	1
Same band	59	21	53	57
One band higher	36	61	33	37
Two bands higher	5	16	4	5
Three bands higher	0	2	1	0
Total	100	100	100	100

analysis is likely to result in over-representation of low-value dwellings in our imputed FES sample. However, it is worth noting that, in some respects, the distribution of the FES sample is closer to that of the population than that of the BSMS sample. This is particularly true for the lower council tax bands in England and Wales, where in the BSMS sample, 53% and 69% respectively, are in Band A. This compares with 32% and 45% respectively in the FES, and 26 and 20% in the population. The distributions of dwellings in the two samples in Scotland look rather strange in comparison with the distribution of the population of dwellings: the BSMS distribution is concentrated in Bands A and D, and the FES distribution's mode is at Band B rather than at Band A; neither bears a close resemblance to the distribution of dwellings in the Scottish population.

To compensate for the over-representation of dwellings in the lower council tax bands in the imputed FES sample, and the mis-representation of dwellings in Scotland, we calibrate the proportions of households in each council tax band so that they match aggregate totals. Therefore, since Table 7.9 shows that 26% of the population of dwellings in England fall into Band A, and 1% fall into Band H, we place the bottom 26% of dwellings in our 1991 FES distribution of imputed house values into band A, and the top 1% in band H, and so on. This means that purchase prices as estimated in POLIMOD are not directly used to determine council tax banding of households, only to rank them. Table 7.10 shows that overall, 57% of households remain in the same council tax band after calibration, 37% move up one band and 5% move up two bands. Households in England experience the least change as a result of this calibration, while households in Wales experience the most. The effect of calibration on council tax levels for households is examined in the next section.

Table 7.11. *The calculation of average council tax in a local authority group*

Local authority area	Total number of 'Band D equivalent' dwellings	Annual Band D council tax	Total council tax 1994/5
Sedgfield	27,758	£631.12	£17,518,629
Gateshead	64,785	£659.97	£42,756,156
South Tyneside	49,836	£614.25	£14,582,192
Copeland	23,021	£633.43	£14,582,192
Total	165,400		£105,468,740
Average annual council tax for this group: £105,468,740/165,400=£637.66			

Source: CIPFA Statistical Information Service (1993) *Council Tax Demands and Precepts 1993–4*; 1994/5 council tax figures courtesy of Department of Environment officials.

Amount payable per band

In all three countries, the amount of council tax payable in respect of a dwelling in any LA area varies between bands in the following proportions:

Band A	6/9	Band E	11/9
Band B	7/9	Band F	13/9
Band C	8/9	Band G	15/9
Band D	9/9	Band H	18/9

The local authority sets the Band D (headline) council tax amount and from this the liability of each dwelling is calculated. The local authority has no discretion to vary these proportions, or the bands described in Table 7.5.

POLIMOD models exemptions for households where the head and spouse are aged less than 18, and reductions from the full amount (25%) where there is only one adult in the dwelling, as well as transitional reductions. Reductions for students apply if all household members are students.

Calculating council tax using FES and other data

As with rates and community charge, we calculate average headline (Band D) council tax in each LA group from CIPFA data[8] (average Band D council tax weighted according to the number of dwellings and their council tax valuation band in each LA area). Table 7.11 shows how this is

Table 7.12. *Average annual council tax liability in 1996/7 by region and by tenure (£s)*

	(A) Council tax bands as derived from BSMS	(B) Council tax bands calibrated to population	(B)/(A)
Region			
Northern England	430.56	440.44	1.02
Yorks & Humberside	430.04	457.08	1.06
North West	464.36	496.08	1.07
East Midlands	416.00	436.28	1.05
West Midlands	436.80	461.24	1.06
East Anglia	372.32	388.44	1.04
Greater London	474.76	536.12	1.13
South East	464.36	532.48	1.15
South West	464.36	517.40	1.11
Wales	244.40	290.16	1.19
Scotland	528.32	567.32	1.07
Tenure			
Local authority rented	388.44	401.96	1.03
Privately rented	353.08	374.40	1.06
Owned with mortgage	485.16	539.76	1.11
Owned outright	458.64	509.08	1.11
Total council tax liability			
(millions)	8,511	9,356	1.10
as % of Blue Book estimate	87.0	95.7	

Note: Aggregate council tax benefit entitlement simulated by POLIMOD is subtracted from aggregate council tax liability for comparison with the Blue Book estimate. This equals £8,511m −£1,636m (uncalibrated) and £9,356m −£1,732m (calibrated).

Sources: FES 1991: own calculations. Blue Book estimate: Central Statistical Office (1996), Table 7.2. Total council tax receipts in 1995=£8,989m, updated to April 1996 using council tax element of the Retail Price Index, Department of Employment (1994) and Office for National Statistics (1996), Table 6.2.

done for 1994/5 in one local authority area. Council taxes for 1994/5 are updated to 1996/7 using the Retail Prices Index for local taxes. Estimated council tax amounts are then applied to each FES household, according to the council tax band in which their dwelling falls.

Table 7.12 shows estimated average annual council tax liability by region and by tenure, both before and after we calibrate council tax band membership to match that of the population in England, Scotland and Wales.

As we should expect, in each case calibration results in an increase in average liability. This increase is greatest in Greater London, the South East, the South West and Wales, and for households who own their homes, either with a mortgage or outright. For example, in the South East, the difference between the two methods amounts to 15%, or £68.12 per year. At the other end of the scale, the difference for households living in local authority rented accommodation is relatively small: only 3% on average, or £13.52 per year.

Comparison with the Blue Book estimate of council tax liabilities in Table 7.12 suggests that council taxes calculated from calibrated bands produce better estimates of total liability than council taxes calculated from uncalibrated bands. The uncalibrated estimate is 87% of the Blue Book figure, while the calibrated estimate is 95.7% of the Blue Book figure. Therefore, calibration does not result in an over-estimate of aggregate liabilities but, rather, a slight under-estimate.

7.6 Conclusions

To improve the method of modelling the three recent regimes of local tax, or to assess alternative schemes, such as property taxes, local income taxes or sales taxes (see Ridge and Smith, 1991), more precise data on the local authority areas in which FES respondents reside are required. Improvements in property value-based taxes would also require better data on the value of dwellings in the survey, or better methods of imputing these values. Also of considerable benefit in this area would be additional information on the size, age and type of dwelling occupied by survey respondents. In part, answers may lie in later versions of the FES, which include data on respondents' council tax bands and purchase prices for owner occupiers. However, after 1991 the FES does not report rateable values. With more recent data, it may therefore become more difficult to model rateable-value-based local tax schemes, such as domestic rates.

Notes

1 POLIMOD calculates *liability to* rather than *payment of* local taxes. Non-payment of taxes is not modelled. POLIMOD assumes that all households are liable to local taxes unless they are recorded in the FES data as exempt from payment, or liable for reduced payments.
2 Chartered Institute of Public Finance and Accountancy (CIPFA) Statistical Information Service (various years).

3 We are grateful to the Analytical Services Division of the Department of Social Security for allowing us access to these LA codes.

4 Redmond (1996) shows how local authorities are grouped.

5 Sources – England and Wales: CIPFA Statistical Information Service (1992) *Community Charge Demands and Precepts 1992–3*; Scotland: CIPFA Scottish Branch (1992).

6 Both Hills (1991) and Davies and Rajah (1992) report that the differences between the BSMS sample with rateable values and that without are not significant.

7 Redmond (1996) considers some alternative models.

8 CIPFA Statistical Information Service (1994) *Council Tax Demands and Precepts 1994–5*.

8 Future directions: non-means-tested social security benefits

8.1 Introduction

At present, POLIMOD does not simulate entitlement to a retirement pension and other non-means-tested benefits. It simply takes amounts of reported receipt and updates these to the year of interest. This is because the Family Expenditure Survey (FES) does not supply all the information we need *fully* to simulate entitlement. To carry out a full simulation of entitlement to retirement pension, for example, we need information about an individual's National Insurance contributions, in some cases we need information about the contributions of their spouse or their former or deceased spouse, and we need to know whether or not they deferred retirement. None of this information is collected and, particularly in the case of contributions, respondents are unlikely to know or to have access to the details that simulation would require. What the FES does provide is a variable that records the total amount of each benefit received by each respondent. About one quarter of all FES respondents report receipt of one or more non-means-tested benefit. The greatest number (2,904 out of all 17,089 respondents to the 1991 survey) report receipt of retirement pension.

This chapter demonstrates the method whereby sufficient information to allow *partial* simulation of non-means-tested benefits can be imputed from these variables and from other information about respondents, taking retirement pension as an example. The broad approach can also be applied to other non-means-tested benefits.[1] Introduction of partial simulation of non-means-tested benefits into POLIMOD would have two main advantages: it would permit simulation of changes in the rates of different elements of benefit payments; and it will entail correction for misreporting, miscoding, and imputation and thereby improve estimates of caseload and expenditure for non-means-tested and means-tested benefits.

Section 8.2 sets out the dissaggregation method. Section 8.3 presents the results of a trial simulation of retirement pension receipt based on the new variables created. The final section concludes.

8.2 Disaggregation method

Retirement pension rules

The retirement pension is a contributory National Insurance benefit payable to persons over state pension age (60 for women, 65 for men), who have retired, and who have made sufficient contributions during their working lives. Widows and married women may be paid retirement pension on the basis of their spouse's contributions. The total amount of pension a person receives is comprised of several elements, each of which is the sum total of several, possibly offsetting, components:

(i) *Basic pension*. This is the flat rate component of contributory retirement pension, payable in respect of the claimant.[2] The basic pension can be increased or reduced by any or all of the following:[3]

an increase for a dependent partner
an increase for each dependent child
a reduction to the basic pension for insufficient contributions
a reduction to the increase for a dependent partner for insufficient contributions
a reduction where over-lapping benefits are received
an increment for deferred retirement.

If the claimant is a married woman, she can receive basic pension on the basis of her own contributions, her husband's, or both. If she claims on the basis of her own contributions, she is entitled to the standard rate of basic pension, subject to the additions and deductions set out above. If she claims on the basis of her husband's contributions, she will be paid a lower married woman's rate at 60% of the standard rate. If she claims on the basis of her own contributions as well as on the basis of her husband's, the combined amount of basic pension she receives cannot be more than the married woman's rate. She can only claim on the basis of her husband's contributions if he is in receipt of retirement pension. The married woman's rate of basic pension may be reduced if the husband made insufficient contributions, and may be increased by increments if the husband deferred his retirement or if the married woman claiming deferred her retirement. A widow or widower can inherit the full, standard rate basic pension of her or his former spouse.

(ii) Earnings-related pension from the State Earnings Related Pension Scheme (SERPS). SERPS can be received regardless of whether a basic pension is received, and may be increased by increments for deferred retirement. It is based on the level and duration of contributions made by the claimant since the introduction of the scheme in April 1978. If a claimant has been contracted out of SERPS for any period, the SERPS he or she receives in retirement is reduced by the amount of the guaranteed minimum pension or protected rights pension earned in those periods. A person who was contracted out for the entire contributory period will have a guaranteed minimum pension which reduces their SERPS entitlement to zero.

A woman who made only reduced rate contributions in her working life and claims on the basis of her husband's contributions receives no SERPS in her own right. Prior to May 1977, married women and some widows could elect to pay reduced rate contributions which provided no entitlement to contributory benefits. This option was revoked from that date but the right to make reduced rate contributions for those who had already made the election was maintained. A woman who reversed her reduced rate election and paid standard rate contributions for at least part of her working life may receive some SERPS. A woman can only receive SERPS based on her own contributions. This may be paid in addition to her married woman's rate of basic pension or her own standard rate basic pension. A widow or widower may claim the full amount of the SERPS earned by her or his deceased spouse.

(iii) Graduated pension. This is payable on the basis of contributions made between 1961 and 1975 to the earnings-related state pension scheme that predated the SERPS. Like SERPS, graduated pension may be reduced by contracting out, or increased by increments for deferred retirement. A widow can only inherit half of her deceased partner's graduated pension.

(iv) Non-contributory retirement pension (formerly old person's pension). This is payable to a person who has made insufficient contributions to receive a full basic pension who is aged 80 or over. It is a flat rate weekly payment of 60% of the standard Category A basic pension. It may be reduced where over-lapping benefits are received.

(v) Age addition. An addition of 25 pence per week in 1991 is payable to any claimant aged 80 or over. A qualifying claimant who has a non-claimant wife aged 80 or over will receive two age additions.[4]

FES data

The 1991 FES-derived data set gives us one variable on receipt of retirement pension: *B338*.[5] For those in receipt of retirement pension at the time of their interview, this is our variable *PEN*.

For most respondents, we have no way of discerning for certain whether the amount they report is, for example, a reduced basic pension plus SERPS and graduated pension or a full basic pension with increments and additions for dependants but no SERPS or graduated pension. Moreover, we have no way of cross checking whether respondents or interviewers have included in *PEN* amounts of attendance allowance or invalidity allowance that are included in their weekly payment but are not part of retirement pension. We have no way of identifying for certain cases where weekly payments that include an income support top-up have been recorded in their entirety as retirement pension. Our approach to disaggregation of *PEN* is therefore necessarily crude. We use *PENR*, retirement pension last received by those in receipt at the time of interview, recoded for benefit confusion and over-lapping benefits,[6] and take a step-wise approach to breaking it down into its component parts.

Dependants and age additions

An addition for a dependent adult can be made to the basic pension subject to a test of the earnings and benefit income of the dependant.[7] The addition can be paid in respect of the partner of the claimant or the person who looks after the children of the claimant. We assume that for the FES respondents, an adult addition is only paid in respect of a person who is married or in a marriage-like relationship. A woman can only claim an addition for her partner if she received one with a state benefit received immediately prior to reaching pension age. Here, we have no information about past benefit receipt and assume that only men receive the addition. Claimants are assumed to be receiving an adult addition (*PENAD*=1) if: they are male; they are married or in a marriage-like relationship; their partner is resident with them in the same benefit unit; their partner does not receive retirement benefit or any other earnings replacement state benefit; and their partner has earnings below the earnings limit. Twenty-eight *PENR* claimants (1%) are attributed with an adult addition.

A child addition (*PENCH*>0) is attributed for each dependent child if: the claimant's partner does not receive a state benefit; and the partner has earnings that do not exceed set limits for each additional child. Where both partners in a couple receive state benefits, the partner who receives child benefit is credited with the child addition.

Every claimant aged 80 or over receives an age addition of 25 pence per week. A qualifying male claimant who has a non-claimant partner aged 80 or over receives two age additions. We apply these rules to all claimants and attribute additions ($AGEAD=1$ or 2) to those who qualify.

No restrictions are placed on the level of $PENR$ at which elements of the total entitlement can be interpreted as adult and child additions. We do, however, assume that all additions are paid at the full rate. In fact, the addition for an adult dependant may be reduced in the same way as the basic pension for the claimant if he or she has made insufficient contributions. Additions for dependent adults and dependent children may not be paid or may be reduced if an over-lapping benefit includes a dependant's addition.

Miscoded income support

Respondents may confuse retirement pension with income support. For those who receive an income support top-up to their retirement pension, the two benefits are received as a single payment through an order book that does not record the detailed breakdown of the retirement pension amount.[8] Because retirement pension entitlements may be very close to the level of the income support entitlements for the elderly, we are conservative in our recoding. We only assume that miscoding has taken place if there is an exact match between the full pension amount (before reductions on account of over-lapping benefits) and our estimate of their income support entitlement.

In 37 cases (1.2% of the FES sample of pension claimants), there is an exact match between $PENR$ and one of our estimates of their possible income support entitlement. In 9 of these cases, respondents report receipt of a small amount of income support. We assume that reported income support is the amount of the income support top-up, and deduct this amount from $PENR$ to arrive at an estimate of their actual retirement pension payment, $IPENR$. In the remaining individual match cases, we set $IPENR$ equal to the rate of basic pension, plus age additions for those aged 80 or over, and assume that the difference is the amount of the income support top-up. In all cases, the respondent is single and has no dependent children.

Comparing the pension amounts before and after this recoding suggests that miscoding or misreporting resulted in over-estimation of retirement pension receipt by an average of £2.85 per week for the recoded cases, and by £0.04 per week for the entire FES sample of retirement pensioners. This estimate is probably conservative: in assuming that the full basic pension is received in cases where no income support is reported, we are likely to over-estimate the pension component of the payments.

Basic pension category

The next step of the disaggregation is to try to work out the amount of SERPS and graduated pension paid to a claimant, whether their basic pension is reduced for insufficient contributions or not, and, if the claimant is a married woman, whether she receives the standard rate of basic pension or the married woman's rate of basic pension. To do this we first split off the elements that we have attributed so far to derive an estimate of pension entitlement that comprises solely (i) basic pension for the claimant net of deductions for insufficient contributions, (ii) SERPS, (iii) graduated pension, and (iv) increments to each of these for deferred retirement. We call this *BPMOD1*.

AD = rate of adult addition
CH = rate of child addition
AG = rate of age addition

for each claimant

$$BPMOD1 = IPENR - (PENAD \times AD) - (PENCH \times CH) - (AGEAD \times AG)$$

We use *BPMOD1* to decide whether a married woman whose husband is in receipt of retirement pension is in receipt of the married woman's rate of basic pension or the standard rate. This is one of the most arbitrary parts of our approach. In the absence of any sound basis for deciding status, we opt for a method that is transparent and consistent: claimants with *BPMOD1* that is closer to the married woman's rate than the standard rate of basic pension are assumed to claim the married woman's rate ($CAT=2$); claimants with *BPMOD1* closer to the standard rate are assumed to claim the standard rate ($CAT=1$). CAT is set equal to 1 for all men and all women who are either unmarried or married to a man who is not in receipt of retirement pension.

Earnings-related pension and basic pension

Using *BPMOD1* and *CAT*, we derive estimates of the ratio of the basic pension received to the standard rate of basic pension (*PENRAT*) and the amount of earnings-related pension received (*ERP*) as follows.

If *BPMOD1* is greater than the relevant basic pension (the standard rate of basic pension if *CAT* is equal to 1, the married woman's rate of basic pension if *CAT* is equal to 2), we attribute the difference to earnings-related pension and earnings-related pension increments (*ERP*). Implicitly, we assume that either the full rate of basic pension without deductions for insufficient contributions and without basic pension increment for deferred retirement is in payment, or the size of basic pension deductions exactly offsets basic pension increments and leaves a net payment exactly equal to the full rate of basic pension (*PENRAT*=1).[9] If *BPMOD1* is not greater than the relevant basic pension, we assume that no earnings-related pension and earnings-related pension increments are received (*ERP*=0). *PENRAT* is calculated as the ratio of *BPMOD1* to the relevant basic pension.

We do not allow for the possibility that a claimant may receive a full basic pension and basic pension increments – *PENRAT* cannot be greater than one. In addition, we do not allow for the possibility that a person receives a reduced basic pension *and* an earnings-related pension.[10]

Recategorisation and minimum reduced basic pension

With an estimate of *PENRAT* for all claimants we are now in a position to revisit the category of pension allocated to married women. A woman on married woman's rate has her basic pension reduced by the same proportion as her husband's basic pension if he made insufficient contributions. By examining the *PENRAT* of women whom we assume receive the married woman's rate, and the *PENRAT* of their partners, we can recode where our method has produced amounts for husbands and wives that are inconsistent. We exercise some caution. Both the husband and wife may be receiving SERPS in addition to a reduced-rate basic pension which we have been unable to identify. We recategorise only if the *PENRAT* of a woman on the married woman's rate is less than that of her husband by more than 5 percentage points. This shifts 42 respondents from the married woman's rate to the standard rate.

Finally, no basic pension is payable if the number of qualifying years is less than one quarter of the required minimum number of qualifying years. To model this, if *PENRAT* is less than 0.25, we interpret all the pension after deduction of additions as *ERP*. *PENRAT* is set to zero. This is done for the entire FES sample of *PENR* claimants. It affects 63 respondents.

Comparison with Department of Social Security data

We now have our final estimates of the three variables we need to simulate entitlement: *CAT*, the basic pension category for each claimant; *PENRAT*, the proportion of the full rate of basic pension received, net of deductions for insufficient contributions and increments for deferred retirement, but before additions for dependants and age and before deduc-

Table 8.1. *Sex and pension categories*[a]

	DSS		FES weighted		FES unweighted	
	num. (000s)	%	num. (000s)	%	num. (000s)	%
All claimants	10,016	100	9,458	100	2,904	100
Men	3,512	35.1	3,300	34.9	1,040	35.8
Women: standard rate	4,412	44.0	4,303	45.5	1,307	45.0
Women: married rate	2,092	20.9	1,855	19.6	557	19.2

Note:
[a] FES estimates are for the UK. DSS estimates are for GB including those resident overseas from a 10% sample of claimant records as at 30 September 1991. They exclude non-contributory retirement pension, graduated pension only and additional pension only cases.
Sources: Department of Social Security, 1992, Table B1.01; FES: own calculations.

tions for over-lapping benefits; and *ERP*, the amount of SERPS, graduated pension, and SERPS and graduated pension increments for deferred retirement received. The distribution of these measures can be compared with Department of Social Security (DSS) estimates for the total retirement pension claimant population based on a 10% sample of claimant records. The figures are not strictly comparable. The DSS figures are for Great Britain and include some groups, such as those resident overseas and those living in hospitals or residential care, that are excluded from the FES sample. The FES estimates include Northern Ireland respondents.

Table 8.1 compares the numbers in each sex and basic pension category group. The proportions in each category closely match those reported by the DSS.

Table 8.2 compares the weighted percentage of claimants in receipt of basic pension and weighted estimates of *PENRAT* from our disaggregation of the FES pension variable with similar estimates from the DSS sample of claimants. The proportions of all retirement pensioners in receipt of basic pension are reasonably comparable. However, we under-estimate the proportion of men receiving a full basic pension (*PENRAT*=1). We should expect the reverse to be the case: in our calculations we lean towards interpreting amounts of pension as basic pension rather than SERPS where there is doubt; in addition, our figures include the effect of basic pension increments on the proportion of the full basic pension received while the

Table 8.2. *Basic pension receipt*[a]

	Men		Women: standard rate		Women: married rate	
	DSS	FES	DSS	FES	DSS	FES
Number receiving retirement pension (000s)	3,287	3,300	4,342	4,296	1,965	1,862
% receiving basic pension	99.8	98.9	96.0	96.0	99.3	99.8
Of those receiving basic pension, % receiving						
100%	96	90	84	71	98	93
90–99%	1	6	2	7	1	7
80–89%	1	1	2	3	0	0
70–79%	1	0	2	1	0	0
<70%	1	3	11	17	1	1

Note:
[a] FES estimates are for the UK. DSS estimates are for GB excluding those residing overseas from a 10% sample of claimant records as at 30 September 1991. They exclude some cases with age related widow's retirement pension. FES estimates are weighted and use the rates current at the date of interview.
Sources: Department of Social Security, 1992, Table B1.08; Retirement Pension published tables September 1991; FES: own calculations.

DSS figures do not. The proportions of men in receipt of at least 90% of the full pension rate are close however (97% versus 96%).

For women on the standard rate of pension, we under-estimate the proportion receiving the full rate of pension without deductions (our estimate is 71%, the DSS estimate is 84%). As with the men, however, the proportions with more than 90% are closer. For women on the married woman's rate, we under-estimate the proportion receiving 100% of basic pension. This may be caused by our method of attributing the married woman's rate. Women whose pension payment is less than the married woman's rate are always allocated the married woman's rate of basic pension (unless they can be recoded on the basis of comparison with their husband's *PENRAT*). It may be that these are cases on their own pensions with reductions. Again, the proportions in receipt of at least 90% of basic pension are closer.

Finally, we contrast our estimates of the amount of earnings-related pension received by FES retirement pension claimants with DSS estimates for the Great Britain claimant population. This is more problematic than the comparisons above. On one side of the comparison, we do not have sufficient information from the FES to disaggregate our measure *ERP* (the combined amount of net SERPS, graduated pension and SERPS and graduated pension increments) any further. On the other side, the published and unpublished DSS tables available do not allow us to aggregate the DSS figures for net SERPS, graduated pension, and SERPS and graduated pension increments. What we can do is compare our distribution of *ERP* with the distribution of net SERPS. This is done in Table 8.3. The comparison can be aided by the information on the proportion of the DSS sample in receipt of graduated pension set out at the top of the table and the fact that average graduated pension for those in receipt is £2.87 per week for men, £1.11 for all women, and £0.72 for women on the married woman's rate.[11]

If we assume that those who receive SERPS are a subset of those who receive graduated pension, then for men our estimate of the proportion of claimants in receipt of earnings related pension is a reasonable approximation of the proportions estimated by the DSS. The approximation is not as good for women. We over- and under-estimate respectively the proportions of married woman's rate and standard rate claimants in receipt of earnings-related pension. The difference between the distribution of SERPS received by the DSS sample of men and the distribution of earnings-related pension received by the FES sample of men can be explained by the inclusion of graduated pension and increments – most men receive SERPS, so the main effect of the inclusion is an upward shift in the distribution of payments. The main effect for women is to bring many who receive only graduated pension into the group and cause more intense clustering of our estimates of *ERP* in the £0.00–4.99 range.

Table 8.3. *Earnings-related pension receipt*[a]

	Men		Women: standard rate		Women: married rate	
	DSS	FES	DSS	FES	DSS	FES
Number receiving retirement pension (000s)	3,512	3,300	4,412	4,296	2,092	1,862
% receiving SERPS	60.8	n.a.	26.1	n.a.	4.1	n.a.
% receiving graduated pension	86.7	n.a.	77.4	n.a.	44.2	n.a.
% receiving ERP	n.a.	87.5	n.a.	67.9	n.a.	57.6
Of those receiving SERPS (DSS) or ERP (FES), % receiving						
£0.00–4.99	56	46	60	72	81	93
£5.00–9.99	24	30	23	16	13	6
£10.00–19.99	13	16	13	8	4	1
£20.00+	7	9	3	4	1	0

Note:
[a] FES estimates are for the UK. DSS estimates are for GB including those resident overseas from a 10% sample of claimant records as at 30 September 1991. FES estimates are weighted and use the rates current at the date of interview.
Sources: Department of Social Security, 1992, Table 1.01 and B1.21; FES: own calculations.

8.3 Results of a trial simulation

This section describes the results of a trial simulation using the new variables. To obtain results that are comparable with DSS out-turns and estimates, the simulation is done on a fiscal year basis. This entails using 1991/92 benefit rates and uprating income and work expenses assessed in the crediting of adult and child additions by the difference between average earnings in the years ending December 1991 and March 1992. The simulation is for Great Britain respondents only. FES-based expenditure estimates are calculated from the estimates of caseload and average payment per person by multiplying by 53 (the number of benefit payment weeks in 1991/92).

We should not expect the two sets of estimates to match perfectly for at least four reasons.

(i)   The FES is only a sample and as such is broadly representative of the population as a whole; but it may be less representative of particular subgroups of the population. While we correct over all for under- and over-representation of different family types and age groups by using different family type weights to gross-up to aggregate population estimates, for the smaller subsamples in the population these weights vary in their effectiveness in correcting for non-representativeness. Jones, Stark and Webb (1991) found that family type weights produced relatively accurate over-all estimates of caseload and expenditure for 'demographically determined' benefits such as retirement pension. They may, however, be less successful in producing accurate estimates of numbers in receipt of and expenditure on SERPS or particular categories of retirement pension.

(ii) There are sampling frame differences. The FES does not sample people who do not live in private households. This leads to substantial under-counting of retirement pension recipients. Nor does the FES survey people who receive state benefits but do not reside in the United Kingdom. While we have adjusted the DSS estimates to exclude those resident overseas and those resident in hospitals, the adjustment is incomplete (see Appendix 8.1). We are unable to obtain data on numbers of recipients in non-household dwellings other than hospitals (such as residential care homes).

(iii) There are timing differences that differentiate the two sets of estimates. The DSS-based estimates of caseload are the average of numbers in receipt at or around the end of the fiscal years 1990/91 and 1991/92. The FES estimates are based on a continuous calendar year sample to December 1991, grossed-up by family weights to popula-

Table 8.4. *Retirement pension: DSS* versus *original and simulated estimates*[a]

| | | FES-based | |
	DSS-based	original	simulated
Expenditure (£m)	24,749	23,926	23,889
Number in receipt (000s)	9,367	9,226	9,210
Average weekly payment (£s)	49.85	48.93	48.94

Notes:
[a] Fiscal year estimates for GB only. FES estimates are weighted and based on 1991/92 benefit rates. DSS figures are adjusted to exclude recipients resident overseas or in hospital and to exclude expenditure on them. See Appendix 8.1 for further detail.
Source: DSS, 1994c, Tables 1 and 6; FES: own calculations.

tion totals. The average caseload implied by the FES will be different from the DSS-based average if there is any trend over the period.
(iv) The simulation does not capture accurately the effects of over-payments, under-payments, and back-payments of benefit. In attributing surplus payment over and above the basic payment to an earnings-related additional pension, and payments below to reduced rate payments, we are likely to capture the effect on the total but mis-allocate the effect on the components of retirement pension.

Table 8.4 compares the estimates of caseload, expenditure and average pension obtained from our simulation with the original estimates that result from simply uprating and grossing-up reported receipt of retirement pension, and with DSS-based estimates.

Simulation makes little difference to the over-all average weekly payment and caseload estimates. The slight drop in numbers in receipt is due to our overlapping benefit calculation. We still slightly under-estimate average weekly payment compared to DSS data.

What is interesting is the comparability of estimates for the components of retirement pension that emerge from the simulation shown in Table 8.5. The proportionate under-estimation of numbers in receipt of basic pension and earnings-related pension is similar to that for the over-all retirement pension caseload. It is notable that our estimate of expenditure on earnings-related pension is reasonably close to that which can be calculated from the *Social Security Statistics* (SSS) sample-based estimates of average payment and numbers in receipt of earnings-related pension, but

Table 8.5. *Components of retirement pension:* DSS *versus simulated*[a]

	DSS-based[b]	Simulated
Basic pension element		
Expenditure (£m)[c]	23,692	21,928
Number in receipt (000s)[d]	9,180	9,014
Average payment for recipients (£pw)	48.69	45.90
Earnings-related element		
Expenditure (£m)[e]	1,057 (GEP)	1,960
	1,794 (SSS)	
Number in receipt (000s)[d]	6,838	6,750
Average payment for recipients (£pw)	2.92 (GEP)	5.48
	4.95 (SSS)	

Notes:

[a] Fiscal year estimates for GB only. DSS-based estimates other than those from the *Social Security Departmental Report* are based on a 10% sample of retirement pensioner as at 30 September 1991 grossed-up by a factor of 10. FES estimates are based on 1991/92 benefit rates and grossed-up and weighted using family-type weights.

[b] DSS figures are adjusted to exclude recipients resident overseas or in hospital and to exclude expenditure on them.

[c] DSS estimates are out-turns reported in the *Social Security Departmental Report*, adjusted (see previous note). The amount of basic pension expenditure includes contributory basic pension expenditure and non-contributory retirement pension but excludes Christmas bonus payments.

[d] The DSS estimate of total number in receipt is that contained in Table 6 of the *Social Security Departmental Report*, adjusted (see note (b)). Estimates of numbers in receipt of basic pension and earnings-related pension are derived using the figures on proportions in receipt in *Social Security Statistics* tables and applying these to the *Social Security Departmental Report* estimates of average total number of recipients in the year. The proportion in receipt of basic pension is 0.98. The proportion in receipt of earnings-related pension is 0.73, assumed to be equal to the proportion in receipt of graduated pension (Table B1.23).

[e] The GEP estimate is based on out-turns reported in the *Social Security Departmental Report*, adjusted (see note (b)). The SSS estimate is derived by multiplying average payments by caseload estimates for the three components of earnings-related pension reported (graduated pension (Table B1.23), net additional pension (Table B1.20) and additional pension increments (Table B1.14)), multiplying by 53 to obtain an annual expenditure estimate, and then adjusting to exclude expenditure on those not resident in GB households by the proportionate share in total expenditure. The unadjusted SSS estimate is 1.857.

Sources: Department of Social Security 1994c, Tables 1 and 6; Department of Social Security, 1992; FES: own calculations.

Table 8.6. *Proportions with additions to retirement pension: DSS versus simulated[a]*

	DSS Sept. 1991		Simulated	
	num. (000s)	%	num. (000s)	%
Receiving retirement pension	10,016	100	9,210	100
with adult additions	100	1.0	297	3.2
with child additions	16	0.2	3	—

Notes:
[a] For GB only. DSS estimates are as at 30 September 1991, based on a 10% sample of retirement pensioners and uprated by multiplying by 10. FES estimates are weighted and based on 1991/92 benefit rates. DSS figures are not adjusted to exclude recipients resident overseas or in hospital.
Sources: Department of Social Security, 1992, Table B1.04; FES: own calculations.

almost twice that based on the estimate derived from the *Social Security Departmental Report* of the Government's Expenditure Plans (GEP). Like our disaggregation, the GEP estimate is based in part on a system of apportioning payments for which there are no exact data on the amount that is SERPS, basic pension, income support or another benefit. The SSS sample-based estimates are possibly the more reliable comparator because they are estimated from known receipts. If this is the case, our method of estimating earnings-related pension produces a moderate (roughly 11%) over-estimation of average earnings-related pension received. This may be due to the under-sampling of the older elderly in the FES.[12] Or it may be due to the crudeness of our method of attributing earnings-related pension and the possibility that we have interpreted as earnings-related pension amounts that are in fact either miscoded other benefits, increments to basic pension, or over-payments or back-payments of retirement pension.

A comparison of the numbers with dependant's additions that result from our simulation with DSS estimates is shown in Table 8.6. We under-estimate numbers with child additions and over-estimate numbers with adult additions.

8.4 Conclusions

In this chapter we have described the method used to impute new information that can provide a basis for the simulation of retirement pensions by disaggregating and recoding the FES variables that record total receipt. Our method of disaggregation provides a reasonable, if not entirely accurate basis for simulation.

One of the major benefits of simulating retirement pension and other non-means-tested benefits, and in particular the correction for miscoded income support payments, is the improvement in FES-based simulation of income support receipt. When all non-means-tested benefits are simulated on the basis of the disaggregations described here and in Wilson (1995a), trial estimates of the number of FES benefit units in receipt of income support increase from 1,317 to 1,404. When weighted and grossed-up to estimates for the entire UK population, this represents an increase from 4.4 million families to 4.7 million families. This raises simulated receipt of income support from 90% to 95% of the actual average number of UK families in receipt in 1991–92 estimated from official statistics.[13, 14]

On a more cautious note, it is important to bear in mind the limits of the information made available. Because we do not get right back to the basis for entitlement (contributions or incapacity, for example), the new information is not sufficient to allow simulation of the effects of changing the rules of entitlement for non-means-tested benefits. In general, the new variables only permit simulation of the effects of changes in financial parameters. Even then, the range of financial policy parameters that can be altered is limited. For example, the payments regime of the State Earnings Related Pension System cannot be altered. An assumption about the effect of such a policy change on SERPS payments overall can be simulated, but the underlying relationship between contributions and payments cannot. An implication of this constraint is that we are limited in our ability to project forward.

So long as these limits are recognised, and so long as general problems regarding the small size and the representativeness of some of the FES subsamples are borne in mind, it would appear from this preliminary work that there are gains to be made from simulating non-means-tested benefit receipts.

Appendix 8.1 Adjustments to DSS caseload and average payment estimates to exclude those not resident in GB households

To obtain estimates of caseload, expenditure and average weekly payment with which to compare FES-based estimates and simulations, we use official estimates reported in the *Social Security Departmental Report*, and adjust where possible to exclude recipients who do not dwell in households in Great Britain and are therefore outside the FES sampling frame. Ideally, this would involve adjusting to exclude those who are homeless, in residential care, in hospital, living in some other non-private household residence or living overseas. We only have estimates of the numbers of recipients who are in hospital or who reside overseas and their average payments. We are unable to adjust to exclude those residing in other non-household settings. Tables 8.A1.1, 8.A1.2 and 8.A1.3 show the adjustments we are able to make.

Table 8.A1.1 *Adjustments to DSS caseload estimates*

| | Number in receipt (000s) | | | | | |
	End 1990–91[a]	End 1991–92[a]	Average 1991–92[a]	Resident overseas	In hospital	Average 1991–92	Adjustment factor
Retirement pension	10,003	10,048	10,026	609[b]	50[b]	9,367	0.9343

Notes:

[a] Caseload figures are from Table 6 of Department of Social Security, 1994c. The average is an estimate of the number in receipt as at 30 September 1991 derived using linear interpolation.

[b] As at 30 September 1991.

Sources: Department of Social Security, 1994c, Table 6; DSS Analytical Services Division, unpublished data.

Table 8.A1.2 *Adjustments to DSS expenditure estimates*

| | Expenditure out-turns for 1991–92 (£m pa) | | | |
	Unadjusted[a]	Resident overseas	In hospital	Adjusted factor	Adjustment
Retirement pension	25,625	823[a]	54[b]	24,749	0.9658

Notes:

[a] Expenditure figures are 1991–92 out-turns reported in Table 1 of Department of Social Security, 1994c.

[b] Calculated on the basis of a 53-week expenditure year: average payment is (expenditure/average caseload)/53×1000. Average payment is calculated before rounding of adjusted caseload and expenditure so the figures reported may differ slightly from those that can be calculated from expenditure and caseload reported in these tables.

Sources: Department of Social Security, 1994c, Table 1; DSS Analytical Services Division, unpublished data.

Table 8.A1.3 *Adjustments to DSS average payments estimates*

| | Average payment per person in receipt (£s per week)[a] | | | | |
	Overall unadjusted	Resident overseas	In hospital	Overall adjusted	Adjustment factor
Retirement pension	48.22	25.49[b]	20.25[b]	49.85	1.0337

Notes:
[a] Calculated on the basis of a 53-week expenditure year: average payment is (expenditure/average caseload)/53×1000. Average payment is calculated before rounding of adjusted caseload and expenditure so the figures reported may differ slightly from those that can be calculated from expenditure and caseload reported in these tables.
[b] As at 30 September 1991.
Sources: Department of Social Security, 1994c, Tables 1 and 6; DSS Analytical Services Division, unpublished data.

Notes

1 A more detailed method of disaggregating retirement pension than ultimately employed is described in Wilson (1995a).

2 Here, we use the term claimant to refer to a person who is in receipt of a benefit or pension. The term is used regardless of whether the benefit was claimed or paid automatically.

3 Prior to October 1989, basic pension could also be reduced if the claimant received earnings over a given limit under the earnings rule.

4 We draw heavily on the information on rules of eligibility and entitlement contained in Matthewman (1990, 1991), Lakhani and Read (1990), Rowland (1990, 1991) and Rowland and Webster (1991). Without these accessible and rich sources our work would have been much more arduous and time-consuming. None of the guides bears responsibility for any errors in application of the rules that appear here.

5 The raw data set gives four additional variables that provide information on SERPS from the payment book used by those who do not receive their retirement pension together with income support. These variables record, for the last payment: amount of additional pension before the deduction of guaranteed minimum pension (*NIPNAPAM*), amount of guaranteed minimum pension (a deduction) (*NIPNMPAM*), amount of additional pension increments (*NIPNAPIN*), and amount of uprating of guaranteed minimum pension increments (*NIPNMPIN*). At least one of these variables is recorded for 292 of the 2,904 respondents who record positive amounts of *B338*. Wilson (1995a) documents an approach to disaggregating *B338* that makes use of these variables. In addition, the raw data set supplies *NIPEN* which records whether a person receives NI retirement pension only (*NIPEN*=1), or old person's pension (non-contributory retirement pension above) only (*NIPEN*=2). The variable is very unreliable, however, with large numbers of respondents who would be ineligible for non-contributory retirement pension by age recording receipt.

6 Entitlement to non-means-tested benefits is governed by a host of 'over-lapping benefits' rules concerning receipt of multiple benefits and the effects of receipt of one benefit on the level of another. We investigate whether these rules are adhered to and recode in some way where receipt of two or more benefits to which a person can have no statutory or practical right is recorded. We also recode where a legitimate over-lap is recorded so that information is held on the full amount of each benefit and over-lapping benefit rules can be applied as part of the simulation of non-means-tested benefits.

7 The definition of earnings for the purposes of means testing additions is common to all NI benefits and pensions. It includes the following: gross wages or salary and income from self employment (less National Insurance contributions but not tax), gross fees or commission, regular tips, some benefits in kind, and income from taking in boarders or lodgers, less non-reimbursed work-related travel costs and a range of other work-related costs such as the costs of meals, childcare, and care for a person with disabilities. We assume that all expenditure on season tickets for the claimant's household is undertaken by the

earning spouse if there is one present, unless there is more than one benefit unit in the household, or there are children present in the benefit unit. We do not attempt to model the remaining allowable work-related expenses.

8 See ESRC Data Archive (1992), Vol. 1, Instructions to Interviewers, p. 176.

9 If we have an estimate of *ERP* from the over-lapping benefits calculation, and if it is greater than the estimate calculated here, then this amount is used and and *PENRAT* is recalculated accordingly.

10 Unless we have an estimate of *ERP* from the over-lapping benefits calculation.

11 DSS, 1992, Table B1.23, as at 30 September 1991.

12 This is corrected for in part by the use of differentiated grossing-up weights for families headed by a person aged 75 and over, but the under-sampling of the older elderly within the group aged 75 and over is not corrected for.

13 The average of average numbers receiving income support at any point in time for 1990–91 and 1991–92 for GB and Northern Ireland is 4.952 million families (Northern Ireland Office, 1993; DSS, 1994c, Table 6). These figures are not adjusted to take account of non-take-up or to exclude those not resident in private households which may explain parts of the remaining discrepancy.

14 The simulation assumes 100% take-up and therefore produces higher caseload estimates than POLIMOD, which adjusts for real world non-take-up.

Part Four
Model validation

9 Validation: methods and findings

9.1 Introduction

To a very large extent, the usefulness of a model like POLIMOD depends on the degree to which it can replicate what happens in the 'real world', and project from there the possible distributional effects of changes to tax and benefit policies. This part of the study is devoted to the validation of POLIMOD output. This chapter describes the validation methods that are available and the approach to validation that is adopted in the remaining chapters and discusses sources of inherent difference between POLIMOD and other sources that must be taken into account before a valid reconciliation can be carried out. A summary of the main findings is also provided.

9.2 Validation methods

A range of internal and external checks on the reliability of model inputs, model procedures, and model outputs can be undertaken. These include:

1 *Model inputs.* POLIMOD's principal input consists of microdata from the 1991 Family Expenditure Survey (FES). Validation of the reliability of the underlying microdata could involve internal checks such as an assessment of the degree of estimation and imputation in responses to individual questions of the type described by Kemsley *et al.* (1980, pp. 49–50). Alternatively, they could involve external checks such as the comparison of grossed up aggregates or distributions with official data of the type carried out by Kemsley *et al.* (*ibid.*, p. 51), or Atkinson and Micklewright (1983), both of which validate FES data against external sources.
2 *Model procedures.* Validation of the reliability of the *simulations* could involve internal case-by-case testing of simulated entitlements and liabilities against legally correct outcomes such as those described by Lambert *et al.* (1994, pp. 30–31) for Australia. Or it could involve exter-

nal comparisons such as those in Giles and Webb (undated) which compare the taxes and benefits simulated for the same individuals and families by two UK models.

3 *Model outputs.* The results of the simulations could be validated internally by comparison with recorded entitlement or liability taken directly from the microdata. Or they could be validated externally. This could entail a comparison of the simulated revenue impacts of policy reforms produced by different models such as that carried out by Hope (1988), or a comparison of simulated aggregates and distributions for actual policy in force with official statistics or forecasts such as those contained in Jones, Stark and Webb (1991) and Lambert *et al.* (1994). Alternatively, validation of model outputs could involve a study of the effect of sampling error on the reliability of outputs such as that conducted by Pudney and Sutherland (1994), or sensitivity testing of key assumptions, for example, those made with regard to take-up of benefits or equivalence scales, such as that undertaken in Chapter 4.

Our objective in Chapters 10 to 12 is to carry out a validation of the reliability of POLIMOD's *model outputs*. The intention is to provide a guide to POLIMOD's comparability with official data on incomes and on taxes and benefits, with other models, and with the micro-data on which it is based.

Chapter 10 validates POLIMOD's income tax simulations. Income tax is central to the simulation of household incomes both directly, and indirectly through its knock-on effect on other liabilities and entitlements. To be confident that POLIMOD is producing reliable and useful results in almost any respect, therefore, requires an assessment of its treatment of income tax. Chapter 10 demonstrates two approaches to validating model outputs: the first an internal comparison of the income tax liabilities that POLIMOD simulates for the survey year with amounts of income tax that respondents report paying in the FES; the second an external comparison of POLIMOD simulations of the revenue impacts of various policy changes with 'Ready Reckoner' calculations published by HM Treasury.

Chapters 11 and 12 demonstrate a third approach to validating model outputs: external comparison with estimates from official statistics. Chapter 11 offers a detailed examination of the comparability of POLIMOD's simulations of the aggregate amounts of income, benefits received and taxes paid and of aggregate numbers of persons or families in receipt of and paying each with external official data. Chapter 12 examines the comparability of a small selection of POLIMOD's simulated distributions with outside sources. The validation against official statistics presented in these two chapters is mainly confined to aggregates, owing to the lack of external distributional data for comparison. POLIMOD uses microdata from the FES because it is currently the richest source of information on the distribution of income and expenditure available. That there is often no better source against which to validate much of POLIMOD's output is an inevitable consequence of this.

In the next section of this present chapter we discuss the general reasons why we might expect POLIMOD to produce results that are different from those from official sources. The chapters that follow then provide a more detailed discussion of issues specific to each element of model output and our method of making adjustments to improve comparability.

9.3 Issues of comparability

There are a number of reasons why we should not expect POLIMOD outputs to match exactly estimates from alternative sources in any particular comparison.

1 *Updating.* POLIMOD generally uses FES data from a past year to simulate policy in a current or future year. To do this, it updates each item of income and expenditure by a factor that captures the average movement of that item between the survey and modelled years. Only earnings are updated by disaggregated factors that take account of the time of year in which the respondent was surveyed, his or her sex, and the level of his or her earnings in the survey year. For all other items, the assumption implicit in not taking account of these factors is that the distribution of income or expenditure is the same in the survey and modelled years, both over the year and across individuals. For some parts of the validation exercise, we use simulations of 1991 policy and this allows us to avoid any error that might be introduced from updating the data to 1996/7, and to focus on other aspects of comparability.

2 *Structural change.* There may also be changes between the survey year and the modelled year that are not captured by the methods that are used to gross-up survey respondents to represent the population as a whole in the modelled year. There may, for example, be a change in unemployment rates or in patterns of tenure which would be expected to cause some deviation between the simulated and actual estimates of items of income or expenditure such as benefits or housing costs. There may be structural changes in the volume of some income streams such as those from the State Earnings Related Pension Scheme (SERPS). However sophisticated the grossing-up technique that is used, the method will be unable to capture all the complexity of structural shifts that occur. Again, for some parts of the validation, this particular source of error is avoided for the purposes of this validation by anchoring our comparisons in 1991, the survey year.

3 *Incomplete coverage.* Coverage of the FES is incomplete. It is a survey of

household income and expenditure in the UK, and only samples people who live in private households. It does not cover those resident in hospitals, residential and nursing homes, hotels, student halls of residence, prisons and army barracks nor those with no residence. Nor does it survey people who receive state benefits or pay United Kingdom taxes but do not reside in the United Kingdom, such as some retirement pensioners, HM Forces posted overseas, and members of the diplomatic service. The FES population is therefore a particular one that is close to, but rarely exactly the same as, populations from which external aggregates are taken. In some instances, notably expenditure on certain items, non-household populations can greatly influence aggregates reported in external sources, such as those in the Blue Book (Central Statistical Office, 1993b).[1] Foreign tourists, for example, spend heavily on accommodation in the UK. Such expenditure is not accounted for in the FES. In some parts of the validation, we attempt to adjust to take account of this source of deviation, but the data available do not allow us to be completely comprehensive or completely accurate.

4 *Differential response.* The FES is a sample survey and as such is broadly representative of the population as a whole but may be less representative of the sub-groups of the population targeted by particular taxes and benefits. The grossing-up weights used in POLIMOD address some but not all dimensions in which there is over- and under-representation.

5 *Annualising method.* For most items, the FES collects data for a time period that is less than a year. For example, most expenditure is recorded in a diary that households keep for only two weeks, and is annualised by multiplying total weekly amounts by 52. In annualising expenditure in this way, we are assuming that had the diary-keeping period been different (say in June instead of January), the pattern of expenditure would have been the same. We make similar assumptions regarding income. Clearly, most people's experience (and evidence from the British Household Panel Study, see Ashworth and Walker, 1994) would suggest that this is unlikely to be the case for any one household, but if sampling is randomly and evenly spread throughout the year, it may be a reasonable assumption to make for *categories* of household. The success of this method in matching annualised amounts from the FES with those from external sources therefore rests on the assumption that the distribution of income, expenditure, taxes and benefits over the year for all respondent households is accurately captured by the aggregation of individual respondent households.

6 *Incomplete microdata.* The FES does not contain all the information that is needed in order to apply the rules of the tax and benefit systems.

In some cases, this means that the characteristics upon which entitlement or liability rests are imputed. The process of imputation in the FES starts when the data are being coded by CSO, and continues when they are being interpreted by users. Some data have been imputed directly by the Microsimulation Unit for use in POLIMOD, but others have been imputed by the Office for National Statistics, and are not fully documented. We do not, therefore, know the full extent of imputation in the FES, nor its effect on results.

7 *Miscoding and misreporting.* Information in the FES may be misreported or miscoded and this may introduce error into the POLIMOD simulations. For example, there is evidence to suggest that some respondents confuse one benefit with another. There is also evidence to suggest that, on average, respondents under-report income from self-employment and investment income (see Atkinson and Micklewright, 1983).

8 *Simulation.* There are at least three ways in which simulation itself may introduce differences with reported data. (i) In some cases, the absence of the microdata on which the rules of the tax and benefit system depend means that parts of the real world calculations are ignored altogether. (ii) Simulation does not capture the effects of over-payments, under-payments, and back-payments of benefits and income taxes. The rules of the tax and benefit system are applied as if there were never any deviation between legal entitlement or legal liability and actual current payments of benefits and taxes.[2] Deviations due to avoidance, evasion, accruals, refunds, non-take-up or administrative error are sometimes captured by administrative data but not by POLIMOD. (iii) Errors can be made in simulation and may go undetected.

9 *Definition and data collection differences.* The available external data may include different elements from POLIMOD outputs. In addition, the timing and nature of data collection may differ in ways that affect amounts. An example is the New Earnings Survey (NES),[3] which can be used to validate the distribution of employee earnings generated by POLIMOD. Earnings data in the NES are collected from employers whereas earnings data in the FES are collected from employees. Therefore, while NES gross earnings should exclude tips and gratuities which are extra to employee wages, FES earnings should include them. Similarly, the NES covers persons who are not resident in private households, while the FES does not.

10 *Errors and imputation in external data.* Like the FES, data from external sources are also subject to imputation, errors in reporting or collating information, and sampling error where the data are taken from

surveys. Some income and expenditure data in the external sources are subject to a large degree of estimation. This is a particularly awkward problem for which there is no solution. In comparing an FES aggregate with an external measure, we are making the implicit assumption that the external measure is superior, or a truer reflection of the real population, but we can never be certain that this is the case. Therefore, wherever possible in this chapter, we quantify the confidence intervals that are associated with external aggregates, and discuss likely sources of error. External data sources used in this part of the study are discussed in more detail in Chapter 11, Appendix 11.1.

9.4 Summary and conclusions

An important adjunct to any model is the provision of information on the reliability of its outputs. This part of the study supplies such information for POLIMOD based on comparison with figures from external sources. In making the comparison, we are in some instances limited in our ability to draw firm conclusions by the difficulty in isolating the precise contribution of the non-household population to each income, expenditure and tax item, and by the fact that some external data are different because they are not comparable. The main findings of the exercise can be summarised as follows.

1 *Original income.* Compared with the Blue Book, POLIMOD tends to under-estimate aggregate original income. This is to some extent due to data comparability (for example, estimates of income from private pensions appear to compare well with administrative data, but do not compare at all well with the Blue Book figures); it is also due to the particular choice of measure for POLIMOD (use of normal earnings rather than actual earnings, for example), although we can identify some instances in which the differences are clearly due to deficiencies in FES data (for example, the under-representation of those with high taxable incomes in the FES must explain much of the short-fall in POLIMOD aggregate investment income estimates). Estimates of the numbers of original income earners are less problematic. On the distributions side of the validation, the POLIMOD distribution of earnings from full-time employment compares very well with that from the external source, the distribution of taxable investment income is adversely affected by the under-representation of those in the higher income brackets, and the comparison of distributions of taxable self-employment income raises some questions about the most appropriate method of updating and counting income for simulation of income tax and National Insurance contributions.

2 *Non-means-tested benefits.* In the comparison of non-means-tested benefits, we find both under- and over-estimation of caseload and aggregate income relative to external sources. To some extent, this is associated with under- and over-representation of particular groups (for example, over-representation of widows and under-representation of those receiving benefits on account of incapacity), and to some extent it is associated with misreporting by respondents, or imputation of missing data in the FES. There may also be problems with external data. For example, the Blue Book estimate of widow's benefit expenditure does not tally with figures reported in the *Social Security Departmental Report.*

3 *Direct taxes.* POLIMOD under-estimates aggregate income tax compared with the Blue Book. A comparison of distributions suggest that this is primarily due to the under-representation of those with very high taxable incomes. The limited comparisons of the estimates of policy *change* that are possible suggest that POLIMOD estimates are generally within the range of SPI-based estimates for changes to the rate structure, personal allowances and the main tax reliefs. In contrast, there is over-statement of aggregate National Insurance contributions, for which there are several possible explanations. Local tax estimates are not comparable because no account is taken of non-payment in POLIMOD, and this is reflected in the reconciliation.

4 *Means-tested benefits.* We find varying degrees of under-estimation of aggregate income from income support, family credit and housing benefit in POLIMOD compared with Department of Social Security data. This is partly associated with under-estimation of caseload and partly associated with the fact that the method used to adjust for non-take-up does not allow for differential take-up by size of entitlement. Under-estimation of caseload may be due to under-representation of particular claimant groups in the FES (for example, people who are incapacitated by illness or disability and people who are unemployed), as well as to our inability to adjust fully to exclude the non-household population from the control totals. It may also be due to the over-statement of non-take-up – considerable uncertainty surrounds the DSS point estimates of take-up. In the case of family credit, some of the under-statement is due to the inability of static simulation to replicate fully the assessment and payment systems that apply in reality. Community charge benefit is the one means-tested benefit for which caseload and aggregate income is over-estimated by POLIMOD. This is likely to be due to non-payment. Comparisons of distributions reflect these problems.

5 *Expenditure and indirect taxes.* The overall estimate of expenditure is very close to the adjusted control total, but underlying this is considerable over- and under-estimation for some items. There is some uncer-

tainty about whether the adjusted controls provide an accurate picture of expenditure by households. POLIMOD over-estimates VAT but it is not clear whether this is due to the difficulty of obtaining truly comparable data from external sources or to genuine over-estimation by POLIMOD. The under-estimation of excise duties can be explained by the low estimates of expenditure on items which attract these taxes.

Notes

1 We refer to this publication throughout as the Blue Book.
2 The exception being take-up of income support where POLIMOD applies a random probability of taking up a legal entitlement.
3 The NES is discussed in Appendix 11.1.

10 Income tax

10.1 Introduction

Income tax is quite literally central in the process of the simulation of household incomes. Some elements of the tax–benefit system are taxable (such as unemployment benefit), some may be deductions from the tax base (such as Class 4 National Insurance contributions until 1996/7) and for other elements, such as means-tested benefits, it is income net of tax on which entitlement depends. Thus to be confident that POLIMOD is producing reliable and useful results, in almost any respect, requires an assessment of its treatment of income tax. Section 10.2 discusses in general terms the suitability of the Family Expenditure Survey (FES) data as the basis for modelling income tax. This survey contains recorded information about actual income tax payments and also contains many of the ingredients necessary for the simulation of income tax liabilities. Sections 10.3 and 10.4 demonstrate two approaches to the validation of POLIMOD's income tax simulations. Section 10.3 presents an internal comparison of the differences between simulated 1991 income tax liabilities and the amounts recorded in the 1991 FES. Section 10.4 presents a selection of simulated policy changes which are compared with official 'Ready Reckoner' calculations for 1995/6. Finally, section 10.5 summarises the main points to bear in mind when interpreting the results of income tax simulations from POLIMOD.

10.2 Some general issues

The simulation of income tax liabilities from survey data requires an adequate representation of the tax base as well as sufficient personal characteristics necessary to apply the correct rules, allowances and reliefs. POLIMOD makes use of recorded information in the FES on original incomes and simulated values for other elements of income in order to calculate the tax base. This, plus information on individual characteristics and family composition, is used to simulate income tax liabilities.

FES microdata are well-suited to be input for general policy simulation, because they contain information about many aspects of households and have a sampling frame that is intended to capture all households, not only those participating in a particular regime. However, in some respects they are not ideal for the simulation of income tax alone. As noted by Keenay (1995), there is a strong case for using data collected from administrative sources for the accurate specialised modelling of personal tax. Apart from typically larger sample sizes, samples from income tax returns necessarily contain information in the form that is appropriate for income tax calculations. In particular, the data apply to the relevant time period – a financial year in this case – rather than providing a snapshot at a particular point in the year, as is the case with the FES. The reporting period for FES income data varies with each income source. For earnings, it is the last five weeks or two months. For self-employment income, it is the last year for which accounts are available, which may be several years prior to 1991. For social security benefits, it is the period the last payment covered (typically, a week or a month). For investment income, it is the last year. Little information is given about the pattern of income receipt or economic activity over the *whole* of the preceding year and so we assume that the relatively short time period when we 'observe' each survey respondent in fact represents the situation for the whole of the year.

A second problem with simulating income tax from survey data is that income tax is in fact collected through a number of routes and much of it is collected at source. This means that respondents do not always know how much tax they have paid, nor how much their gross income was, before the deduction of tax. Similarly, where tax relief is allowed at source they may only know about the net payment, after relief of tax. In these cases, the gross income (or payment) must be imputed or itself simulated from the information recorded after tax (or tax relief). The advantage of tax record data, such as the Survey of Personal Incomes (SPI) is that taxpayers are required to enter information regarding gross income amounts. However, as Keenay (1995) points out, the SPI contains only about 60% of investment income taxed at source and the remainder of this, and information on reliefs at source, must be imputed. In POLIMOD, income from all sources is assessed for tax together. To do anything else would require much more detailed information about the flows of income and tax from each source than we have available to us. Tax reliefs are viewed as deductions from tax rather than reduced payments. This is because the standard income measure used by POLIMOD in analyses of the impact of policy –

net disposable income (before housing costs) – should reflect changes in the nature and value of tax reliefs, regardless of their method of deduction or administration. Changes in mortgage payments due to reduced tax relief, for example, would not be captured by our 'before housing costs' income measure if the simulation simply reduced mortgage payments themselves.

Finally, income tax is not only assessed annually, it is assessed cumulatively throughout the year using the Pay As You Earn (PAYE) system under which most earnings from employment and occupational pensions are taxed. Over-payment or under-payment in one period may be corrected in a later period. Indeed, incorrect actual payments in one year will be corrected in a later year, often by adjustment to the taxpayer's tax code for use in the PAYE scheme. Simulated income tax, on the other hand, assumes that the situation observed at one point in the year is the case throughout the year and that no adjustments need be made for past errors or over- or under-payments.

10.3 Simulated and recorded income tax compared

This section provides an assessment of the accuracy of POLIMOD income tax simulations by comparing simulated income tax liabilities with the reported and imputed amounts of tax paid by respondents to the FES. The comparison is made for 1991. This allows us to abstract from the additional complications that arise from the need to update FES data when simulating incomes and income tax for a more recent policy year. Table 10.1 outlines the main features of the income tax system in 1990/1 and 1991/2.

In using FES variables to validate the results of POLIMOD simulations, we encounter the same problem we face when using FES variables as the basis of POLIMOD simulations: some of the information we require is not collected. In particular, amounts of *tax at source* (from, for example, interest on savings) and amounts of *tax relief at source* (on, for example, mortgage interest or life assurance premiums) are not recorded in the FES. To get around this problem, we construct comparable measures of income tax payments as follows.

Simulated income tax

POLIMOD simulates income tax after the deduction of mortgage interest relief at source and relief at source on life assurance premia. To get around the problem of lack of information on these reliefs, their simulated value is

Table 10.1. *Income tax in 1990/1 and 1991/2 (£s per year except where otherwise indicated)*

	1990/1	1991/2
Tax rates		
Standard rate	25%	25%
Higher rate	40%	40%
Above taxable income of	20,700	23,700
Personal allowances		
Single allowance	3,005	3,295
Married couple's allowance	1,720	1,720
Additional allowance (lone parent)	1,720	1,720
Age allowance		
Single allowance (age 65–74)	3,670	4,020
Single allowance (age 75+)	3,820	4,180
Married couple's allowance (age 65–74)	2,145	2,355
Married couple's allowance (age 75+)	2,185	2,395
Income limit	12,300	13,500
Taper	50%	50%
Mortgage interest relief	at marginal rate	at 25%
Composite rate on bank and building society interest?	yes	no

added back into simulated income tax. This gives income tax liability before deduction of reliefs at source, a measure that can be compared with the reported FES tax data. As discussed further below, the adjustment does not *completely* remove the effect of mortgage interest relief on the comparison in the first quarter of 1991, but this is expected to affect only a small number of taxpayers.[1]

Reported income tax

To get around the problem of lack of information on amounts of tax deducted at source, these are imputed from the variables that record income from interest and investments after deduction of tax. Imputed tax at source is added to the FES variables that report amounts of tax paid directly or through PAYE. For those interviewed in the 1990/1 tax year, all investment income is assumed to be taxed at source at the composite rate of income tax. For those interviewed in the 1991/2 tax year, when people with income below the tax threshold could apply for exemption, it is assumed that only those who report tax on other items of income, or have an implied amount of investment income before tax that is greater than the relevant personal and married couple's allowances, are liable for tax at source. The detailed construction of FES income tax from FES codes is shown in Appendix 10.1.

Looking first at the proportions of respondents with simulated and reported tax payments shown below, the proportion of respondents with simulated tax payments is under one percentage point less than the proportion with reported or imputed tax payments. However, there is not an exact match between those with simulated and reported payments: 11% of those with reported tax payments have no simulated tax payments; 9% of those with simulated tax payments have no reported tax payments.

	Reported income tax (FES) (%)		
	no	yes	total
Simulated income tax (POLIMOD) (%)			
no	50.3	4.9	55.2
yes	4.1	40.7	44.8
total	54.4	45.6	100.0

The distribution of differences for those who have either simulated or reported income tax payments (or both) is shown in Table 10.2. While 60% have differences within ±£5, a substantial minority of cases have larger differences.

Table 10.3 shows the distribution of differences expressed as a percentage of simulated income tax, for those cases which have non-zero simulated income tax. For over one-third of these cases the amount of reported and imputed income tax is within 5% of the simulated amount.

Not surprisingly, once grouped by range of simulated income tax, those with income tax close to the mean have the closest match. Almost 45% have reported and imputed income tax within 5% of simulated income tax compared with 25% of those with payments less than half or more than twice the mean. Those with simulated income tax liabilities of less than half the mean are more likely to have differences in the range of 100% – most of the cases for whom POLIMOD simulates an income tax liability but have no reported or imputed liability have small simulated income tax liabilities. There are a number of reasons why we should not expect simulated and reported income tax to match perfectly. In what follows, we set out the factors that we expect to cause differences, and

Table 10.2. *Distribution of differences in income tax payments (reported or simulated) for all individuals*

Reported *less* simulated (£s per week)	All with either simulated or reported income tax (%)
< −10.00	12.8
−10.00 to −5.01	6.3
−5.00 to −1.01	11.5
−1.00 to 1.00	32.5
1.01 to 5.00	16.2
5.01 to 10.00	8.0
>10.00	12.7
Mean absolute difference	12.71
Total number	8,492

Note: Percentages may not sum owing to rounding.
Sources: 1991 FES; POLIMOD.

attempt to isolate respondents for whom the comparison is likely to be affected by each. The aim is to strip away layers of complication so that we can both quantify the effects of each factor, and examine the distribution of differences for a subset for whom we can identify no reason for deviation.

Usual versus *last earnings*

First, we should expect differences to arise from the difference between the earnings measure that POLIMOD uses to simulate income tax and the earnings to which reported amounts of income tax relate. While the FES gives us gross earnings on both a usual and last-time-paid basis, income tax deducted from gross earnings is only reported for gross earnings the last time paid. POLIMOD uses gross usual earnings which for 20% of respondents is not the same as the last pay.

Column (2) in Table 10.4 shows the distribution of proportionate differences between reported and simulated income tax for respondents who are earners, whose last pay was not usual and for whom there is a non-zero amount of simulated income tax. Compared to the distribution for all respondents shown in column (1), the differences are much greater.

Table 10.3. *Distribution of proportionate differences in income tax payments*

Reported in rela-tion to simulated income tax	Grouped by range of simulated income tax				
	All (%)	<1/2 mean	1/2 mean− mean	mean− 2×mean	>2×mean
Within 5%	35.9	25.6	43.9	45.1	25.0
Within 10%	47.0	43.9	55.5	56.6	41.2
Within 20%	60.1	44.9	66.3	74.0	61.4
Within 40%	72.8	54.8	81.1	86.5	80.3
Within 80%	83.1	66.7	91.9	94.2	90.2
Within 100%	95.2	90.4	97.8	98.4	97.8
Number	7,655	2,773	2,257	1,965	660

Sources: 1991 FES; POLIMOD.

In most cases, tax simulated on the basis of usual earnings is less than reported tax. This corresponds with the finding that for those employed at the time of their interview, usual earnings are lower, on average, than earnings the last time paid (see Wilson, 1995).

Lags in reporting income from self-employment

Income from self-employment is updated for use in POLIMOD to compensate for the amount reported being from some time in the past (respondents are asked to report their net profits in the most recent 12-month period for which they have information). No such adjustment is made to the FES variable that records income tax paid by those with self-employment income. This means that the comparison is between simulated income tax paid on an updated amount and reported income tax paid on the original amount. In addition, while for many cases it is likely that both the reported profit and the reported tax relate to the same time period, as it is usually the tax assessment exercise that formalises the calculation of each, in some cases the reported profits that we use to simulate income tax and the reported income tax paid may relate to different time periods.[2]

Column (3) in Table 10.4 shows the comparison for those who report receiving income from self-employment and who have a non-zero amount of simulated income tax. For 50%, the difference is greater than 80% of simulated income tax.

Table 10.4 *Distribution of proportionate differences in income tax payments for sub-groups*

Reported in relation to simulated income tax	(1) All	(2) Unusual last pay	(3) Taxable income includes income from self-employment	(4) Irregular or interrupted employment or recent retirement	(5) Direct payments of tax made but no income from self-employment	(6) Possibility of mortgage interest relief in PAYE tax
Within 5%	35.9	8.3	4.9	22.4	13.1	18.1
Within 10%	47.0	16.8	9.9	30.6	23.2	45.8
Within 20%	60.1	32.5	16.1	41.7	40.1	59.7
Within 40%	72.8	54.5	29.3	53.5	61.2	77.8
Within 80%	83.1	78.7	50.1	67.5	77.6	91.7
Within 100%	95.2	89.7	93.1	94.6	81.0	97.2
Number	9,655	1,169	728	927	237	72
Mean simulated income tax (£s pw)	46.57	46.60	63.57	32.71	112.48	176.65
Mean absolute difference (£s pw)	12.70	22.78	42.40	12.32	46.00	67.68

Table 10.4 (*cont.*)

Reported in relation to simulated income tax	(7) Pay slip not consulted	(8) Possibility of transfer of married couple's allowance	(9) More than 90% non-benefit taxable income is investment income	(10) In receipt of occupational pension, report no tax on it	(11) In receipt of occupational pension	(12) In receipt of maintenance payments
Within 5%	25.5	9.3	13.5	4.9	22.5	1.2
Within 10%	37.1	14.6	15.0	11.4	36.0	11.0
Within 20%	51.9	24.5	24.6	16.7	52.8	35.8
Within 40%	66.7	41.1	37.1	23.6	66.0	48.1
Within 80%	78.2	55.6	52.1	35.8	77.4	67.9
Within 100%	94.9	78.1	85.9	93.5	93.8	96.3
Number	372	151	313	246	738	81
Mean simulated income tax (£s pw)	42.68	21.24	28.79	18.54	28.66	28.19
Mean absolute difference (£s pw)	13.18	8.51	11.97	10.35	7.54	10.32

Source: 1991 FES; POLIMOD.

Inter- and intra-year cumulative tax labilities and overpaid tax

An unpaid tax liability or an amount of overpaid tax can be carried over from one year to the next. This means that respondents in the 1991 FES may be paying income tax for which they became liable in 1990 (or a previous year), or enjoying tax credits which they accumulated by overpaying tax in 1990 (or a previous year). Or they may be overpaying or underpaying tax in 1991 and accumulating a tax liability or tax overpayment. In all of these instances, the respondent's tax payments would not match their tax liability on their 1991 income and this may be reflected in reported tax but not in POLIMOD simulations.

In addition, tax liabilities or overpaid tax accumulated in one part of a tax year can be squared in the next part. As explained in section 10.2, this is something that simulations using FES microdata cannot easily capture. For most income items, the FES collects data for a time period that is less than a year (such as the last pay period or the last fortnight). Because income tax liabilities are assessed annually, we need to extrapolate from these amounts to construct a picture of annual income for each respondent. To do this, POLIMOD uses information on income in the current or most recent week and annualises by multiplying weekly amounts by 52. This is not problematic for respondents who remain continuously employed or continuously not employed with the same level of wage and non-wage income for the modelled year, but for those for whom this is not the case, we might expect simulated and actual income tax to deviate.

We should expect inter-year and intra-year accumulations of tax liabilities and tax credits to arise if a respondent has had irregularities in his or her income due, for example, to periods of unemployment or to leaving the paid workforce for retirement, domestic work, illness or study. We should also expect them to arise from irregular earnings within employment, such as irregular subsidiary employment, or from irregular income from self-employment or from investments.

We can identify the former sources of irregularity – those that relate to transitions in and out of employment. We identify employed respondents who have not been in employment for all 52 weeks of the past year, unemployed respondents who have not been unemployed for all 52 weeks of the past year, retired respondents who retired in the last 12 months, recipients of statutory sick pay, sickness benefit, statutory maternity pay, maternity allowance, and unemployment benefit, all of whom must have had interrupted employment within the last 12 months in order to be receiving benefit, and recipients of income support in receipt for less than 52 weeks.[3] Column (4) in Table 10.4 shows the comparison for this subsample. Compared with column (1), a smaller proportion of respondents have small percentage differences, and a larger proportion have differences in the region of 100% of simulated income tax. POLIMOD tends to simulate greater income tax payments than respondents report. This is consistent with over-payment of tax on past income resulting in the enjoyment of a current tax holiday, or entry into employment part-way through a tax year resulting in enjoyment of enhanced weekly allowances.

We can also assume that if a person makes a direct payment of tax but reports no income from self-employment, this payment relates to under-payment of tax over some period in the past. Column (5) in Table 10.4 shows the distribution of proportionate differences between simulated and reported tax for this group. For 19%, reported and imputed income tax is more than twice simulated income tax. The average absolute difference is £46 per week.

Because we do not have information from the FES about people's future income irregularities, we are not able to make the corresponding comparison for respondents who overpay tax at the time of their interview.

Incomplete adjustment to exclude mortgage interest relief

The comparison may still include some of the effects of mortgage interest relief. As noted above, in the first quarter of 1991, mortgage interest relief for higher rate tax payers was delivered partly though the PAYE system and through direct repayments of income tax. Column (6) in Table 10.4 shows the distribution of differences for the subsample of respondents interviewed in the first quarter of 1991 who have simulated mortgage tax relief, and taxable income in the higher rate tax bracket. While the proportion with reported and imputed income tax within 5% of simulated income tax is lower than overall, the proportion that match within 10% is similar. The average absolute difference is several times greater than the overall average. Because of the large tax burdens of those affected, residual mortgage interest relief has a large absolute but small relative effect on the comparison.

Estimation in response

We might expect that simulated and reported income tax would differ for those who do not consult records when asked for details of their income and tax payments but make a rough guess or estimate. This can be checked for respondents who have earnings from employment. If the respondent consults a pay slip for details of his or her net pay and income tax and other deductions, he or she is asked to supply the gross pay stated on the pay slip. If a respondent has a non-zero amount of earnings from employment and has no gross pay recorded, we assume that he or she has not consulted a pay slip.[4] Column (7) in Table 10.4 shows the distribution of differences for this group. A larger proportion have differences in the range of 80 to 100% of simulated income tax. This might suggest that those who do not consult a pay slip are more likely to report zero income tax where a positive amount is simulated on the basis of their stated income. For most, however, it appears that if there is estimation in responses, it alters the comparison only slightly, lowering the proportion that match within 5%. The average difference is similar to the overall figure.

Transfer of the married couple's allowance

POLIMOD simulations assume that in couples where there are two earners, where the husband does not use all or any of the full amount of the married couple's allowance, the unused portion is always transferred to the wife. If, for example, POLIMOD observes a married couple with an unemployed male partner and an earning female partner, it credits her with the whole of the married couple's allowance. In practice, this does not happen automatically, but depends on decisions made by the couple concerned. If the husband's unemployment was not expected to be prolonged, the couple may not elect to transfer the allowance, for example. For couples for whom the transfer assumptions are not valid, we should expect reported and simulated tax payments to differ. Column (8) in Table 10.4 shows the distribution of proportionate differences for members of married couples in which the male partner has taxable income below the combined level of the personal and married couple's allowances appropriate to his age and the female partner has some taxable income. Average simulated tax is correspondingly low and the difference between reported and simulated income tax is large. Less than 25% of cases have reported and imputed income tax within 20% of simulated income tax.

Imputation of tax on income from interest

Income tax paid on some elements of investment income needs to be imputed both for the purposes of simulation and for the purposes of deriving a comparator for simulation results. The methods used are necessarily crude (we would need a full simulation of income tax to attribute tax on interest more accurately) and this may affect the comparison. Column (9) in Table 10.4 shows the comparison for the group for whom we expect the effects of imputation to be particularly problematic – those who do not have wage or self-employment incomes for whom a large proportion of taxable income other than state benefits is investment income. One third have differences in the range of 100%.

Occupational pensions

Income from occupational pensions tends to be taxed at source. FES respondents are asked the amount of pension they receive, whether their pension is taxed at source, and the amount of the deduction at source. Column (10) in Table 10.4 shows that of those who report receipt of an occupational pension but do not report an amount of tax, just over one third have reported income tax within 80% of simulated income tax. In most cases, POLIMOD simulates an income tax liability where none is reported or imputed. Column (11) in Table 10.4 shows the distribution of differences for all cases in receipt of occupational pensions. It is possible that many of those who do report an amount of tax deduction at source report amounts that do not match their simulated liability.

Non-taxation of maintenance payments

Maintenance payments received from a former spouse or partner are included in taxable income. They may not, however, be reported as taxable income, or they may be received regularly but give rise to irregular payments of tax that are not captured by the tax variables in the FES. In either case, we would expect reported and simulated tax to depart. Column (12) in Table 10.4 shows that this is indeed the case. Only one respondent out of 81 who receive maintenance and who have a simulated tax liability also has reported tax within 5% of their simulated tax. One third of cases have no reported or imputed tax.

Table 10.5 shows the comparison for the cases that remain after excluding those identified as likely to be problematic for any of the reasons listed above and whose reported income tax is not within 10% of their simulated income tax.

For 60% of the remaining observations, reported income tax is within 5% of simulated income tax. This is the case for 36% of *all* payers of simulated income tax shown in Table 10.3. The mean absolute difference is reduced from £12.70 to £4.16 per week. The concentration of larger proportionate differences among those with simulated income tax less than half and more than twice the overall mean is not entirely eliminated, although differences in excess of 80% of simulated income tax are almost entirely concentrated among those with simulated income tax less than half the overall mean.

Table 10.6 compares the distribution of absolute differences before and after the exclusion of the problem cases, for all cases with either simulated or reported tax. Where overall less than one third of cases have differences between simulated and reported and imputed income tax payments of £1 or less per week, the exclusion leaves us with about one half of cases with differences of this magnitude. Over 80% of the remaining cases have

Table 10.5. *Distribution of proportionate differences in income tax payments for remaining cases*

Reported in relation to simulated income tax	All (%)	Groups by range of simulated income tax			
		<1/2 mean	1/2 mean– mean	mean– 2×mean	>2×mean
Within 5%	59.8	53.8	65.4	64.2	42.6
Within 10%	78.3	73.4	82.7	80.5	70.3
Within 20%	87.7	81.2	89.3	92.2	87.6
Within 40%	94.5	87.0	96.7	98.5	96.6
Within 80%	96.9	90.6	99.4	99.5	98.9
Within 100%	99.3	97.7	100.0	100.0	100.0
Number	4,598	1,318	1,513	1,380	387

Sources: 1991 FES; POLIMOD.

differences between simulated and reported and imputed income tax payments of £5 or less per week.

The outstanding differences may reflect any of a number of different factors coming into play. Firstly, the exclusion of cases for whom we expect less than a perfect match is not complete: it would not be possible to exclude all those for whom the comparison is affected by imputation and adjustment of investment income because they are so numerous, and it is not possible to identify all those affected by accumulating tax liabilities and tax credits. Secondly, no account has been taken of imputation undertaken in the preparation of FES derived data set. Imputation of income tax paid on some items of income is by all accounts fairly common, and the differences that arise in the comparison may be associated with the contrasting methods that the FES and POLIMOD employ. Lastly, the differences may reflect income tax evasion or unrecorded avoidance by FES respondents.

10.4 Validating modelled changes to income tax

Validation of POLIMOD simulations of policy changes is not a straightforward exercise since it requires comparable estimates of the effects of the same policy changes using independent information. Simulations using Survey of Personal Incomes (SPI) data are the most promising source of such information. Comparison of the underlying distribution of simulated tax with the distributions in the Survey of Personal Incomes for the same period (the last 9 months of 1991) show that the two compare well, with the exception of the top of the distribution. Here, the FES simulations

Table 10.6. *Distribution of differences in income tax payments after exclusion of problem cases*

Reported *less* simulated (£s per week)	All with either simulated or reported income tax (%)	Cases remaining after exclusion of problem cases (%)
<−10.00	12.8	4.0
−10.00 to −5.01	6.3	3.5
−5.00 to −1.01	11.5	12.0
−1.00 to 1.00	32.5	48.6
1.01 to 5.00	16.2	19.8
5.01 to 10.00	8.0	6.3
>10.00	12.7	5.9
Mean absolute difference	12.71	4.16
Total number	8,492	5,435

Note: Percentages may not sum owing to rounding.
Sources: 1991 FES; POLIMOD.

under-estimate the number of taxpayers paying more than £10,000 per year by approximately 19% (see Chapter 12). This would lead us to expect that many policy options might be simulated with reasonable precision but that those targeted on the highest-income taxpayers would be expected to be under-estimates. This section compares POLIMOD simulations for 1995/6 with some SPI-based estimates calculated by the Treasury (HM Treasury, 1994a, 1995b).

Rate structure and personal allowances

The Treasury publishes 'Ready Reckoner' calculations from the Inland Revenue simulation model based on SPI data in such a way that no direct comparison is possible with POLIMOD results. As explained in Section 10.2, POLIMOD simulates income tax as though tax payments were made on an accruals basis and each element of income was taxed in the current year according to the current rules. Each summer, the Treasury makes calculations for the next tax year and the following one using the current tax structure as the base. In each case, the base tax system is indexed by one or two years according to current inflation forecasts. Thus in 1994, the figures were based on the 1994/5 tax system uprated to 1995/6 and 1996/7 levels. A year later, the 1995/6 structure is uprated to 1996/7 and 1997/8 levels. These four sets of estimates, set out in Table 10.7, are made on bases

Table 10.7. *Comparison of POLIMOD simulations with Treasury figures (£m per annum)*[a]

	Treasury[b]				POLIMOD[c]	
	1995/6	1996/7(a)	1996/7(b)	1997/8	gross	net
Change lower rate by 1p	770	660	850	720	778	765
Change standard rate by 1p	1,770	2,100	1,600	2,000	2,002	1,992
Change higher rate by 1p	300	520	240	560	361	359
Change personal allowance by £100	490	630	430	640	604	593
Change married couple's allowance and additional personal allowance by £100	120	150	110	160	150	145
Change age allowances by £100	45	60	45	60	73	71
Change lower rate band by 10%	250	320	240	350	326	322
Decrease basic rate limit by 10%	740	1,050	580	1,100	932	930
Change age allowance limit by £500	6	11	8	14	0	0
Relief on occupational pension contributions	7,500	—	—	—	2,546	2,539
Relief on life insurance premia	160	—	—	—	158	158
Relief on mortgage interest	2,800	—	—	—	3,137	3,032
Exemption of child benefit[d]	700	—	—	—	629	594

Notes:

[a] All changes are increases unless otherwise stated. Presentation of estimates to the nearest £ million should not be taken as indicating that POLIMOD results are significant to this level of precision.

[b] Treasury estimates are made as follows:

1995/6: *Rates* and *allowances* are calculated in July 1994 using the 1994/5 system indexed to 1995/6 as the base (HM Treasury, 1994a). These are 'first year' estimates and do not capture all the effects of the change, some of which occur the year after the change is made. *Reliefs* (last 4 rows) are estimates made in July 1995 (HM Treasury, 1995b).

1996/7(a): These are estimates made in July 1994 using the 1994/5 system indexed to 1996/7 (HM Treasury, 1994a). They are 'full year' estimates, capturing the full effect of a change introduced in April 1995.

1996/7(b): These are 'first year' estimates made in July 1995 using the 1995/6 system indexed to 1996/7 as base (HM Treasury, 1995b).

1997/8: These are 'full year' estimates made in July 1995 using the 1995/6 system indexed to 1997/8 (HM Treasury, 1995b).

[c] POLIMOD estimates are given gross and net of consequential changes to means-tested benefit entitlements. Levels of allowances and thresholds are not rounded. All estimates are on a full year basis with the 1995/6 system as base.

[d] POLIMOD estimate does not include exemption of income tax on one parent benefit; Treasury estimates do.

Sources: HM Treasury, 1994a; HM Treasury, 1995b; POLIMOD updated to 1995/6.

that are most similar to 1995/6 POLIMOD estimates but which differ in the following respects:

1995/6 in 1994

(i) The Treasury estimates are based on the 1994/5 structure except where changes had already been announced for 1995/6 at the time the calculations were made. In particular, the new levels of the married couple's allowances and additional personal allowance, and the rate at which they were to be allowed against tax, are incorporated in the base. Other structural changes that are not incorporated include the widening of the lower rate band and increases to the single age allowances (because they had not been announced at the time the calculations were made).

(ii) Forecast inflation in July might be different from the index used to uprate allowances at the Budget in November. In this case the index derived from forecast inflation was 2.75% but the index actually used to uprate allowances in the November 1994 Budget was 2.20%.

(iii) The Treasury figures are 'first year' estimates and do not allow for the full impact of all the changes. For example, incomes which are not taxed at source will not be affected until they are taxed the following year.

1996/7 in 1994

Points (i) and (ii) above apply. In addition:

(iv) Incomes and the tax system have been indexed a further year beyond the POLIMOD estimate. But these estimates are on a 'full year' basis.

1996/7 in 1995

As in POLIMOD, the 1995/6 system is used as the base. However, point (iv) applies: income levels and the tax system have been indexed beyond the POLIMOD estimate. And (iii), the estimates are on a first year basis.

1997/8 in 1995

A further year of forecast inflation has been introduced but the estimates are on a full year basis.

Some of the differences affect some policy changes more than others. The distinction between full-year and first-year has more significance for higher rate tax than for standard rate tax, for example. At the very least we should expect POLIMOD estimates to come within the range of the four Treasury estimates given in the table.

Treasury estimates are all calculated without allowing for consequential effects on entitlements and liabilities in other parts of the tax–benefit system. POLIMOD estimates are given in two ways: gross of these 'knock-on' effects (particularly on means-tested benefit entitlements), and net, after these effects are taken into account. The differences between net and gross tend to be small compared with the differences between POLIMOD and the Treasury estimates. Again, however, it should be pointed out that the magnitude of the differences depends on the type of policy change. Changes affecting lower-income groups (and therefore means-tested benefit receipt) such as changes to the lower rate band or to child benefit, introduce the most difference between the two POLIMOD estimates.

Two of the POLIMOD estimates shown in Table 10.7 are outside the range provided by the Treasury Ready Reckoners. Both relate to age allowances. Changing the age allowance income limit by a relatively small amount affects no cases in this particular FES database. Such small numbers are bound to be estimated with low levels of confidence using a sample of the size of the FES, and it is probable that even an estimate within the Ready Reckoner range would be insignificantly different from zero. The impact of changing the level of the age allowance is over-estimated by POLIMOD in comparison with the SPI simulation. Again, the numbers involved in the relevant range of income are small. Such comparisons serve to remind us that all results based on FES are subject to sampling error and that estimates relating to small numbers of cases may not be statistically significant.

The one comparison that relates particularly to high incomes is the change in the higher rate of income tax by one percentage point. Here, we see that although the POLIMOD estimates are within the range of all four Treasury figures, they are substantially lower than the two full-year estimates. This confirms our prediction that under-representation of very high incomes in the FES is likely to lead to low estimates of the effect of changes on high incomes. However, it should be pointed out that the shortfall in the data appears to be of people with the *very* highest incomes rather than those throughout the whole higher rate tax bracket. Thus changes to the basic rate threshold, for example, are fairly accurately estimated according to the comparison in Table 10.7. At the same time, we might expect POLIMOD to substantially under-estimate the revenue effects of changes such as the introduction of a new high rate band on very high incomes.

Reliefs and exemptions

The lower half of Table 10.7 compares the total value of selected reliefs and exemptions from tax from POLIMOD and from the 1995 Ready

Reckoner. These latter figures are based on estimates from a number of sources and are not forecasts. As we have no reason to believe that the basis on which they are made is very different from POLIMOD, the most relevant comparison is with the figures for 1995/6. Figures are quoted for a small selection of those provided in the Ready Reckoner. Many of the smaller reliefs are not possible to simulate using FES data.

At first sight, the comparison of estimates of the cost of relief on occupational pension contributions suggests that the POLIMOD estimate is only a third of the value it should be. However, the Treasury figure includes the cost of tax relief for employers' contributions 'on the basis that under the present arrangements employers' contributions are not taxable as a benefit in kind of the employee' (note 3 in the 1994 Ready Reckoner table). Aggregate figures indicate that employer contributions are approximately twice the size of employee contributions (Central Statistical Office, 1993b, Table 4.10). This suggests that POLIMOD's estimate of the value of the tax relief that falls directly on the employee is fairly accurate.

The cost of relief on life insurance premia compares extremely well across the two sources. However, given the difficulties we have in capturing the effect of phasing out of the relief (see Appendix 2.2), it is likely that the proximity of the two figures is coincidental.

The cost of mortgage interest tax relief is somewhat over-estimated by POLIMOD for 1995/6. Comparison of National Accounts figures for 1991 with a POLIMOD simulation for the same year shows the opposite to be the case: mortgage relief is then under-estimated by POLIMOD (see Chapter 11). This suggests that the updating procedure that we apply to gross mortgage interest fails to capture all the changes that have resulted in the fall in the cost of this relief over the period (£5.6 billion in 1991 and £2.8 billion in 1995/6). The procedures by which gross mortgage interest is imputed and updated are described in the Appendix following Chapter 12. Although changes such as those to the rules regarding the tax relief and changes in the interest rate are captured by these procedures, it is likely that structural shifts in the composition of mortgage interest, the distribution of mortgage debt in particular, have not been taken fully into account. This possibility is difficult to confirm, since independent information on the current distribution of outstanding mortgages is not available. Although the comparison shown in Table 10.7 is reasonable, it is probable that certain sorts of policy changes to mortgage tax relief would not be well-estimated by POLIMOD for 1995/6. Changes to the limit on capital are an example of a change that is likely to be poorly estimated, since the impact of this would be highly dependent on the size distribution of loans.

The Treasury also provides estimates of the cost of personal allowances and the exemption of income from certain sources. Since these are based on SPI data which excludes most people with incomes below the current tax threshold, it is not able to capture the cost of reliefs and personal allowances that are received by non-taxpayers and which contribute to keeping them from paying tax. In some cases, the cost of relief may have been fairly reliably estimated in conjunction with other sources: mortgage tax relief is an example. But this is less easy to do with personal allowances and so we do not make these comparisons. However, Table 10.7 does include a comparison of the cost of making child benefit tax-free, although it should be remembered that some degree of imputation will have been necessary to come to the SPI-based estimate.

10.5 Summary

This chapter has demonstrated that, given the difficulties in making comparisons, POLIMOD simulations compare well with SPI-based estimates of the revenue cost of selected policy changes and existing reliefs. However, evaluation of POLIMOD income tax simulations should bear the following points in mind:

• POLIMOD assumes that the information provided in the FES for each case applies to a whole year: thus tax simulations do not take account of possible changes in income over the tax year. Section 10.3 has shown that recorded and simulated tax can be substantially different in many cases. While general explanations for this situation can be found, reconciliation of the two measures is not possible on a case-by-case basis.
• Having recognised that simulated tax is a different concept from that of recorded tax, it is then clear that we cannot expect POLIMOD estimates to provide a similar picture to that obtained using recorded information. Comparisons with information on full-year tax liabilities, such as from the SPI, may be more appropriate, in spite of the differences between the data sources.
• Comparisons of the distribution of simulated tax with the SPI distribution for 1991 suggest that high income taxpayers are under-represented in POLIMOD but that otherwise the distributions are similar. The limited comparisons of the estimates of policy *change* that are possible also suggest that POLIMOD estimates are generally within the range of SPI-based estimates for changes to the rate structure, personal allowances and the main tax reliefs.
• However, all estimates are subject to sampling error and particular care should be taken in using results for changes which affect small numbers of cases.
• Updating cannot capture all the structural and compositional changes in the underlying income distribution between the survey year and the

modelled policy year. Thus care should be taken in interpreting results from simulations involving characteristics subject to recent or current shifts (such as home ownership).

- POLIMOD simulations assume that no tax evasion or avoidance takes place (beyond that which is reflected in under-reporting in the FES income data used as inputs to the simulations).
- POLIMOD is based on data from a UK household survey: the income-tax liabilities of UK taxpayers not resident in the UK or not resident in households will not be captured in the simulations.
- Income tax is central to the tax–benefit calculations for most house-holds. Any problems with estimates of income tax may have consequential effects on the simulations of other components of the system.

Appendix 10.1 Calculation of FES reported and imputed income tax

Income tax paid is calculated by (i) summing the FES variables that record PAYE and direct payments of tax and tax deducted from annuities, occupational pensions and trust income, and (ii) adding to this an imputed amount of income tax deducted at source from interest and other investment income.

The variables that record income tax payments are as follows:

B387 (amount of income tax paid direct)
B349 (amount of tax deducted from public or private pension)
B347 (amount of tax deducted from annuity/trust/covenant)
B305 (income tax deduction – PAYE amount – main job) added if *A250*=1 (last pay in main job was last week or last month)
B310 (tax deducted from pay in subsidiary job) added if *A255*=1 (last pay in subsidiary job was last week or last month).

Tax deducted at source from interest and other investment income is imputed if either an amount of tax paid is recorded by one of the variables listed above, or if the amount of interest and other investment income recorded is above the level of the personal and married couple's allowance appropriate to the person's age and marital status, and depending on the number of hours worked by his or her partner. (For simplicity, it is assumed that the male partner has the married couple's allowance unless he has zero recorded income tax in which case it is transferred to the female partner.)

The variables that are summed to calculate investment income fall into two groups. Those in the first group report before tax income.[5] They are

B399 (building society before-tax interest received)
B401 (high street bank before-tax interest received).

Those in the second group report after tax income. They are grossed-up at the basic or composite rate of tax to give gross income if either there is a positive amount of tax reported elsewhere, or the implied total amount of investment income is greater than the personal and married couple's allowances. If there is no reported tax and if the combined amount is less than the allowances, there is assumed to be no tax. The variables are:

B400 (building society after-tax interest received)
B402 (high street bank after-tax interest received)
B374 (other savings bank/building society interest received)
B378 (stocks/shares etc. interest/dividends after tax)
B409 (gilt-edged stock and war loan interest).

Notes

1   In the first quarter of 1991 mortgage interest relief was paid at the marginal rate of tax and relief was only applied at source at the basic rate, so that higher rate tax payers were credited with the remaining relief to which they were entitled either directly or through the PAYE system. It is not possible to make the data completely comparable because, on the one hand, POLIMOD does not distinguish between at source and direct and PAYE relief and, on the other, amounts of direct and PAYE relief cannot be identified from income tax amounts reported in the FES. As a result, we should expect POLIMOD simulated income tax to overstate income tax before deduction of reliefs at source for higher rate tax payers interviewed in the first quarter of 1991 who have a mortgage. From April 1991, mortgage relief was limited to the basic rate and relief was administered at source, so that the FES and POLIMOD amounts of tax are comparable.

2.   While an adjustment is made in POLIMOD to self-employment income to correct for under-reporting, it is assumed that under-reported income is not declared for tax purposes so this does not affect the income tax simulation.

3   A person is assumed to have had irregular income if $A200=1$ or 2 (employed or self-employed) and *WKSWEMP* (weeks employed in the last year (raw data set))$\neq52$, or $A200=3$ (unemployed) and *WKSWUNEM* (weeks unemployed in the last 12 months (raw data set))$\neq52$ or $A200=6$ (retired) and $RETL12M=1$ (retired in the last 12 months (raw data set)) or $A223>0$ (receiving unemployment benefit) or $A225>0$ (receiving sickness benefit), or $A240=1$ (receiving maternity allowance), or $A279=1$ (receiving statutory sick pay), or *SMP-BENPR*$=1$ (receiving statutory maternity pay (raw data set)) or $A229=1$ (receiving income support at present) and *A228* (weeks receiving income support)<52.

4   The raw data set variable is *GROSSPAY*.

5   It appears that, in almost all cases, people who report interest from building societies and high street banks report either before-tax amounts or after-tax amounts. There are 53 cases in which respondents have positive amounts of both *B400* and *B399* and 35 cases in which respondents have positive amounts of both *B401* and *B402*. Of these cases, the difference between the before-tax and after-tax amounts is within 10% of the hypothetical tax that would be paid to arrive at the after-tax amount for only one respondent. This suggests that the amounts tend to relate to different bank accounts. In five cases, however, the before-tax and after-tax amounts are identical which suggests that they relate to the same account and are not taxed. For these cases, to avoid double counting, the gross amount is set to zero.

11 Aggregates

11.1 Introduction

As part of its output, POLIMOD produces summary tables that show aggregate money amounts and headcounts from each simulation, that is, the amount of money received in income from various sources, raised by a tax or paid in a benefit in a year, as well as the number of individuals, families or households who are affected. For example, if we were to simulate 1991 policy these output tables might tell us that 22 million individuals in the grossed-up FES sample received a total of £260 billion in earnings and paid £14.7 billion in Class 1 National Insurance contributions on these earnings. If we were to model changes to Class 1 contributions, these tables would also show how much was paid in Class 1 contributions after the policy change, and the overall impact of the change on net income.

POLIMOD calculates liability to personal taxes and eligibility to benefits in an order, described in Figure 11.1, that mimics eligibility and liability calculations that actually take place. First, non-means-tested benefits are added to original income (income before direct government intervention). From this total, taxable income and income for National Insurance contribution purposes are derived (some parts of this total, such as child benefit, are not taxable, and only earnings are subject to National Insurance contributions), and liability to income tax and National Insurance contributions is calculated. Next, local taxes are deducted and eligibility to means-tested benefits are calculated. Finally, payment of indirect taxes on household consumption is estimated. In this chapter, following the sequence of this process of calculation, we compare POLIMOD estimates of income amounts, taxes paid and benefits received, and the number of people who pay or receive them, with estimates from external sources. We start with a description of our method of comparison.

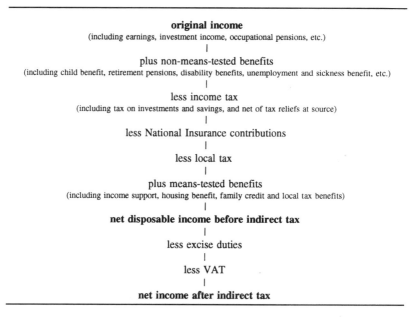

original income
(including earnings, investment income, occupational pensions, etc.)
|
plus non-means-tested benefits
(including child benefit, retirement pensions, disability benefits, unemployment and sickness benefit, etc.)
|
less income tax
(including tax on investments and savings, and net of tax reliefs at source)
|
less National Insurance contributions
|
less local tax
|
plus means-tested benefits
(including income support, housing benefit, family credit and local tax benefits)
|
net disposable income before indirect tax
|
less excise duties
|
less VAT
|
net income after indirect tax

Figure 11.1   The components of net income after indirect tax

11.2 Method of comparison

To abstract from differences that might arise from the need to update FES data or from structural changes, the comparison is made between simulations and official statistics for 1991, the survey year. The following information is obtained for each of the income, benefit, and tax items of interest.

POLIMOD output

During 1991, UK households and individuals were subject to two different regimes of income tax, National Insurance contributions and indirect tax. For example, in April 1991, income-tax thresholds and allowances were increased, and the standard rate at which VAT is charged was raised from 15% to 17.5%. In addition, three regimes of benefits applied during the year: pre-April, when benefit rates for the fiscal year 1990/1 applied; April to October, when benefit rates were increased for the fiscal year 1991/2; and October onwards, when child benefit and non-means-tested benefit rates and some premiums for means-tested benefits were increased. Taxes and benefits for each respondent are simulated according to the regime in force when the household was interviewed.

For the purpose of comparing POLIMOD output with statistics from official sources, the model's simulations are presented in two ways using two different methods of grossing-up the FES data to represent the UK population as a whole. The first uses uniform weights to gross-up – one family in the FES grosses-up to 3,362 families in the simulated population. The second uses differential family weights that adjust for over- and under-representation of different types of families in the FES. These weights are discussed more fully in the Appendix to this book.[1]

Control figures from external sources

External control figures for validation are obtained from various sources. These are discussed in more detail in Appendix 11.1. For aggregate income, expenditure, and taxes, much use is made of Blue Book estimates of the income and expenditure of the household sector for 1991. For aggregate counts (of taxpayers and benefit recipients, for example), statistical reports of the relevant government departments, the Labour Force Survey (LFS) and the Survey of Personal Incomes (SPI) are used.

Blue Book data always refer to the entire UK. Therefore, it has a similar reference group to that of POLIMOD. Data from other government sources, however, such as those of the Department of Social Security (DSS) (1993c, 1994b) refer only to Great Britain, that is, England, Wales and Scotland but not Northern Ireland. As a result, at several points in this analysis, we compare administrative data from England, Scotland and Wales only with POLIMOD output that excludes Northern Ireland, or we adjust by a factor calculated from data for Great Britain only. In so doing, we are making the implicit assumption that Northern Ireland data have similar characteristics to data in the rest of the UK. Where we believe that Northern Ireland data are significantly different from data for the rest of the UK, we bring this to the reader's attention.

Adjusting control figures from external sources to FES population totals

Blue Book estimates, departmental statistics and other official data are often estimated for non-household and non-UK resident populations which are not covered by the FES. The Blue Book household sector income and expenditure estimates, for example, include private trusts and individuals living in institutions (Central Statistical Office, 1985, p. 47). Where possible, we adjust the external data by a factor that approximates

Table 11.1. *Subgroups of the non-household and total population from the 1991 Census*

	(A) Total population (000s)	(B) Non-household (000s)	100×(B)/(A) Adjustment factor %	name
Age 16 or over				
Economically active:				
employed	24,292.3	277.30	1.14	EMP
unemployed	2,484.5	43.60	1.75	UMP
students	1,676.8	183.90	10.97	STD
Economically inactive:				
permanently sick	1,799.0	200.10	11.12	PSK
retired	8,314.7	433.60	5.21	RET
other inactive	5,297.9	93.50	1.76	OTH
Total	43,865.1	1,232.00	2.81	TOT
Aged under 16	11,023.7	34.60	0.31	CHD

Note:
Persons who are visitors or guests to hotels, boarding houses, hostels and other common lodging houses are excluded. Children under the age of 16 present in residential educational establishments and in NHS and non-NHS hospitals are excluded. In the FES, absent household members who consider the address to be their main residence are included as members of the household, as are children aged under 16 who are away at boarding school.
Sources: Column (A): Office of Population Censuses and Surveys (1993c), Table 8 and Table 2. Column (B): Office of Population Censuses and Surveys (1993b) Volume 2, Table 5 and Volume 1, Table 3.

the amount of difference in coverage between the FES and external data sources. In practice, this means adjusting mostly for the non-household UK population, although some other minor adjustments are also occasionally made, and these are reported in the text.

Table 11.1 shows the total number of individuals resident in England, Scotland and Wales (column A), and the total number of individuals present in these countries who are part of the non-household population (column B), as reported in the 1991 Census.[2] Separate adjustment factors are derived for seven categories – the employed (EMP), the unemployed (UMP), students (STD), the permanently sick (PSK), retired people (RET), other inactive people (OTH) and people aged under sixteen (CHD). The third column in Table 11.1 shows the adjustment factors that can be applied to statistics that are representative of the entire population to estimate their value for the household population only. Given that the adjustments do not compensate completely for the differences between the Census coverage and the FES, and given that the proportions in each group may be different in Northern Ireland,[3] they should be viewed as approximate. Where more precise adjustments can be made on the basis of actual payments data or other information, they are described below.

These adjustment factors are used to adjust different estimates. The RET adjustment factor (5.21%) obtained for the retired population, for example, is applied to adjust external data on numbers in receipt of occupational, private and state pensions. The factors are also used to adjust aggregate income and expenditure estimates from the Blue Book. In doing this, we are making two assumptions: firstly, that the incidence of different elements of income and expenditure is the same across the household and non-household population and, secondly, that average income and expenditure among those in the FES population is the same as that among those who are outside it. These assumptions are a potential source of error. Evans (1995) suggests that there is a different pattern of income receipt among the non-household population compared with people who live in private households. Using 1989 data, he estimates that mean *total income* for those outside the sampling frame of the FES is between 77% and 93% of mean income of those included.[4] Therefore, it is likely that the population-based adjustment factors shown in Table 11.1 slightly understate total income that can be attributed to the household population. However, the opposite may be the case with particular *components* of income.

11.3 Original income

In POLIMOD, original income is defined as market and other income received before any direct intervention by government. It includes wages and salaries from employment, income from self-employment, investment income from interest on savings, rent and dividends, income from occupational pensions and annuities, and other items of income such as allowances from other family members, maintenance and so on. These parts of the POLIMOD output are not simulated. They may be adjusted where there are lags in the data (as in the case of income from self-employment), and they may be adjusted where there is systematic under-reporting (as in the case of the adjustments made for under-reporting of investment and self-employment income), but in general they are drawn directly from the 1991 FES data, grossed-up to represent the UK household population.[5]

Employee earnings

Table 11.2 shows that aggregate gross employee earnings from POLIMOD are 94% of adjusted Blue Book aggregate wages and salaries on both a uniform weighted basis and on a family weighted basis. This is similar to, but at the lower end of, the range of deviation found by Atkinson and Micklewright (1983) for the period 1970–77.[6] The CSO gives income from employment an A reliability grading. This corresponds with a 90% probability that the true value of the figure lies within ±3% of the reported figure (Central Statistical Office, 1985, p. 62). The POLIMOD estimate lies outside this margin.

On the Blue Book side of the comparison, there are a number of possible reasons for the shortfall which are discussed in detail by Atkinson and Micklewright (1983). The Blue Book figure for wages and salaries is derived from a 1% sample of Pay As You Earn (PAYE) income tax records. Therefore, since income tax records exist only for those whose incomes are above the tax threshold, for those whose earnings are too low to incur income tax they are estimated using FES data. In addition, income not covered by the PAYE system (such as that from tips and gratuities) is estimated, and income from employment that is not declared for tax purposes is also estimated and added in, the adjustment being 0.3% of total wages and salaries in 1980 (Central Statistical Office, 1985, pp. 55–6).

On the POLIMOD side, the FES earnings measure used by POLIMOD is *normal* gross weekly earnings. For male and female full-time employees in the 1991 FES, average normal earnings were some 5% less than average *actual* earnings from the FES (£269.40 compared with £282.60) and some 4% less than average actual earnings from the New Earnings Survey (£280.80).[7]

Kemsley *et al.* (1980) found that FES respondents tend to estimate their normal earnings over several months preceding their interview, which may mean that they are lower because of lags caused by wages growth. Alternatively, normal hours of work may be lower than actual hours of work (Atkinson, Gomulka and Sutherland, 1988), or unusual additional earnings may be greater, on average, than unusual earnings deficits (Wilson, 1995b). Normal earnings are used in POLIMOD because they appear to provide a more accurate picture of the distribution of earnings about the median when compared with the distribution of NES earnings (see Wilson, 1995b), and because they are a more appropriate measure for simulation of means-tested benefits. This choice may explain much of the shortfall in aggregate earnings.

The numbers of earners from the Labour Force Survey (LFS) (Office of Population Censuses and Surveys, 1992) and POLIMOD shown in Table 11.2 are remarkably similar. This is not surprising, since the LFS and the

Table 11.2. *Employee earnings: aggregate amounts and number receiving (estimates from external sources* versus *POLIMOD, 1991)*

	External sources		POLIMOD uniform weights		POLIMOD family weights	
	unadjusted	adjusted	reported	as % of adjusted external sources	reported	as % of adjusted external sources
Total amount (£m)	280,469	276,178[a]	260,470	94	260,230	94
Number receiving (000s)	21,863	22,382[b]	22,250	99	22,300	100

Notes:

Adjustment factors applied to external sources are calculated from Labour Force Survey data for 1991. These data produce slightly different estimates of the number of employees from those produced by the Census (see Table 11.1). Northern Ireland is included in published LFS tables for some analyses, and this information is used below to create adjustment factors to be applied where information on Northern Ireland is omitted. Therefore, in Tables 11.2 and 11.3, LFS data are used to calculate adjustment factors for Northern Ireland, while Census data from Table 11.1 are used to calculate adjustment factors for the non-household population.

[a] Total earnings

The Blue Book estimate of total wages and salaries includes those of people not living in households (see EMP from Table 11.1) and members of HM Forces living overseas. On 1 July 1991, there were 89,300 of the latter, representing 0.393% of the Blue Book estimate, if we assume that average earnings in this group were the same as average earnings in the population as a whole. If we make the same assumption for earnings in the non-household population, the adjustment factor to exclude the earnings of the two groups not covered by the FES is:

$$1.14 + 0.393 = 1.53\%$$

[b] Number of employees:

Adjustment for Northern Ireland (*Source:* OPCS, 1992, Table 6.22):

	UK (000s)	Northern Ireland (000s)
Number of economically active persons	28,592	689
Number of unemployed	2,385	83
Working (economically active less unemployed)	26,207	606

$606/26,207 = 0.0231 =$ adjustment factor for Northern Ireland of 2.31%
Number of UK employees: NI adjustment factor×GB employees (OPCS, 1992, Table 6.8)

$$1.0231 \times 21,863 = 22,368.0 \text{ thousand}$$

The Labour Force Survey reports that some respondents who were in employment did not give their employment status (14,000 in GB). We assume those in employment who did not give their employment status to be employees.
Total LFS-based number of employees in the UK:

$$22,368 + (14.0 \times 1.0231) = 22,382.3 \text{ thousand}$$

Sources: Number of persons with earnings: Office of Population Censuses and Surveys, 1992, Table 6.8, full and part-time employees, Spring 1991. Number of HM Forces serving overseas: Central Statistical Office, 1995, Table 7.6. POLIMOD estimates: 1991 FES. Employee earnings: Central Statistical Office, 1993b, Table 4.9, wages and salaries (includes pay in cash of HM Forces).

FES have similar sampling frames – they are both surveys of private households. However, published LFS tables for numbers of employees refer only to England, Scotland and Wales, and therefore the adjusted figure compensates for this by taking account of employment in Northern Ireland. Sampling error in the LFS is discussed in Appendix 11.1. For estimates of numbers of employees, this is likely to be extremely low – less than 0.5% given a significance level of 0.05.

Income from self-employment

Historically, income from self-employment has proved difficult to measure from survey data for two reasons. Firstly, self-employed respondents to surveys on incomes often find it difficult to assess what their incomes are (Eardley and Corden, 1994). Secondly, there is often a problem of non-response and under-reporting in surveys of incomes of self-employed people. In this respect, the FES is no exception. Both the FES and the Blue Book estimates of income from self-employment, therefore, have high margins of error.

In the FES, there is a high proportion of estimated and 'don't know' responses to questions on incomes from self-employed respondents (Kemsley *et al.*, 1980, p. 50). Studies of non-response for the 1981 and 1991 FES years carried out by the Office for Population Censuses and Surveys find that the probability of response is significantly lower than average for households headed by a self-employed person (Redpath, 1986; Foster, 1994). We might therefore expect both misreporting of income by those surveyed and under-counting of the self-employed population to affect POLIMOD estimates. A 19.5% adjustment is made within POLIMOD for undeclared self-employment income in the FES in an attempt to counter the former effect.[8]

The CSO gives the Blue Book estimates of income from self-employment a C rating (this corresponds to a 90% probability that the true value of the figure lies within 10 to 20% of the reported figure). The POLIMOD estimate is within this margin of error at 86% of the adjusted Blue Book (which excludes non-household persons in employment). In addition to the possibility of measurement error in the Blue Book estimates, there may also be contrasting definitions and measurement methods that contribute to the difference.[9]

Table 11.3 shows that the POLIMOD count of numbers in self-employment lies at 91% of the adjusted LFS count on both a uniform and a family weighted basis. However, response rates in the FES among the self-employed give some cause for concern. The response rate for households headed by a self-employed person in the 1981 FES was 65% compared with 74% overall (Redpath 1986). If we re-weight the 1991 POLIMOD

Table 11.3. *Income from self-employment: aggregate amounts and number receiving (estimates from external sources* versus *POLIMOD, 1991)*

	External sources		POLIMOD uniform weights		POLIMOD family weights	
	unadjusted	adjusted	reported	as % of adjusted external sources	reported	as % of adjusted external sources
Total amount (£m)	49,788	49,355^a	42,770	87	42,540	86
Number receiving (000s)	3,316	3,393^b	3,100	91	3,080	91

Notes:
Adjustment factor applied to external sources:
[a] income from self-employment: 0.87% (to exclude non-household population of employed persons *less* those serving in HM Forces, who are, by definition, employees).
Total number of employed persons in the non-household population is 277,300 (see Table 11.1). Of these, the total serving in HM Forces is 66,500 (see Appendix 11.3). Therefore, the total who could be either employees or self-employed is 210,800. $100 \times (210.8/24,292.3) = 0.87\%$ (24,292.3 = total number of employed persons in 1991 Census – see Table 11.1).
[b] numbers with income from self-employment: 2.31% (to include Northern Ireland – unadjusted figure excludes Northern Ireland – see notes to Table 11.2).
Sources: Income from self-employment: Central Statistical Office, 1993b, Table 4.9, income from self-employment after deducting interest payments, depreciation and stock appreciation. Number of persons with income from self-employment: Office of Population Censuses and Surveys, 1992, Table 6.8, Persons in full and part-time self-employment, Spring 1991. POLIMOD estimates: 1991 FES.

count to compensate for differential non-response, the gap between LFS and FES totals can be explained, even if we take into account sampling error in the LFS. However, it must be emphasised that POLIMOD totals for self-employment, like data on self-employment from most other sources, are particularly problematic and difficult to validate.

One can only speculate why response among the self-employed is low in the FES. It may be that the self-employed are less willing to participate in a financial survey. It may also be that many self-employed people are not yet able to make a true estimate of their profits and losses because their business is a relatively new one, for example, and are therefore treated as non-respondents on account of their inability to provide income information.

Investment income

The POLIMOD estimate of investment income in Table 11.4 incorporates a 19.5% adjustment for under-reporting.[10] In spite of this, it falls short of the adjusted Blue Book figure by over 20% on a family weighted basis and is

Table 11.4 *Income from investments: aggregate amounts and number receiving (estimates from external sources* versus *POLIMOD, 1991)*

	External sources		POLIMOD uniform weights		POLIMOD family weights	
				as % of adjusted external		as % of adjusted external
	unadjusted	adjusted	reported	sources	reported	sources
Total amount (£m)	45,839	44,551[a,b]	35,520	80	34,700	78
Number receiving (000s)	23,725	32,149[a,c]	28,450	88	28,150	88

Notes:
Adjustment factors applied to exclude non-household population from external sources:
[a] income from investments and numbers in receipt of income from investments: 2.81% (TOT on Table 11.1).
[b] Because FES respondents are asked their investment income over the last 12 months, the Blue Book estimate of investment income is adjusted to a comparable basis by taking the average of 1990 and 1991 estimates. The 1993 Blue Book figure for 1990 is £47,235 million. The 1993 Blue Book figure for 1991 is £45,839 million, as shown in the unadjusted column.
[c] The unadjusted external total for numbers in receipt of investment income refers only to those with taxable investment income who have total taxable income above the tax threshold in 1991/92. The adjusted figure is adjusted by the ratio of the family weighted number of POLIMOD cases with investment income (28,150,000) to the family weighted number of POLIMOD cases with taxable investment income who have income above the tax threshold (20,190,000).
Sources: Income from investment: Central Statistical Office, 1993b, Table 4.9, rent, dividends and interest (gross receipts). Number of persons with income from investments: Board of the Inland Revenue, 1994, Table 3.6; 1993, Table 3.5, interpolated from estimated numbers with total investment income in 1990–91 and 1991–92. POLIMOD estimates: 1991 FES.

outside the confidence interval given by the CSO. Investment income, like self-employment income, has a C rating – 90% probability that the true value of the figure lies within 10 to 20% of the reported figure. Part of the difference can be attributed to the estimated shortfall in numbers with investment income. In addition, the household sector Blue Book estimates include private trusts. More so for investment income than for any other item, private trusts may account for a sizeable share of income and their inclusion in the Blue Book figures may account for a significant proportion of the shortfall. Atkinson and Micklewright (1983), who adjust to exclude investment income of private trusts, find a somewhat greater shortfall for 1970–77 (around 50%) than that observed for 1991 (around 40% before the POLIMOD adjustment for undeclared income). The difference was thought to be associated with under-statement and non-reporting of investment income by respondents, and possibly the under-representation of those with very high investment incomes in the FES. It seems reasonable to suggest that this continues to be a problem in the 1991 FES. However, it may also be that the FES does not capture small amounts of investment income for a large number of respondents who 'forget' to report them, thus adding to the overall shortfall.

POLIMOD also under-states numbers in receipt of investment income relative to the adjusted Inland Revenue estimate. The unadjusted Inland Revenue figure is based on the Survey of Personal Incomes (SPI) which excludes people who have total incomes below the income-tax threshold. This is adjusted according to the ratio of all POLIMOD respondents who report investment income to those with investment income whose total incomes are above the income tax threshold.[11] The Inland Revenue estimates the numbers with investment income (primarily bank and building society interest and dividends from UK companies) that are missing from its survey, and warns that the margin of error that accompanies its estimates is large, but does not attempt to quantify this error (Board of the Inland Revenue, 1994, p. 32).

Occupational and private pensions

Table 11.5 shows that POLIMOD estimates of aggregate income from occupational and private pensions fall well short of the Blue Book estimate. One possible reason for this is that Blue Book estimates include lump sums paid on death and on retirement and repayment of contributions on withdrawal from pension schemes. While in the 1991 FES interviewers are not explicitly instructed to exclude lump sum payments, this may be the practice. On the basis of information for private sector occupational pensions in 1991 shown, only 72.5% of scheme payments were regular pensions. The remainder were mainly lump sums.[12]

If irregular payments have not been captured by the FES, then roughly half the shortfall is explained. Other items included in the Blue Book figure, but likely to be excluded from the POLIMOD measure, may explain some of the remaining difference. These include redundancy payments paid by employers, *ex gratia* payments and other non-pension payments, as well as employer's liability insurance claims.[13]

Evidence from the SPI certainly supports the thesis that total occupational pensions as reported in the FES may be a reasonable representation of total occupational pensions paid to households in the UK. If we compare the occupational pension component of the POLIMOD amount (£19,610 million) with an estimate of total taxable income from occupational pensions for 1991–92 made from the SPI (£18,500 million),[14] it

Table 11.5. *Income from occupational and private pensions: aggregate amounts and number receiving (estimates from external sources* versus POLIMOD, *1991)*

	External sources		POLIMOD uniform weights		POLIMOD family weights	
				as % of adjusted external		as % of adjusted external
	unadjusted	adjusted	reported	sources	reported	sources
Total amount (£m)	47,980	45,480[a]	21,080	46	20,540	45
Number receiving (000s)	6,500	6,161[a]	6,100	99	5,890	96

Notes:
Adjustment factors applied to exclude non-household population from external sources:
[a] income from and numbers receiving occupational and private pensions 5.21% (RET on Table 11.1).
Sources: Income from occupational and private pensions: Central Statistical Office, 1993b, Table 4.9, pensions and other benefits from life assurance and pension schemes. Number receiving occupational and private pensions: Government Actuary's Department, 1991, 'Occupational Pension Schemes 1991: p. 14, estimated number of occupational pensions only. POLIMOD estimates: 1991 FES.

appears that POLIMOD slightly over-estimates income from occupational schemes. However, it is likely that some of this over-estimate represents occupational pensions that are not taxed, and therefore not included in the SPI.

Table 11.5 compares numbers of people in receipt of occupational pensions only, as there are no readily available data on numbers in receipt of private pensions. These are the majority of non-state pension recipients – just under 8% of those in receipt of an occupational pension or private pension in POLIMOD receive a private pension only. Numbers of occupational pensioners compare well. Note that the source for numbers in receipt of occupational pensions in Table 11.5 is not the SPI, but a survey of occupational pensions by the Government Actuary. According to the SPI, 4.48 million people in 1991/2 were receiving occupational pensions of £3,295 a year or over – this is the level at which they became liable for income tax in that year.

Other income

Other original income from POLIMOD includes regular allowances (from relatives or from a charity, for example), income from babysitting, foster-

Table 11.6. *Other original income: aggregate amounts (estimates from external sources* versus *POLIMOD, 1991)*

	External sources		POLIMOD uniform weights		POLIMOD family weights	
	unadjusted	adjusted[a]	reported	as % of adjusted external sources	reported	as % of adjusted external sources
Total income (£m)	11,873	11,539	4,590	40	4,550	39

Notes:
Adjustment factors to exclude non-household population from external sources:
[a] 2.81% (TOT on Table 11.1).
Sources: Central Statistical Office, 1993b, Table 4.9, other transfers. POLIMOD estimates: 1991 FES.

ing allowances from local authorities and other organisations, maintenance, income from odd jobs, children's income, private benefits and income from covenants. It also includes student grants and student loans, which are not strictly original income but play a minor role in the overall income picture. Other income from the Blue Book is the 'other transfers' item in the household income and expenditure table (Central Statistical Office, 1993b, Table 4.9) which includes income from non-profit making bodies and transfers from overseas but excludes transfers *between* households such as maintenance payments. This item is given a C rating by the CSO. There are, therefore, comparability and estimation problems that we expect would adversely affect the comparison.

The POLIMOD estimate in Table 11.6 falls far short of the Blue Book estimate, and well outside the 10–20% margin for error indicated by the C rating. One possibility is that this reflects the exclusion of irregular amounts of income from POLIMOD. Lump sums are only included if they are regularly received. No attempt is made to find a control total for numbers in receipt of other income.

Total original income

Table 11.7 summarises the differences between total original income from the FES and from external sources. Total original income from the FES is 85% of adjusted total original income for the household sector from the Blue Book on the basis of uniform weighted total, and 86% of the Blue Book total on the basis of the family weighted total.

Table 11.7. *Total original income: aggregate amounts (estimates from external sources versus POLIMOD, 1991)*

	External sources		POLIMOD uniform weights		POLIMOD family weights	
	unadjusted	adjusted	reported	as % of adjusted external sources	reported	as % of adjusted external sources
Total income (£m)	435,949	427,187	364,430	85	365,774	86

Notes:
Total original income equals total direct money income from work and property plus pensions and other benefits from life assurance and pension schemes (it excludes income in kind and state benefits). This table represents the sum of income reported in each column (unadjusted and adjusted External sources and POLIMOD) in Tables 11.2 to 11.6. The implicit adjustment factor to exclude the non-household population from the external sources is 2.01%.
Sources: See sources for income amounts on Tables 11.2 to 11.6. POLIMOD: 1991 FES.

11.4 Non-means-tested benefits

Tables 11.8 to 11.16 show POLIMOD estimates of aggregate receipt of non-means-tested benefits compared with control totals from the Blue Book where these are available and from other sources where they are not (see Appendix 11.2). The CSO gives all Blue Book estimates of benefit expenditure an A rating (which corresponds to a 90% probability that the estimate is within ±3% of the true value). With the exception of child benefit and one parent benefit, which are modelled or estimated, the POLIMOD amounts shown are simply amounts of current benefit receipt from the FES, grossed-up to represent benefit receipt of the population as a whole.

Child benefit

Table 11.8 shows that, grossed-up using uniform weights, POLIMOD slightly over-estimates the number of families in receipt of child benefit. This reflects the over-representation of families with dependent children in the FES. Once reweighted using family weights, the POLIMOD estimate of numbers of families in receipt of child benefit is exactly equal to the adjusted estimate based on DSS statistics. In contrast, reweighting shifts

Table 11.8. *Income from child benefit and number receiving (totals from external sources* versus *P O L I M O D, 1991)*

	External sources		POLIMOD uniform weights		POLIMOD family weights	
	unadjusted	adjusted	estimated	as % of adjusted external sources	estimated	as % of adjusted external sources
Total income (£m)	5,228	5,212	5,370	103	5,000	96
Number of families receiving (000s)	7,031	6,958	7,390	106	6,980	100

Notes and sources: See Appendix 11.2.

the estimate of aggregate income from child benefit from slightly above to slightly below the adjusted control total. This may be due to the effects of over- and under-representation in the FES that is not corrected for by the family weights used by POLIMOD. For example, these weights do not distinguish between lone parent families with different numbers of children. Nor do they distinguish between two parent families with three and more than three children. The reconciliation suggests that, while the weights produce a good estimate of the total number of families with dependent children in the UK, the underlying estimate of the total number of children in respect of whom child benefit is payable is not as accurate.[15]

One parent benefit

Compared with data from official sources, POLIMOD over-estimates income from one parent benefit and numbers in receipt in Table 11.9. POLIMOD's simulated total is roughly one and a half times the aggregate income and caseload reported by official sources. There may be two reasons for this. Firstly, non-take-up of one parent benefit is not taken account of in POLIMOD. There is no financial incentive to claim one parent benefit while in receipt of income support and, while those who were lone parents before they received income support have no reason to drop their claim to one parent benefit, those who were not have no reason to make a claim. There may also be non-take-up due to lack of knowledge of the payment among those who are not in receipt of income support. Secondly, POLIMOD assumes that the characteristics of families and individuals do not change over time. This means that it does not allow for non-take-up of benefits

Table 11.9. *Income from one parent benefit and number receiving (totals from external sources* versus POLIMOD, 1991)

	External sources		POLIMOD uniform weights		POLIMOD family weights	
	unadjusted	adjusted	estimated	as % of adjusted external sources	estimated	as % of adjusted external sources
Total income (£m)	252	251	360	143	380	151
Number of families receiving (000s)	827	818	1,240	152	1,290	158

Notes and sources: See Appendix 11.2.

such as one parent benefit by lone parents whose status is a relatively new one, or a changing one, or who expect their status to be temporary.

Retirement pension

Table 11.10 shows the Blue Book estimate of expenditure on retirement pension, adjusted to exclude the non-household population by the 5.21% factor (RET) derived in Table 11.1.[16] Grossed-up with uniform weights, the POLIMOD estimate is slightly higher than the adjusted Blue Book figure. Grossed-up with family weights that compensate for the over-representation of the younger elderly, it is slightly below. Both POLIMOD estimates are within the confidence interval for the Blue Book estimates.

DSS counts of numbers in receipt of retirement pension shown in Table 11.10 are adjusted to exclude an estimated 620,000 recipients resident overseas,[17] and the assumed 5.21% not resident in private households within the UK. On an unweighted basis, the grossed-up POLIMOD caseload is 107% of the control figure. Re-weighted using family weights, the POLIMOD estimate is 104% of the control.

It should be borne in mind that the adjustment factor applied to both aggregate income and caseload is approximate. It is possible that the share in aggregate income of the non-household population of retirement pensioners is somewhat less than 5.21% because of the reductions in benefit that would apply for those who are in non-private hospitals for more than a short period. It is also possible that the proportion of retirement pensioners in the non-household population is somewhat smaller than the overall proportion of the elderly. Given the degree of uncertainty, POLIMOD aggregates compare reasonably well.

Table 11.10. *Income from retirement pensions and number receiving (totals from external sources* versus *P O L I M O D, 1991)*

	External sources		POLIMOD uniform weights		POLIMOD family weights	
				as % of adjusted external		as % of adjusted external
	unadjusted	adjusted	reported	sources	reported	sources
Total income (£m)	25,191	23,879	24,350	102	23,440	98
Number receiving (000s)	10,231	9,108	9,760	107	9,440	104

Notes and sources: See Appendix 11.2.

Widow's pension

P O L I M O D estimates of widow's benefit caseload are some 136% and 124% of adjusted DSS estimates on a uniform weighted basis and a family weighted basis respectively (Table 11.11). Over-representation of widows in the FES was also found by Atkinson *et al.* (1988) and Jones *et al.* (1991). The estimates of aggregate expenditure shown in Table 11.11 deviate by a proportionately greater amount, implying a higher average payment for the P O L I M O D sample. This was not found in the comparison of reported widow's benefit from the FES with expenditure out-turns from the DSS Departmental Report (Department of Social Security, 1994c) described in Wilson (1995a). Indeed, the 1991 Blue Book widow's benefit estimate for the UK is well below out-turns for either 1990/91 or 1991/92 for Great Britain alone. The reason for the difference between the two sources is not clear.

Unemployment benefit

While the family weighted P O L I M O D estimate of unemployment benefit caseload is 92% of adjusted DSS caseload in Table 11.12, P O L I M O D aggregate income from unemployment benefit is 74% of the adjusted Blue Book unemployment benefit expenditure. If it assumed that all unemployment benefit claims commence immediately employment ceases, then 12% of those who report receipt of unemployment benefit in the 1991 FES have been out of work for a length of time that suggests that the amount reported as unemployment benefit is more likely to be income support. The true under-estimation of caseload, therefore, may be somewhat

Table 11.11. *Income from widow's pension and number receiving (totals from external sources* versus *POLIMOD, 1991)*

	External sources		POLIMOD uniform weights		POLIMOD family weights	
	unadjusted	adjusted	reported	as % of adjusted external sources	reported	as % of adjusted external sources
Total income (£m)	865	841	1,220	145	1,130	134
Number receiving (000s)	361	331	450	136	410	124

Notes and sources: See Appendix 11.2.

Table 11.12. *Income from unemployment benefit and number receiving (totals from external sources* versus *POLIMOD, 1991)*

	External sources		POLIMOD uniform weights		POLIMOD family weights	
	unadjusted	adjusted	reported	as % of adjusted external sources	reported	as % of adjusted external sources
Total income (£m)	1,486	1,460	1,060	73	1,080	74
Number receiving (000s)	564	554	490	88	510	92

Notes and sources: See Appendix 11.2.

greater than it appears from FES data. This may be associated with under-representation of the unemployed in the FES.

Maternity allowance

POLIMOD estimates of maternity allowance caseload and aggregate income both fall short of the control figures (Table 11.13). Given the extremely small size of the underlying sample (4 cases report receipt of maternity allowance), little confidence can be placed in these estimates.

Statutory maternity pay

Caseload estimates for statutory maternity pay from POLIMOD compare well with the adjusted DSS control figure (Table 11.13). There is, however,

Table 11.13. *Income from sickness and maternity benefits and number receiving (totals from external sources* versus *POLIMOD, 1991)*

	External sources		POLIMOD uniform weights		POLIMOD family weights	
	unadjusted	adjusted	reported	as % of adjusted external sources	reported	as % of adjusted external sources
Maternity allowance						
Total income (£m)	39	39	30	77	30	77
Number receiving (000s)	18	18	10	56	10	56
Statutory maternity pay						
Total income (£m)	362	358	240	67	230	64
Number receiving (000s)	81	80	80	100	80	100
Sickness benefit						
Total income (£m)	263	260	370	142	380	146
Number receiving (000s)	128	127	150	118	150	118
Statutory sick pay						
Total income (£m)	788	779	460	59	450	58
Number receiving (000s)	349	345	180	52	180	52

Notes and sources: See Appendix 11.2.

a sizeable under-estimation of expenditure. This may result from the under-representation of those in receipt of earnings related statutory maternity pay, or from the imputation procedures employed in the FES. Respondents are not actually asked the level of their payments, but are asked whether or not they receive an earnings-related payment.

Sickness benefit

Table 11.13 also shows that POLIMOD overstates sickness benefit caseload and aggregate income compared with control totals. This may be a function of the small underlying FES sample size (44 cases report receipt), and the consequently large confidence interval that surrounds the POLIMOD figure.

Statutory sick pay

Caseload and aggregate income estimates for statutory sick pay from POLIMOD are roughly half the level of the control totals (Table 11.13). This is entirely plausible, given that many people who receive statutory

Table 11.14. *Income from invalidity benefit and number receiving (totals from external sources* versus P O L I M O D, *1991)*

	External sources		POLIMOD uniform weights		POLIMOD family weights	
	unadjusted	adjusted	reported	as % of adjusted external sources	reported	as % of adjusted external sources
Total income (£m)	5,203	4,624	3,990	86	3,950	85
Number receiving (000s)	1,389	1,235	1,080	87	1,070	87

Notes and sources: See Appendix 11.2.

sick pay may not be aware that they are getting it, as it is often combined with occupational sick pay to make up a normal salary amount. Therefore, many of these people may just report receiving their earnings. However, the small sample size (55 observations) for receipt of this benefit in the FES means that gross and average receipt in POLIMOD must be subject to wide confidence intervals.

Invalidity benefit

Table 11.14 shows that POLIMOD invalidity benefit caseload is 87% of DSS caseload, after deduction of the assumed 10% non-household population. A similar degree of shortfall is found for expenditure when compared with adjusted Blue Book figures. DSS figures on average payments per person are £73.48 (Department of Social Security, 1993c). These compare well with average figures from the FES: £73.15. It is most likely, therefore, that the under-estimation in POLIMOD is due to low response associated with incapacity.

Severe disablement allowance

Table 11.15 shows that the most remarkable contrasts between POLIMOD output and official control totals are observed in the comparison of severe disablement allowance caseload (with around 180% over-estimation) and aggregate income (with around 250% over-estimation). This is not specific to the 1991 FES. Jones *et al.* (1991) found marked over-statement of grossed-up receipt when using the 1987, 1988 and 1989 surveys. Evans and Sutherland (1992) suggest that the cause may be confusion of severe dis-

Table 11.15. *Income from severe disablement allowance and number receiving (totals from external sources* versus *POLIMOD, 1991)*

	External sources		POLIMOD uniform weights		POLIMOD family weights	
	unadjusted	adjusted	reported	as % of adjusted external sources	reported	as % of adjusted external sources
Total income (£m)	578	514	1,300	253	1,270	247
Number receiving (000s)	308	274	490	179	480	175

Notes and sources: See Appendix 11.2.

ablement allowance with disability premia payable with income support. This possibility is explored in Wilson (1995a) where it is estimated that recoding for this and other confusion and simulation of entitlements reduces the degree of over-estimation of aggregate income and caseload to under 115%.

Invalid care allowance

There is moderate over-statement of the number of recipients of invalid care allowance in POLIMOD (Table 11.16). This may be because people who are caring for relatives are more likely to respond to the survey, or it may reflect a degree of misreporting or benefit confusion with, for example, invalidity allowance. Amounts of invalid care allowance in the FES are imputed assuming that all respondents receive the basic rate of payment with no additions for dependants. Given this, it is surprising that the proportionate over-statement of aggregate income from invalid care allowance is greater than the over-statement of caseload. Rather, we would expect the FES to under-state average payment of invalid care allowance.

Other disability-related benefits

With the exception of industrial injuries disablement benefit, most other disability-related benefits on Table 11.17 reflect varying degrees of under-representation of the relevant populations in the FES. This is likely to be associated with the severity of incapacity on which each is contingent. Estimated caseload for industrial injuries disablement benefit is similar to but slightly higher than the adjusted control figure.

Table 11.16. *Income from invalid care allowance and number receiving (estimates from external sources* versus *POLIMOD, 1991)*

	External sources		POLIMOD uniform weights		POLIMOD family weights	
	unadjusted	adjusted	reported	as % of adjusted external sources	reported	as % of adjusted external sources
Total income (£m)	280	280	280	100	280	100
Number receiving (000s)	153	153	180	118	170	111

Notes and sources: See Appendix 11.2.

Other benefits

Total income from the residual 'other benefits' category from POLIMOD, also given in Table 11.17, compares well with the DSS control. It must be recognised, however, that this healthy comparison may be no more than coincidental, given the vague nature of the category. No attempt is made to reconcile numbers in receipt of other benefits.

11.5 Direct taxes

Tables 11.18, 11.19 and 11.20 show comparisons of amounts of direct taxes paid by households from the Blue Book and from POLIMOD, and contrast counts of the numbers of direct tax payers from POLIMOD with counts from other sources.

Income tax and MIRAS

POLIMOD estimates of income tax are biased by two offsetting effects. On the one hand, POLIMOD annualises income by assuming that respondents' annual incomes are 52 times the weekly amounts reported or estimated. It is assumed that there is no part-year working or part-year receipt of income. While this assumption produces a reasonable approximation of aggregate income, the existence of annual tax allowances means that it is biased towards over-estimation of aggregate income tax liabilities and numbers of tax payers.[18] In addition, POLIMOD updates incomes reported by the self-employed in the FES to 1991 levels so that these incomes are comparable with incomes from other sources. However, in 1991 self-employed FES respondents would have paid income tax on incomes from

Table 11.17. *Income from other benefits and number receiving (estimates from external sources* versus *POLIMOD, 1991)*

	External sources		POLIMOD uniform weights		POLIMOD family weights	
	unadjusted	adjusted	reported	as % of adjusted external sources	reported	as % of adjusted external sources
Attendance allowance						
Total income (£m)	1,692	1,504	1,100	73	1,080	72
Number receiving (000s)	991	881	670	76	660	75
Mobility allowance						
Total income (£m)	1,041	925	780	84	750	81
Number receiving (000s)	678	603	560	93	540	90
Industrial injuries disablement benefit						
Total income (£m)	591	514	350	68	340	66
Number receiving (000s)	211	184	190	103	190	103
War disablement benefit						
Total income (£m)	795	707	300	42	290	41
Number receiving (000s)	249	210	150	71	140	67
Other benefits						
Total income (£m)	323	314	350	111	320	102

Notes and sources: see Appendix 11.2.

a previous year that might have been lower (although this is not necessarily the case), or may not have paid income tax at all if their business was a new one. While our updating method makes sense for the calculation of current income, it may also result in an over-estimate of current income-tax liability.

On the other hand, the FES under-states original income and this leads to a bias towards under-estimation of tax liabilities. We should expect the second effect to dominate for estimates of aggregate tax payments: The amounts of income tax produced by the first effect are smaller than amounts of income tax omitted by the second effect (being associated with the under-representation of those with very high taxable incomes – see Chapter 12). We would expect the first effect to dominate for estimates of numbers of tax payers: The number of additional tax payers produced by the first effect is greater in number than the number of omitted tax payers responsible for the second.

This is borne out in the tables. Table 11.18 shows that POLIMOD estimates of income tax after deduction of tax relief at source (mortgage inter-

Table 11.18. *Income tax and income tax reliefs (estimates from external sources* versus *POLIMOD, 1991)*

	External sources		POLIMOD uniform weights		POLIMOD family weights	
	unadjusted	adjusted[a]	estimated	as % of adjusted external sources	estimated	as % of adjusted external sources
Income tax (net of reliefs at source)						
Total liability (£m)	61,775	60,830	57,800	95	57,440	94
Number of payers (000s)	25,800	25,405	27,500	108	27,410	108
MIRAS						
Total amount (£m)	5,628	5,628	5,400	96	5,300	94
Number receiving (000s)	9,675	9,675	10,070	104	9,910	102

Note:
[a] Adjustment factors applied to exclude the non-household population are as follows: Income tax liability and number of payers: 1.53% (see notes to Table 11.2. SPI figures include non-household members and HM Forces based overseas); MIRAS 0.0% (only payable to private householders); unadjusted figures are derived by summing 0.25 and 0.75 of financial year 1990/91 and 1991/92 figures respectively.
Sources: Income tax (net of reliefs at source): UK taxes on income (Central Statistical Office, 1993b, Table 4.9) less life assurance premiums relieved at source (*ibid.*, Table 9.6) less mortgage interest relieved at source (*ibid.*). Number of income tax payers: Board of the Inland Revenue, 1994, Table 2.1. MIRAS: Central Statistical Office, 1993b, Table 9.6, mortgage interest relieved at source. Number of MIRAS recipients: Board of the Inland Revenue, 1993, Table 5.2, numbers of single people or married couples.

est relief at source (MIRAS) and life assurance premium relief in 1991) fall short of estimates based on the Blue Book by 5%.[19, 20] Part of the difference may also be explained by income tax paid by trusts which is included in the Blue Book estimate but is not simulated by POLIMOD. The number of income tax payers estimated by POLIMOD is 8% greater than the adjusted estimate from the Survey of Personal Incomes on an age and family composition weighted basis.

External control figures on Table 11.18 for the aggregate value of MIRAS and the number in receipt are not adjusted, as it is assumed that mortgage interest relief is only payable to those in private homes. The POLIMOD estimates compare well with the Blue Book figures, with a slight shortfall in the aggregate value of MIRAS and a slightly higher count of numbers receiving. It should be noted that estimates of numbers in receipt of MIRAS contained in the Inland Revenue Statistics are based on SPI data for higher rate tax payers only and are estimated from the FES and from Department of Environment data on new building society loans for others.

National Insurance contributions

Class 1 National Insurance contributions are deducted from employees' earnings. Class 2 National Insurance contributions are a flat rate amount paid by self-employed persons whose earnings are above a certain threshold (£2,900 in 1991/2). Class 4 National Insurance contributions are also paid by self-employed persons whose earnings are above a given threshold (£5,900 in 1991/2). Class 3 contributions are paid voluntarily. POLIMOD does not simulate Class 3 contributions since no person is liable to pay them and the total amount of contributions is very small – £38 million were paid in voluntary contributions during 1991/2 (Department of Social Security, 1994b, p. 314).

The Blue Book provides breakdowns of the aggregate amounts of contributions paid by employees and the self-employed during 1991. These are shown in Table 11.19. POLIMOD appears to over-state the amount of employee (Class 1) contributions by 10% when compared with the Blue Book figure. This is despite the fact that POLIMOD slightly understates employee earnings (see Table 11.2). There may be several reasons for this discrepancy. Firstly, it is possible that the proportion of respondents with each type of Class 1 contribution is misspecified in POLIMOD. But POLIMOD is more likely to under-state, rather than over-state, the numbers of contributors to the Not Contracted Out regime, which is the most expensive of the three regimes available to employees (see Chapter 6). It is perhaps more likely that for 1991, during which unemployment was rising and employment falling, the method used by POLIMOD to annualise incomes in general, and earnings in particular, results in an over-estimate of contributions paid. It is possible that some FES respondents who were employed at the beginning of the year, subsequently became unemployed, and paid lower contributions over the whole year than are simulated in POLIMOD.

The over-estimation of Class 1 contributions by POLIMOD contrasts with the under-estimation of the number of Class 1 contributors. This reflects a problem of comparability between the POLIMOD estimate and the control total. The POLIMOD estimate is lower because it is a summary of the situation of each respondent at a single point in the year. The control total is an estimate of the total number of people who contributed to the Class 1 regime at any time in the year.

The over-estimate of Class 2 and 4 National Insurance contributions of the self-employed by POLIMOD is even greater. The reasons why we should expect some over-estimation of employee contributions also apply

Table 11.19. *National insurance contributions (estimates from external sources* versus *POLIMOD, 1991)*

	External sources		POLIMOD uniform weights		POLIMOD family weights	
	unadjusted	adjusted	estimated	as % of adjusted external sources	estimated	as % of adjusted external sources
Class 1 NI contributions						
Total liability (£m)	13,733	13,523	14,690	109	14,730	109
Number of payers (000s)	21,870	21,535	19,280	90	19,420	90
Class 2 and Class 4 NI contributions						
Class 2 liability (£m)			600		600	
	1,175	1,165		124		123
Class 4 liability (£m)			840		830	
Number of payers (000s)	2,350	2,330	2,310	99	2,310	99
Total NI contributions						
Total liability (£m)	14,918	14,690	16,130	110	16,160	110
Number of payers (000s)	25,010	24,627	23,450	95	23,580	96

Notes:
Adjustment factors applied to exclude the non-household population are as follows: amounts of Class 1 National Insurance contributions and numbers of contributors: 1.53% (see notes to Table 11.2). Amounts of Class 2 and Class 4 National Insurance contributions, and numbers of contributors: 0.87% (see notes to Table 11.3). Unadjusted figures are derived by summing 0.25 and 0.75 of financial year 1990/91 and 1991/92 figures, respectively.
Sources: Class 1 NI contributions: Central Statistical Office, 1993b, Table 7.5, contributions from employees. Class 2 and 4 NI contributions: *ibid.*, contributions from self-employed. Total NI contributions: *ibid.*, total contributions excluding £40 million from non-employed persons. Number of NI contributors: Central Statistical Office, 1995a, Table 3.12. For year ending April 1992, Class 2 includes 0.3 million who pay both Class 1 and Class 2 contributions.

to those of the self-employed, but there are additional reasons why the over-estimate might be much greater. One of these is updating. Earnings of the self-employed are reported in the FES as profits for the full year. In most cases, therefore, these profits relate to 1990 or 1989. POLIMOD updates these profits to the middle of 1991 to make them comparable with income from other sources. But it is likely that self-employed people pay contributions on the basis of last year's profits. Therefore, while updating of income from self-employment to make it comparable with income from other sources makes sense for the calculation of current income, it may also result in an over-estimate of the income on which most people pay contributions.

The contrast between estimates of the number of contributors among

Table 11.20. *Community charge (estimates from external sources* versus *POLIMOD, 1991)*

	External sources		POLIMOD uniform weights		POLIMOD family weights	
	unadjusted	adjusted	estimated	as % of adjusted external sources	estimated	as % of adjusted external sources
Total liability (£m)	8,249	8,068[a]	9,560	118	9,460	117
Number of payers (000s)	41,594	40,679[a]	42,580	105	42,080	103

Note:

[a] The community charge adjustment factor is the estimated proportion of those liable for community charge in England who are in the non-household population. The estimated number of non-household persons with community charge liabilities in England is 777,263. This is the number present in community dwellings in England (1,300,772), less the number of visitors and guests present in communal dwellings who are not UK resident (76,709) (see Appendix 11.3), less the estimated number of non-household residents who are exempt community charge (446,800) (from *Hansard*, Written Answers, 15 November 1989, column 240, exempt persons in hospitals and homes plus exempt persons in detention). The estimated total number with charge liabilities in England is 35,664,900. This is the resident population aged 18 or over (36,442,000) (from Office of Population Censuses and Surveys, 1993d, 1991 Census: Sex, Age and Marital Status, Table 1), less the estimated number exempt from community charge (777,100) (from *Hansard*, Written Answers, 15 November 1989, column 240, the number of exempt visiting forces is excluded).

Sources: Community charge liability: Central Statistical Office, 1993b, Table 4.9 plus rates (*ibid.*, Table 8.1). Number of community charge payers: Office of Population Censuses and Surveys, 1993d, 1991 Census: Sex, Age and Marital Status, Table 1.

the self-employed can be explained in a similar way as that between the number of contributors who are employees – the methods used to produce the POLIMOD and external totals are very different, and therefore the figures are not directly comparable.

Local taxes

In 1991, domestic rates were levied in Northern Ireland and the community charge was levied in Great Britain. Rates and community charge amounts in the Blue Book are *after* the off-setting effects of rates rebates, and community charge benefit. To facilitate comparison, the amount of community charge benefit simulated by POLIMOD is therefore deducted from simulated community charge. Rates rebates for Northern Ireland amounting to £20 million included in housing benefit simulations are also deducted. Table 11.20 shows the resulting estimates. On this basis, local taxes simulated by POLIMOD grossed-up with family weights are 17% greater than Blue Book estimates. The Blue Book estimates are liabilities rather than receipts and are calculated on accrual basis; as such, they are comparable with the simulated estimates produced by POLIMOD. They do, however, include an adjustment for non-payment and non-collection which is not taken account of in POLIMOD. This may explain the difference observed.

An official count of the number of actual community charge payers in 1991 is not readily available. In its place, we construct an estimate of the number of individuals with community charge liabilities based on Census data and on estimates from *Hansard* of the numbers exempt from the charge. The POLIMOD estimates compare reasonably well, the uniform weighted estimate being 105% of the control figure, and the family weighted estimate being 103% of the control figure. The actual number of payers is likely to have been somewhat lower. However, there is no readily available estimate of the ultimate number of non-payers of 1991 community charge liability against which to assess the degree of over-statement. It is worth emphasising that, as with all taxes, POLIMOD models *liabilities* rather than actual payments, and therefore with any tax (such as community charge) where there is believed to be a high degree of non-compliance, POLIMOD's estimates are likely to over-state the true figure.

11.6 Means-tested benefits

Tables 11.21 to 11.24 compare POLIMOD aggregate income and caseload estimates for means-tested benefits with adjusted estimates from external sources. The adjustments that are applied to exclude the non-household population from the control totals are documented in Appendix 11.3. In the case of income support, adjustments made to exclude expenditure on the largest relevant non-household populations – those in residential care and those in nursing homes – are based on administrative data. It should be emphasised once more that the adjustments are approximate.

Income support

Table 11.21 shows that POLIMOD estimates of aggregate income from income support fall short of the Blue Book figure, adjusted to exclude the non-household sector, by approximately one third. This is in part related to under-counting of caseload in POLIMOD (the caseload shortfall being just under one quarter of the adjusted DSS estimate) and in part related to lower average income support payments from POLIMOD simulations than from the external data.

Table 11.21. *Income support (external sources* versus *POLIMOD, 1991)*

	External sources		POLIMOD uniform weights		POLIMOD family weights	
	unadjusted	adjusted	estimated	as % of adjusted external sources	estimated	as % of adjusted external sources
Total amount (£m)	11,155	10,193	6,840	67	6,780	67
Number receiving (000s)	4,816	4,484	3,450	77	3,460	77

Notes and sources: see Appendix 11.4.

Part of the under-estimation of average payments is associated with the method that is used to take account of non-take-up in POLIMOD. In practice, an estimated 20% of eligible families did not claim their income support entitlements in 1991 (Department of Social Security, 1994a, p. 30). POLIMOD adjusts for this by randomly assigning non-take-up to 20% of all families in the FES. Those with low entitlements have a higher probability of non-take-up, take-up of total expenditure being an estimated 86% in 1991 (*ibid.*). The adjustment takes no account of this, which causes POLIMOD to under-estimate average payments. There is also considerable variability in the estimated take-up rates of different claimant groups, the highest being 95% for lone parents and the lowest being 72% for pensioners (*ibid.*). Average rates of income support payment in 1991 were highest for lone parent claimants at £62.53 per week and lowest for those aged 60 or over at £34.16 per week (Department of Social Security, 1992a, Table A3.05). That there is this coincidence of high take-up and high average payment means that in adjusting for non-take-up in equal measure, some under-statement of average payment may arise.

Part of the under-statement of income support caseload may be associated with the take-up adjustment. There is a significant margin of error attached to the DSS estimates of take-up, the range attached to the 80% point estimate for 1991 being 77% to 90%. It is possible that true take-up is somewhat greater than 80%. However, even if 100% take-up is assumed, the POLIMOD caseload estimate is below the control total by some 4%. This suggests that there are other factors that explain the difference. The under-estimation of both average payments and caseload is consistent with under-representation in the FES of those with high payments such as those with disabilities (suggested by the reconciliation of non-means-tested benefits) and the older elderly (found by Redpath, 1986 and Foster, 1994). The under-estimation of caseload may also be associated with the

Table 11.22. *Family credit (external sources* versus *POLIMOD, 1991)*

	External sources		POLIMOD uniform weights		POLIMOD family weights	
	unadjusted	adjusted	estimated	as % of adjusted external sources	estimated	as % of adjusted external sources
Total amount (£m)	629	627	440	70.2	440	70
Number receiving (000s)	360	359	310	86	300	84

Notes and sources: see Appendix 11.4.

under-representation of the unemployed, as suggested by the under-estimation of unemployment benefit caseload described above.

In addition, POLIMOD grossly over-estimates caseload for one parent benefit, receipt of which is likely to have the effect of reducing simulated income support. In making no adjustment for non-take-up of one parent benefit, we shall be under-estimating income support. Work undertaken to disaggregate and recode non-means-tested benefit receipt reported in the FES suggests that there is a substantial amount of confusion of income support with non-means-tested benefits such as retirement pension and severe disablement allowance. Correcting for this would increase the income support caseload and expenditure simulated by POLIMOD (see Chapter 8).

A further explanation may be the method by which POLIMOD simulates receipt of family credit (discussed below). POLIMOD does not permit simultaneous receipt of family credit and income support, which is possible in practice if a family credit entitlement, assessed while in employment, continues to be paid into a period of unemployment. In no instance is family credit included in the assessment of means for income support. This may cause over-estimation of income support entitlement for some respondents.

Family credit

Table 11.22 shows the comparison of simulated family credit with control totals. To an even greater degree, eligible families tend not to take up their family credit entitlements. POLIMOD randomly assigns non-take-up to 38% of benefit units. This is based on the point estimate of non-take-up produced by the DSS for 1991 (Department of Social Security, 1994a, p. 23). After adjusting for non-take-up, POLIMOD caseload falls short of the DSS estimates by around 16%, and aggregate income falls short of DSS

Table 11.23. *Community charge benefit (external sources* versus *POLIMOD, 1991)*

	External sources		POLIMOD uniform weights		POLIMOD family weights	
	unadjusted	adjusted	estimated	as % of adjusted external sources	estimated	as % of adjusted external sources
Total amount (£m)	1,392	1,360	1,750	129	1,720	127
Number receiving (000s)	6,314	6,169	7,470	121	7,340	119

Notes and sources: see Appendix 11.4.

expenditure estimates by 30%. As is the case with income support, the corresponding under-estimation of average family credit payment is in part associated with the fact that, in POLIMOD, non-take-up is assigned without regard to the level of entitlement – in practice, smaller entitlements tend not to be taken up.

We should expect POLIMOD to produce low estimates of caseload and aggregate income for family credit because of the way that the benefit is administered.[21] Once a family credit assessment has been made, the payments continue regardless of further changes in circumstances or earnings for six months. This does not lend itself well to simulation using the static methods employed by POLIMOD. When POLIMOD simulates entitlement, it does so on the basis of current circumstances only. For that proportion of actual claimants who were eligible but whose circumstances have recently changed in such a way as to make them ineligible for family credit (for example, children leaving home, changes in earnings or hours of work), POLIMOD simulates no family credit entitlement. Just how much of the caseload short-fall this explains depends on the degree of volatility in circumstances that is experienced by family credit claimants. It is also possible that part of the difference is related to problems with the reporting of self-employment income in the FES (Jones *et al.*, 1991).

Community charge benefit

Table 11.23 shows that community charge benefit is the one means-tested benefit where the POLIMOD aggregates are over-estimates. This is likely to be associated with the fact that no adjustment is made for non-take-up of entitlements (the DSS is unable to produce an estimate of non-take-up on which to base an adjustment). Nor is any adjustment made for non-payment of community charge liabilities. The reconciliation of simulated

Table 11.24. *Housing benefit (external sources versus POLIMOD, 1991)*

	External sources		POLIMOD uniform weights		POLIMOD family weights	
	unadjusted	adjusted	estimated	as % of adjusted external sources	estimated	as % of adjusted external sources
Total amount (£m)	5,946	5,779	5,118	89	5,040	87
Number receiving (000s)	4,142	4,026	4,020	100	3,930	98

Notes and sources: see Appendix 11.4.

community charge with community charge revenue discussed above suggests that this could be substantial. It is possible that many observations for which POLIMOD awards community charge benefit may actually be non-payers.

Housing benefit

Table 11.24 shows that POLIMOD underestimates housing benefit caseload and aggregate income by 2% and 13% respectively. The estimates assume 90% take-up of entitlements based on the point estimate of take-up produced by the DSS (Department of Social Security, 1994a, p. 32). The effect of assuming 100% take-up is to over-estimate caseload (103%) and under-estimate income (91%). As with income support and family credit, the fact that no adjustment is made to take account of higher non-take-up among those with low housing benefit entitlements is likely to explain the proportionately greater under-statement of aggregate income from housing benefit. In addition, the under-estimation of income from housing benefit is possibly due to the flow-on effects of the under-counting of income support caseload – householders who receive income support are automatically entitled to housing benefit that covers 100% of their eligible rent while this is not always the case for claimants who are not in receipt of income support.

In contrast with income support, housing benefit caseload in POLIMOD is similar to the external control total. It is possible that POLIMOD performs better with housing benefit because the comparability problems associated with the non-household population are not as pronounced. Our inability fully to adjust the control totals to exclude the non-household population may account for some of the unexplained difference for income support. What is remarkable is the close match in the distribution of

Table 11.25. *Household tenure type for Great Britain*

	POLIMOD %	1991 Census %
Local Authority/Scottish Homes/housing association rented	23.7	24.6
Private rented	6.8	7.1
Owned with mortgage or rental purchase	43.5	42.6
Owned outright	24.2	23.8
Other	1.8	1.9
Total	100.0	100.0

Note:
'Other' for POLIMOD includes rent free dwellings and for the Census includes dwellings rented with job or business and non-permanent accommodation.
POLIMOD figures are grossed up using family weights.
Sources: Office of Population Censuses and Surveys, 1993a, Part I, Volume 2/3, Table 20; FES 1991.

tenure type between the 1991 FES and the 1991 Census shown in Table 11.25. This may mitigate the problems of over- and under-representation of different claimant types discussed in the context of income support. In addition, the close proximity of mean eligible rents from the DSS sample and POLIMOD for all but non-Local Authority tenants aged under 60 (Table 11.26) suggests that housing costs from the FES are a robust basis for simulation of housing benefit.

11.7 Household expenditure and indirect taxes

Expenditure by households in the FES is measured in two ways. Firstly, respondents are asked to complete a diary of all their expenditures and purchases over a two-week period. Secondly, they are interviewed about certain large purchases that they may have made over a given period (up to a year) preceding the interview (see Chapter 5). Therefore, the reliability of FES-derived aggregates is likely to reflect this data collection strategy – data collected are likely to be more reliable where items are purchased frequently (bread or milk would be obvious examples), or where the respondent has a record of amounts paid (as may be the case with telephone or fuel bills). Conversely, FES data may be less reliable with respect to items that are infrequently purchased, or where the respondent is asked to recall purchases made up to a year ago.[22] It may also be the case that, for some households, the process of diary-keeping actually influences their pattern of expenditure. Anecdotal evidence would suggest that this is likely to be

Table 11.26. *Housing benefit receipt*

	Local Authority tenants in receipt of housing benefit		Non-Local Authority tenants in receipt of housing benefit	
	DSS	POLIMOD	DSS	POLIMOD
Age under 60				
average eligible rent (£pw)	27.92	28.46	40.16	55.89
number (000 households)	1,399	1,380	666	501
Aged over 60				
average eligible rent (£pw)	26.68	25.68	29.35	28.36
number (000 households)	1,539	1,469	418	397

Note:
Aged under 60 refers to households where both the claimant and the partner of
the claimant are aged under 60.
Sources: Department of Social Security, 1992, Tables A3.03 and A3.04 (numbers)
and Tables A4.05 and A4.06 (average eligible rents). POLIMOD (all cases).

the case where respondents feel guilty about purchasing large quantities of
items such as alcohol, cigarettes and chocolate. Therefore, in these cases
the diaries may accurately reflect what has been purchased over the two-
week period, but the 'real' pattern may be distorted by the process of
diary-keeping.

This section is divided into two parts. The first compares Blue Book and
POLIMOD aggregates for different categories of expenditure, and the
second part examines total expenditure and total VAT and excise duties
paid. In POLIMOD, household expenditure is mainly used as a basis for
calculating households' liabilities to indirect taxes. Therefore, in validating
the components of expenditure, we are concerned with how good
POLIMOD would be in modelling the effects of changes to the indirect tax
regimes that cover these components. It is worth emphasising that
although the FES is generally designed in such a way as to enable users to
separate goods into categories on the basis of their VAT rating, some items
are slightly ambiguous. For example, VAT is not collected on the purchase
of second-hand goods, but it is not always possible to identify the purchase
of second-hand goods in the FES, so they may be categorised with new
goods that attract VAT.

Table 11.27 shows data on expenditure on most categories of goods
listed in the Blue Book and modelled by POLIMOD that are exempt from

Table 11.27. *Consumers' expenditure on non-excisable items (Blue Book versus POLIMOD, 1991) (£s million except where otherwise indicated)*

	External sources (Blue Book)		POLIMOD uniform weights		POLIMOD family weights	
	unadjusted	adjusted	estimated	as % of adjusted external sources	estimated	as % of adjusted external sources
Food (household expenditure)	44,048	42,810	42,701	100	42,657	100
Clothing and footwear	21,125	20,531	19,175	93	19,295	94
Rents	12,263	12,263	12,032	98	12,220	100
Rates, sewerage and water charges	3,101	3,101	3,354	108	3,360	108
Maintenance, etc. by occupiers	13,256	13,256	24,910	188	24,755	187
Fuel and power	14,202	14,202	14,871	105	14,840	104
Household goods and services	19,846	19,846	16,410	83	16,308	82
Cars, motorcycles and other vehicles	15,918	15,471	20,276	131	20,705	134
Other running costs of vehicles	13,984	13,591	10,937	80	11,131	82
Public transport	746	7,285	3,702	51	3,783	52
Air travel	4,824	4,688	649	14	657	14
Telecommunications	6,055	5,885	4,836	82	4,847	82
Postage	788	766	650	85	647	84
Recreation and entertainment	23,707	23,041	16,225	70	16,585	72
Books and newspapers	4,842	4,706	4,865	103	4,880	104
Education	4,028	3,915	4,335	111	4,204	107
Pharmaceutical and medical	5,350	5,200	4,694	90	4,646	89
Catering (meals and accommodation)	31,388	30,506	15,581	51	15,859	52

Note:

[a] Adjustment factor used to exclude non-household population is 2.81% (TOT in Table 11.1).

Source: Central Statistical Office, 1993b, Table 4.7. Unadjusted Blue Book figures are for consumers' expenditure. This includes 'personal expenditure consisting of household expenditure on goods and services . . . and final expenditure by profit-making bodies. Excluded are interest payments, all business expenditure and the purchase of land and buildings'. Included is what in FES terms is non-household expenditure, such as that by tourists and people who do not live in private households.

indirect taxes, or liable to VAT only. The adjusted 1991 Blue Book figures reduce the figures set out in the 1991 Blue Book by 2.81% (TOT from Table 11.1), the estimated proportion of people in Britain who do not live in households. In the case of specifically *household* expenditure which we can assume to be wholly attributable to households (such as rent), the Blue Book figures are not adjusted.

Food (household expenditure)

This category includes all food bought in shops including ice cream and confectionery, but not food bought in restaurants or take-away food. The POLIMOD estimate of expenditure on food is almost identical to the adjusted Blue Book figure. The Blue Book estimate is not based on the FES, but mostly on the National Food Survey (Central Statistical Office, 1985, p. 75).

Clothing and footwear

There appears to be a good fit between POLIMOD and Blue Book definitions of clothing and footwear, and the aggregates are also very similar – the POLIMOD estimate is 94% of that of the Blue Book after adjusting for the non-household population. That the POLIMOD figure is slightly smaller is not surprising, given that some of the Blue Book figure includes expenditure by people who do not live in households.

Rents

The Blue Book figure for rents is not adjusted to take account of the non-household population, as it is generally only household members who pay rent. It is not surprising that the Blue Book and POLIMOD figures are so similar, since the Blue Book figure is also based on FES data (Central Statistical Office, 1985, p. 77).

Rates, sewerage and water charges

The POLIMOD estimate of rates, sewerage and water charges is 8% higher than that in the Blue Book. There may be several reasons for this. One is that the sources used are different – the Blue Book uses figures supplied by the Office of Water Services (Central Statistical Office, 1993b, p. 149). Another is that rate rebates (which only occur in Northern Ireland in 1991, and are therefore a very small proportion of the total figure) are deducted from the Blue Book estimate, but not from the POLIMOD figure (Central Statistical Office, 1985, p. 78).

Maintenance, etc., by occupiers

Here, the POLIMOD estimate is almost double that of the Blue Book (which is not adjusted to allow for the non-household population). There does not appear to be a simple reason for the difference. It may be related to sampling error, or it may be that the Blue Book total excludes certain items that are included in the POLIMOD total. However, the literature would suggest that this is not the case (see Central Statistical Office, 1985, p. 68). One possible source of difference in this category is that the Blue Book figure is partly based on retail sales inquiries which may result in a different estimate (although it is also partly based on the FES). It may also be due to other adjustments made in the compilation of the Blue Book. The Central Statistical Office also sometimes makes 'significant additional adjustments . . . to individual categories of consumer expenditure'.[23] It is the CSO policy to align the three measures of GDP (expenditure, income and output). These adjustments change from quarter to quarter.

Fuel and power

Because fuel and power are sold to households, and because of the relative care taken in collecting data on this type of expenditure (respondents are asked about gas and electricity bills in the three months before interview) one might expect that the FES would provide a reasonably good estimate of total expenditure on domestic fuel and power in the UK. The POLIMOD figure is slightly high compared with that reported in the Blue Book, which is calculated from data on energy consumed. The Blue Book figure is not adjusted to take account of the non-household population.

Household goods and services

Here, the POLIMOD estimate is smaller than the Blue Book (which is not adjusted to allow for the non-household population). There does not appear to be a simple reason for the difference.

Cars, motorcycles and other vehicles

In the Blue Book, expenditure on cars, motorcycles and other vehicles (estimated from various trade statistics) is made up of consumers' purchases of new cars, etc., and net purchases of second-hand vehicles, that is, purchases less sales by consumers of second-hand vehicles. In POLIMOD, the equivalent figure is simply a total for the amount spent on vehicles, regardless of income from the sale or exchange of second-hand cars, etc.

Moreover, in the Blue Book, charges on the hire purchase of vehicles are excluded from the total, but these are included in the case of POLIMOD (see Central Statistical Office, 1985, pp. 72–3). Therefore, it is not surprising that the POLIMOD figure is about a third larger than the Blue Book figure. The comparison of vehicle excise duty paid (see below) suggests that estimates for the number of motor cars owned by households from POLIMOD and other sources are similar.

Other running costs of vehicles

With regard to this item of expenditure, the CSO states that 'apart from driving licences, driving lessons, driving tests and the value of private use of company cars . . . the Family Expenditure Survey is used to estimate expenditure in this category' (Central Statistical Office, 1985, p. 78). The 1993 Blue Book adds that the FES does not record expenditure on repairs where the insurance company settles directly with the repairer (Central Statistical Office, 1993b, p. 149). The value of the private use of company cars and the addition of repairs paid directly by insurers could possibly explain the difference between Blue Book and POLIMOD estimates, as the former is a fifth higher than the latter.

Public transport

The POLIMOD estimate for expenditure on public transport (including trains, buses, taxis and sea travel) is about half that of the Blue Book. Blue Book figures are based on passenger receipts for British Rail and statistics from the Department of Transport. Amounts are deducted for general government and business expenditure in this area (Central Statistical Office, 1985, p. 79). The 1993 Blue Book (p. 150) suggests that the FES under-states expenditure on taxis, but no other reason is given in the documentation as to why the Blue Book and POLIMOD estimates might be so far apart.

Air travel

The POLIMOD figure for air travel is considerably smaller than the Blue Book figure (the former is 14% of the latter). There are several reasons for this. Firstly, the Blue Book figure includes an apportionment of package holiday costs, while the POLIMOD figure only includes the amount spent directly by households on airfares. Secondly, the Blue Book figure is likely to include some expenditure by tourists who are excluded from the FES. This non-household expenditure is likely to amount to more than the 2.81% of the total allowed for in this exercise. Thirdly, the Blue Book figure attempts to include the full cost of overseas journeys, rather than just payments for flights immediately to and from the UK (Central Statistical Office 1993b, p. 150). Finally, it is worth noting that both the Blue Book and FES reports estimate high margins of error for this category of expenditure.

Telecommunications

The POLIMOD estimate for expenditure on telephone calls and rental is 82% that of the Blue Book. In the Blue Book, estimates of consumers' expenditure on telephone rentals and calls are prepared quarterly by British Telecom. No attempt is made to apportion the amount of business calls from personal phones, or the amount of personal calls from business phones. It is possible that the POLIMOD estimate is low because of time lags – some bills paid during 1991 would have been incurred during 1990, and any bill incurred before April 1991 would have been subject to a lower rate of VAT. However, these two possibilities are unlikely to explain fully the difference between the POLIMOD and the Blue Book estimates.

Postage

The POLIMOD estimate for expenditure on postage is 15% less than the Blue Book estimate. The Blue Book figure is based on estimates made by the Post Office. The biggest problem with these estimates is that it is difficult to distinguish business mail from consumers' expenditure.

Recreation and entertainment

In the Blue Book, most of the data under this heading are estimated from the FES, supplemented by data from retailers. However, the POLIMOD estimate only amounts to 70% of the Blue Book estimate. There is no obvious reason why this should be so.

Books and newspapers

Consumer's expenditure on books and newspapers in the Blue Book is also estimated from the FES, and the estimate is very close to that in POLIMOD.

Education

In the Blue Book, expenditure on education is estimated from trade associations such as the Independent Schools Information Service, and supplemented by some FES data (Central Statistical Office, 1985, p. 81).

The POLIMOD estimate is reasonably close, being within 10% of the Blue Book estimate. It is difficult to discern a reason, however, why the POLIMOD estimate should be higher.

Pharmaceutical and medical

Much of the Blue Book's estimate under this heading comes from the FES, but is supplemented by data from medical insurance companies on the amount that they pay for treatment. These data are missing in the FES, and therefore in POLIMOD. On the other hand, the POLIMOD data include expenditure on all spectacles, whether NHS or not, while the Blue Book estimate does not. On balance, the POLIMOD estimate, which is 90% of the Blue Book estimate, seems reasonable.

Catering (meals and accommodation)

The Blue Book figure in this category is based on FES data, but is twice that in POLIMOD. There are several reasons for this. Firstly, the Blue Book figure includes additions for expenditure by people not covered by the FES, such as students in tertiary education establishments. Secondly, a very large amount (almost a third of the total) is added to the FES figure to allow for expenditure for foreign tourists. Thirdly, additions are made to expenditure on food in works canteens, to cover the value of employers' subsidies, with extra additions to cover benefits for employees of the catering industry (see Central Statistical Office, 1985, p. 81; 1993a, p. 150). All these adjustments, which have the effect of increasing the Blue Book estimate, leads one to expect that POLIMOD does perhaps approach true direct expenditure by households on meals and accommodation.

Table 11.28 compares POLIMOD and Blue Book aggregates for expenditure on goods which attract excise duties: road fuels, vehicle excise duty, alcohol, tobacco and gambling. Aggregate estimates of expenditure by households on petrol and oil are very similar. Figures in the other three areas are less comparable.

Petrol and oil and vehicle excise duty

Perhaps surprisingly, POLIMOD estimates for households' expenditure on petrol and excise duties are very reliable when compared with the Blue Book, despite the fact that the figures come from different sources in each case. This would suggest that in modelling taxes on motoring, POLIMOD revenue estimates are likely to be quite good.

Table 11.28. *Consumers' expenditure on goods that attract excise duties
(Blue Book versus POLIMOD, 1991) (£s million except where otherwise
indicated)*

	External sources (Blue Book)		POLIMOD uniform weights		POLIMOD family weights	
	unadjusted	adjusted	estimated	as % of adjusted external sources	estimated	as % of adjusted external sources
Petrol and oil	10,793	10,490	10,271	98	10,489	100
Vehicle excise duty	1,879	1,826	1,882	103	1,905	104
Alcohol	23,629	22,965	13,147	57	13,682	60
Tobacco	9,536	9,268	6,247	67	6,339	68
Betting and gaming	3,109	3,022	1,751	58	1,775	59

Note:
[a] Adjustment factor used to exclude the non-household population is 2.81% (TOT in Table 11.1).
Source: Central Statistical Office, 1993b, Table 4.7.

Alcohol

In the case of alcohol, Blue Book totals are based on returns from HM Customs and Excise and trade data (Central Statistical Office, 1985, pp. 75–6), with a certain 'arbitrary proportion' (8%) that is attributed to business expenditure excluded. The difference between the POLIMOD estimate and the Blue Book estimate (the former is 60% the size of the latter) is very large. Some of this difference is likely to be attributable to expenditure by tourists and greater than average expenditure by people who do not live in households (see Chapter 5). However, it is also possible that there is considerable under-statement of expenditure on alcohol by FES respondents, and therefore an under-estimate in POLIMOD of the amount that households spend on alcohol.

Tobacco

Blue Book estimates of consumers' expenditure on tobacco are supplied from trade sources (Central Statistical Office, 1985, p. 76). The POLIMOD estimate is considerably lower, less than 70% of the Blue Book estimate. A proportion of this can be explained by non-household population consumption and by consumption by tourists. However, it is also possible

Table 11.29. *Indirect tax revenue (Blue Book versus P O L I M O D, 1991) (£s million except where otherwise indicated)*

	External sources (Blue Book)		POLIMOD uniform weights		POLIMOD family weights	
	unadjusted	adjusted[a]	estimated	as % of adjusted external sources	estimated	as % of adjusted external sources
Total expenditure	319,711	310,727	310,963	100	308,207	99
VAT	23,192	22,540	24,771	110	24,644	109
Excise duties	17,230	16,746	13,567	81	13,627	81

Note:
[a] Adjustment factor used to exclude non-household population is 2.81% (TOT in Table 11.1).
Sources: Total expenditure: Central Statistical Office, 1993b, Table 4.7. VAT: *ibid.*, Table 7.2. Taxes on expenditure: value added tax (£38,647m), adjusted by the share in total taxes on expenditure that comes from the personal sector from Table 9.5 (50,895/84,816=0.6001). Excise duties: *ibid.*, Table 7.2. Taxes on expenditure: sum of Beer, wines, cider, perry and spirits, Tobacco, Hydrocarbon oils, Car tax, Betting and gaming, Other, and Motor vehicle excise duties (total=£28,712m) adjusted by the share in total taxes on expenditure that comes from the personal sector from Table 9.5 (50895/84816=0.6001).

that some respondents to the FES also under-state their consumption of tobacco.

Gaming and betting

The comparison of gambling aggregates from the Blue Book and POLIMOD is difficult because of the way expenditure on gambling is defined in each case. In the case of POLIMOD, this is simply the total reported expenditure on gambling. However, the Blue Book figure represents expenditure less winnings. In spite of this, the POLIMOD figure is less than 60% of the Blue Book figure.

Overall expenditure, VAT and excise duties compared

Table 11.29 compares POLIMOD's estimate of total expenditure and total VAT and excise duties paid by households with estimates from the Blue Book. It is worth emphasising that these estimates are quite crude, for two reasons. Firstly, total estimates for taxes paid on expenditure in the Blue Book are given for all sectors, including government, business, etc. As the notes to Table 11.29 explain, these are adjusted in a rather crude fashion according to the proportion of taxes on expenditure that are attributable to personal consumption. But we have no way of knowing how robust this adjustment is.

Secondly, it is not possible to get a good match between definitions of total expenditure by households in POLIMOD and in the Blue Book. Some items which POLIMOD counts as expenditure, for example the cash costs associated with purchasing a house, are not included in the Blue Book's definition of consumers' expenditure (see Central Statistical Office, 1993b, p. 140). As noted above, the Blue Book includes insurance payouts for the repair of damaged motor cars, etc., in its total, while POLIMOD does not. Therefore, while both totals are quite close, this is in the context of considerable mismatch between some individual elements, as Tables 11.27 and 11.28 show.

The POLIMOD estimate of total VAT paid by households is actually higher than that in the Blue Book. There is no ready explanation as to why this should be so. Because of the way the Blue Book is set out, it is not possible to separate consumers' expenditure that attracts VAT from expenditure that does not. Therefore, a direct comparison of expenditure in these areas cannot be made. There are two possibilities worth considering: Either the Blue Book estimates of expenditure in areas that attract VAT are lower than those of POLIMOD, or the adjustment factor used to derive the Blue Book estimate is not a valid representation of the private household sector's share of VAT.

POLIMOD's low estimates of expenditure on most goods that attract excise duties are reflected in the low estimate of the excise duties themselves. The POLIMOD figure is about 80% of the Blue Book figure.

11.8 Conclusions

This chapter provides a validation of POLIMOD aggregates based on comparison with figures from external sources. In making this comparison, we are in some instances limited in our ability to draw firm conclusions by the difficulty of isolating precisely the contribution of the non-household population to each income, expenditure and tax item, and by the fact that some external data are different because they are not comparable. (The main findings of the exercise are summarised in the conclusions to Chapter 9.)

Appendix 11.1 Major external data sources used in this analysis

United Kingdom national accounts

The Blue Book describes those activities which constitute the economic life of the UK – production, income, consumption, accumulation and wealth. Its main purpose is to record output, income and expenditure flows, stocks and assets. Thus its purpose is considerably wider than the use to which it is put in this analysis. It is concerned with *national* aggregates rather than household or even personal sector aggregates. Moreover, it is primarily concerned with reconciling output, income and expenditure so that Gross Domestic Product (GDP) can be calculated (see Central Statistical Office, 1993b, pp. 2–3). GDP can be viewed as the total of all incomes earned from the production of goods and services, or the total of all expenditures made (less the cost of imports), or the sum of net output: value added in all activities related to the production of goods and services.

This process of reconciliation, in which data are collected from many sources (see Central Statistical Office, 1985), compared and adjusted, is an attempt to measure what is *actually* happening to output, income and expenditure in the UK. In this sense, it is the perfect data source for making comparisons with the output of a national microsimulation model such as POLIMOD – both the Blue Book and POLIMOD try to measure the somewhat elusive reality of incomes and expenditures in the UK. However, as is shown in this analysis, it also makes for a somewhat problematic comparison. Firstly, since POLIMOD is based on the FES, it is essentially a model of the household-based personal sector, and is not representative of the non-household sector. Secondly, since the Blue Book is interested in 'true' national aggregates, it is not concerned with differentiating between the household and non-household sectors, although it does differentiate between the personal, corporate and government sectors. But the personal sector is not merely the current incomes and expenditures of private households, as it is in the FES, but it includes unincorporated businesses, life assurance and pension funds (that are theoretically owned by their members) and private non-profit making bodies serving the public. Sometimes the personal sector is subdivided into categories that makes comparison with POLIMOD aggregates relatively straightforward. In other cases, large differences have to be reconciled.

Much of the Blue Book is based on sample data, either from surveys or administrative records, and as with the FES these data are subject to sampling error and other kinds of error. The Central Statistical Office (1985) attempts to quantify the reliability of Blue Book estimates in a general way, categorising each estimate as:

A 90% probability that the true value of the estimate lies within 3% of the reported figure
B 90% probability that the true value of the estimate lies within between 3 and 10% of the reported figure
C 90% probability that the true value of the estimate lies within between 10 and 20% of the reported figure
D The true value of the estimate may not lie within 20% of the reported figure

This kind of grading is useful for comparing with POLIMOD results. However, it must be borne in mind that (as in most cases) where the Blue Book figure and the POLIMOD figure are not directly comparable, the value of such a grade must diminish, as the adjustment made to make the two aggregates more comparable (such as to take account of the non-household population) may distort these confidence intervals.

The Survey of Personal Incomes (SPI)

The SPI is a 1% sample survey of tax records, and is carried out annually by the Inland Revenue. Differential sampling is applied in such a way that observations with very high incomes have a proportionally greater chance of selection than those with lower incomes (up to one chance in three, compared with one chance in 2,000 for some with low incomes). It is for this reason, as well as the large overall sample size, that the SPI is arguably one of the better surveys of high incomes in the UK, and it is commonly used by researchers to calibrate incomes in more general purpose surveys such as the FES (for example, see Giles and Johnson, 1994, p. 17). Much of the personal incomes and taxes data presented in the annual *Inland Revenue Statistics* is based on this survey, and sometimes supplemented by data from other sources such as the FES. Explicit confidence intervals are not given for these data, although statistics that are subject to particularly wide margins of error are highlighted. In some cases, it is stated that where sampling error implies a 5% probability of the population value 'lying some considerable way from the estimate given' (Board of the Inland Revenue, 1994, p. 31) then this is noted. This is the case with income from investments, and the number of people receiving income from this source. No confidence intervals or warnings are given for other Inland Revenue statistics used in this paper, and we assume them to be small.

The Labour Force Survey (LFS)

The Labour Force Survey is a survey of households, and is carried out quarterly by the Office of Population Censuses and Surveys for the Department of Employment, mostly in Great Britain, with some subsampling carried out in Northern Ireland in the second quarter of the year, when the total UK sample amounts to about 62,000 households. No questions on income are asked in this survey, and the response rate is high, at over 80% (see Office of Population Censuses and Surveys, 1992).

As a result of the large sampling size, sampling error associated with the aggregates used in Part Four (number of employees and self-employed) is low, with a confidence interval of less than 1% for employees and of less than 2% for the self-employed, given a significance level of 0.05 (see Office of Population Censuses and Surveys, 1992, p. 5).

Social security statistics

Most of the social security statistics reported in this section as external totals are data from the Department of Social Security, often in the form of 1% samples of administrative records, for example, in the case of income support, or in the case of family credit, a 5% sample of administrative records, or in the case of attendance allowance a 100% stock sample (see Department of Social Security, 1992). No confidence intervals are reported for findings produced by the Department that might be subject to sampling error, although as is reported in the main text of this chapter, Blue Book statistics on social security aggregates paid to households are subject to a 3% confidence interval.

The New Earnings Survey

The New Earnings Survey (NES) is a 1% sample survey of employees and their pay in Great Britain, and is carried out in April each year. The main purpose of the survey is to obtain information about the levels, distributions and make-up of earnings of employees in all industries and occupations. It is conducted in England, Wales and Scotland only, although a parallel survey is carried out in Northern Ireland. Questionnaires are sent to employers of employees who have been sampled, and the employers complete the forms. Therefore, the NES is a survey of what employers pay, rather than what employees receive, and does not include information on informal extras such as tips and gratuities.

The survey is based on a 1% random sample of employees who are members of PAYE income tax schemes. Observations are sampled on the basis of National Insurance numbers. The coverage of full-time adult employees in the survey is virtually complete, but the coverage of part-time employees is not comprehensive – this is especially true for those with earnings below the lower National Insurance threshold (see Department of Employment, 1991, and Wilson, 1995b). Response is high (77.9% in 1991).

The Department of Employment warns that results of the NES are subject to sampling error. Wilson (1995b) discusses sampling error in the NES in more detail, but concludes that because of its very large sample size, it is likely to be considerably lower than in the FES, although error may be higher among some groups, such as the very low paid.

Appendix 11.2 Control totals for non-means-tested benefits

Tables 11.A2.1 and 11.A2.2 show the adjustments made to control totals for income from non-means-tested benefits and numbers in receipt of non-means-tested benefits respectively.

Appendix 11.3 Population present in Great Britain by establishment at the 1991 Census

Table 11.A3.1 shows the population present in Great Britain by establishment at the 1991 Census.

Appendix 11.4 Control totals for means-tested benefits

Tables 11.A4.1 and 11.A4.2 show the adjustments made to control totals for income from means-tested benefits and numbers in receipt of means-tested benefits respectively.

Table 11.A2.1. *Derivation of control totals for income from non-means-tested benefits (£m)*

Item	Great Britain 1990/91 out-turns (A)	Great Britain 1991/2 out-turns (B)	Great Britain 1991 (C)	Northern Ireland 1990/91 out-turns (D)	Northern Ireland 1991/2 out-turns (E)	Northern Ireland 1991 (F)	1990/91 out-turns (G=A+D)	1991/2 out-turns (H=B+E)	United Kingdom 1991 (I=C+F)	resident overseas (J)	non-household (K)	adjusted 1991 (L=I−J−K)
Child benefit		4,591	5,189	4,939	175	193	188	466	5,382	5,228	16	5,212
One parent benefit	229	249	234	7	8	8	236	257	252	1	1	251
Retirement pension									25,191	1,312		23,879
Widow's pension									865		24	841
Unemployment benefit									1,486	26		1,360
Maternity allowance									39	0	0	39
Statutory maternity pay									362		4	358
Sickness benefit									263		3	260
Statutory sick pay									788		9	779
Invalidity benefit									5,203	579		4,624
Severe disablement allowance	429	596	554	19	25	24	448	621	578		64	514
Invalid care allowance	208	285	266	12	15	14	220	300	280		0	280
Attendance allowance	1,382	1,706	1,625	60	70	67	1,442	1,776	1,692		188	1,504
Mobility allowance	883	1,062	1,017	21	25	24	904	1,087	1,041		116	925
Industrial injuries disablement benefit	520	587	570	17	19	19	537	606	591	12	65	514
War disablement benefit									795		88	707
Other benefits	308	246	328	15	15	16	323	261	344		9	314

Table 11.A2.1. (cont.)

Sources and Notes

Columns (A) and (B)   Department of Social Security (1993a), Table 9a. Other benefits include industrial death benefit, other industrial injury benefits, guardian's allowance, independent living fund, motability, social fund payments. **Retirement pension expenditure includes non-contributory retirement pension, and excludes Christmas bonus.**

Columns (D) and (E)   Northern Ireland Office (1993) Table 9.22. Other benefits include social fund, independent living fund, transitional payments and guardian's allowance. Retirement pension expenditure includes non-contributory retirement pension, and excludes Christmas bonus.

Columns (C) and (F)   1991 expenditure is calculated by adding 25% of expenditure in 1990/91 to 75% of expenditure in 1991/92.

Column (G) and (H)   These are the sums of expenditure out-turns for Great Britain and Northern Ireland.

Column (I)   These are Blue Book estimates where they are available, and the sum of columns (C) and (F) where they are not. War pension expenditure is from Table 7.2 of the 1993 Blue Book. The remaining Blue Book estimates are from Table 7.5 of the 1993 Blue Book. All Blue Book estimates exclude payments to persons resident overseas. Widow's benefit includes guardian's allowance.

Column (J)   Estimates for Great Britain are based on proportions derived using estimates for those resident overseas supplied by the DSS Analytical Services Division, Newcastle. The adjustment to expenditure is made on the basis of proportions of recipients resident overseas. The calculation is as follows.

Benefit	Date	Overseas (000s)	Total (000s)	Proportion (%)
Industrial disablement benefit	4/4/92	4	204	2.0%

Column (K)   Estimates of expenditure on the non-household population are based on the census-based proportions shown in Table 11.1. It is assumed that carers in receipt of invalid care allowance live in private households. The adjustment proportion applied to each benefit is as follows:

Child benefit	0.31% (CHD)
One parent benefit	0.31% (CHD)
Retirement pension	5.21% (RET)
Widow's pension	2.81% (TOT)
Unemployment benefit	1.75% (UMP)
Maternity allowance	1.14% (EMP)
Statutory maternity pay	1.14% (EMP)
Sickness benefit	1.14% (EMP)
Statutory sick pay	1.14% (EMP)
Invalidity benefit	11.12% (PSK)
Severe disablement allowance	11.12% (PSK)
Invalid care allowance	0.0%
Attendance allowance	11.12% (PSK)
Mobility allowance	1.12% (PSK)
Industrial injuries disablement benefit	11.12% (PSK)
War disablement pension	11.12% (PSK)
Other benefits	2.81% (TOT)

Table 11.A2.2. Derivation of caseload control totals for non-means-tested benefits (000s)

	Great Britain			Northern Ireland						United Kingdom		
	1990/91 caseload	1991/2 caseload	1991 average	1990/91 caseload	1991/2 caseload	1991 average	1990/91 caseload adjusted	1991/2 caseload	1991 average	resident overseas	non-household	1991 average
Item	(A)	(B)	(C)	(D)	(E)	(F)	(G=A+D)	(H=B+E)	(I=C+F)	(J)	(K)	(L=I−J−K)
Child benefit	6,781	6,854	6,800	229	232	231	7,010	7,086	7,031		73	6,958
One parent benefit	790	836	802	24	26	26	814	862	827		9	818
Retirement pension	10,003	10,048	10,014	216	217	216	10,219	10,265	10,231	622	501	9,108
Widow's pension	351	344	349	12	11	11	363	355	361	20	10	331
Unemployment benefit	477	695	550	13	15	14	490	710	564		10	554
Maternity allowance	18	15	17	1	1	1	19	16	18		0	18
Statutory maternity pay	80	85	81				80	85	81		1	80
Sickness benefit	110	138	116	11	12	12	121	150	128		1	127
Statutory sick pay	355	330	349				355	330	349		4	345
Invalidity benefit	1,306	1,439	1,334	53	56	55	1,359	1,495	1,389		154	1,235
Severe disablement allowance	293	302	295	13	13	13	306	315	308		34	274
Invalid care allowance	136	167	144	8	9	9	144	176	153		0	153
Attendance allowance	918	1,059	953	36	38	38	954	1,097	991		110	881

Table 11.A2.2. (cont.)

Item	Great Britain			Northern Ireland			United Kingdom					
	1990/91 caseload	1991/2 caseload	1991 average	1990/91 caseload	1991/2 caseload	1991 average	1990/91 caseload adjusted	1991/2 caseload	1991 average	1991 resident non-overseas household	non-resident overseas household	1991 average
	(A)	(B)	(C)	(D)	(E)	(F)	(G=A+D)	(H=B+E)	(I=C+F)	(J)	(K)	(L=I−J−K)
Mobility allowance	648	699	661	16	18	17	664	717	678		75	603
Industrial injuries disablement benefit	200	204	201	9	10	10	209	214	211	4	23	184
War disablement benefit	248	250	249				248	250	249	12	26	211

Sources and Notes:

Columns (A) and (B) Department of Social Security (1994c) Table 6. (Statutory sick pay and statutory maternity pay numbers are from the 1993–94 to 1995–96 Report)

Columns (D) and (E) Northern Ireland Office (1993) Table 9.26. Child benefit caseload is estimated assuming the average number of children attracting benefit in a family is 2. The weighted average number of children for the 59 Northern Ireland families with children in the FES is 2.1.

Column (C) Average caseload in 1991 is estimated by linear interpolation. Caseload reported by the DSS is as at March except unemployment benefit (at February), sickness benefit, invalidity benefit, maternity allowance, severe disablement allowance and industrial injuries disablement benefit (March/April).

Column (F) Caseload figures for Northern Ireland are arithmetic means of caseload over the year. Average caseload in 1991 is estimated by summing 0.25 of 1990/91 caseload and 0.75 of 1991/92 caseload.

Columns (G), (H) and (I) These are the sums of caseload estimates for Great Britain and Northern Ireland. War Pension, statutory sick pay and statutory maternity pay numbers are only available from published sources for Great Britain. The United Kingdom figure refers only to Great Britain. No attempt is made to estimate caseload for 'other benefits'.

Column (J)   Estimates are based on proportions derived using estimates for those resident overseas for Great Britain supplied by the DSS Analytical Services Division, Newcastle. The calculation of the proportions is as follows:

Benefit	Date	Overseas (000s)	Total (000s)	Proportion
Widow's pension	30/9/91	19	346	5.5%
Industrial disablement benefit	4/4/92	4	204	2.0%
War disability benefits	3/92	12	250	4.8%
Retirement pension	30/9/91	609	10,016	6.1%

Column (K)   Estimates of numbers in the non-household population in receipt of benefits are based on the census based proportions shown in Table 11.1, applied to the UK resident population. It is assumed that carers in receipt of invalid care allowance live in private households. The adjustment proportion applied to each benefit is as follows:

Child benefit	0.31% (CHD)
One parent benefit	0.31% (CHD)
Retirement pension	5.21% (RET)
Widow's pension	2.81% (TOT)
Unemployment benefit	1.75% (UMP)
Maternity allowance	1.14% (EMP)
Statutory maternity pay	1.14% (EMP)
Sickness benefit	1.14% (EMP)
Statutory sick pay	1.14% (EMP)
Invalidity benefit	11.12% (PSK)
Severe disablement allowance	11.12% (PSK)
Invalid care allowance	0.0%
Attendance allowance	11.12% (PSK)
Mobility allowance	11.12% (PSK)
Industrial injuries disablement benefit	11.12% (PSK)
War disablement pension	11.12% (PSK)
Other benefits	2.81% (TOT)

Table 11.A3.1 *Population present in Great Britain by establishment at the 1991 Census*

Type of establishment	Total number	Per cent
Households	*52,628.5*	*97.18*
Hospitals		
NHS	284.6	0.53
non-NHS	19.2	0.04
total	303.8	0.56
Local authority and housing association homes and hostels		
elderly	107.1	0.20
other	45.2	0.08
total	152.3	0.28
Nursing homes and residential homes (non-NHS/LA/HA)		
elderly	281.7	0.52
other	52.3	0.10
total	334.0	0.62
Children's homes	13.1	0.02
Prison service establishments	43.6	0.08
Defence establishments	66.5	0.12
Education establishments	270.0	0.50
Hotels and boarding houses	269.4	0.50
Hostels and common lodging houses (non-HA)	23.0	0.04
Other miscellaneous establishments	40.3	0.07
Persons sleeping rough	2.8	0.01
Campers	1.5	0.00
Civilian ships, boats and barges	7.1	0.01
Total in communal establishments	*1,527.5*	*2.82*
Total staff in communal establishments	97.5	0.18
Total population present	*54,156.1*	*100.00*

Sources: Office of Population Censuses and Surveys (1993a) *1991 Census Communal Establishments Great Britain, Volume 1*, Table A and Table 1.

Table 11.A4.1. *Derivation of control totals for income from means-tested benefits (£m)*

	Great Britain			Northern Ireland					United Kingdom			
	1990/91 out-turns	1991/2 out-turns	1991	1990/91 out-turns	1991/2 out-turns	1991	1990/91 out-turns	1991/2 out-turns	1991	Social fund repayment	non-hh pop'n	adjusted 1991
	(A)	(B)	(C)	(D)	(E)	(F)	(G=A+D)	(H=B+E)	(I)	(J)	(K)	(L=I+J−K)
Income support									11,155	142	1,104	10,193
Family credit	494	626	593	32	37	36	526	663	629		2	627
Community charge benefit	2,161	1,136	1,392				2,161	1,136	1,392		32	1,360
Housing benefit	4,941	6,058	5,779	159	170	167	5,100	6,228	5,946		167	5,779

Sources and Notes:

Columns (A) and (B)   Department of Social Security (1993a) Table 9a.

Columns (D) and (E)   Northern Ireland Office (1993) Table 9.22.

Columns (C) and (F)   1991 expenditure is calculated by summing 25% of expenditure per person per week in 1990/91 and 75% of expenditure in 1991/92.

Columns (G) and (H)   These are the sums of expenditure out-turns for Great Britain and Northern Ireland.

Column (I)   The Blue Book estimate of Income support expenditure (Central Statistical Office, 1993b, Table 7.2) is shown. Expenditure calculated from other official sources is the sum of columns (C) and (F).

Column (J)   Income support out-turns in the *Social Security Departmental Report, The Government's Expenditure Plans* (Department of Social Security, 1994c) are expenditure inclusive of amounts paid as direct payments for housing, electricity, gas and the like, deducted from the payments of recipients, but exclusive of repayments of loans from the Social Fund deducted from the payments to recipients. It is assumed that the Blue Book figures are calculated on the same basis. Because POLIMOD simulates income support before the deduction of repayments to the Social Fund, these amounts must be added back in to the control total. The estimate shown is the sum of 25% of the 1990/91 recoveries and 75% of the 1991/92 recoveries shown in Tables A4.04 and A4.05 of the 1992 Social Security Statistics (Department of Social Security, 1992). It is assumed that all repayments are made by people in receipt of income support.

Table 11.A4.1. (cont.)

Column (K)   Estimates of expenditure on the non-household population are based on (1) the Census-based proportions shown in Table 11.1, (2) data from Table 1.1 of the May 1991 Income Support Statistics Quarterly Enquiry and (3) Table 8.1 of the May 1991 Residential Care/Nursing Home Income Support Statistical Enquiry.

The proportion of expenditure that goes to the non-household population in residential care and nursing homes is estimated to be 124.30 (average income support for those in residential care)+202.30 (average income support for those in nursing homes)×94,000 (number in nursing homes), as a proportion of 46.93 (average overall income support payment)×4,526,400 (total number in receipt of income support) in May 1991.

The proportion of expenditure on non-household unemployed recipients of income support is estimated to be 1,335,000+871,000 (number of unemployed and lone parent recipients in 1991 from Table A2.04 in Department of Social Security (1992)×0.0175 (UMP from Table 11.1) as a proportion of 4,487,000 (total number of recipients in 1991 from Table A2.04 in Department of Social Security (1992).

The proportion of expenditure on non-household disabled recipients of income support is estimated to be 375,000 (number of disabled recipients in 1991 from Table A2.04 in Department of Social Security (1992)×0.1112 (PSK from Table 11.1) as a proportion of 4,487,000 (total number of recipients in 1991 from Table A2.04 in Department of Social Security (1992).

The adjustments applied to the remaining benefits are as follows (all from Table 11.1): family credit, 0.31% (CHD); community charge benefit, 2.3% (see notes to Table 11.20); housing benefit, 2.81% (TOT).

Table 11.A4.2. *Derivation of caseload control totals for means-tested benefits (000s)*

	Great Britain			Northern Ireland			United Kingdom				
	1990/91 averages (A)	1991/2 averages (B)	1991 (C)	1990/91 averages (D)	1991/2 averages (E)	1991 (F)	1990/91 averages (G=A+D)	1991/2 averages (H=B+E)	1991 average (I)	non-hh pop'n (J)	1991 adjusted (L=I−J)
Income support	4,480	5,030	4,618	192	201	199	4,672	5,231	4,816	332	4,484
Family credit	326	352	346	14	15	15	340	367	360	1	359
Community charge benefit	6,519	6,330	6,314	0	0	0	6,519	6,330	6,314	145	6,169
Housing benefit	3,989	4,021	3,997	144	146	145	4,133	4,167	4,142	116	4,026

Sources and Notes:

Columns (A) and (B)   Department of Social Security (1994) Table 6.

Columns (D) and (E)   Northern Ireland Office (1993) Table 9.26.

Column (C)   Average caseload in 1991 is estimated by linear interpolation. Caseload reported by the DSS is as at March for income support, at September for family credit, and at May for housing benefit and community charge benefit.

Column (F)   Caseload figures for Northern Ireland are arithmetic means of caseload over the year. Average caseload in 1991 is estimated by adding 25% of 1990/91 caseload and to 75% of 1991/92 caseload.

Columns (G), (H) and (I)   These are the sums of caseload estimates for Great Britain and Northern Ireland.

Column (J)   Estimates of numbers in the non-household population in receipt of benefits are based on: (1) the Census-based proportions shown in Table 11.1, (2) data from Table 1.1 of the May 1991 Income Support Statistics Quarterly Enquiry and (3) Table 8.1 of the May 1991 Residential Care/Nursing Home Income Support Statistical Enquiry.

The proportion of recipients in residential care and in nursing homes is estimated to be 137,000 (number in residential care)+94,000 (number in nursing homes), as a proportion of 4,526,400 (total number in receipt of income support) at May 1991.

Table 11.A4.2. (*cont.*)

The proportion who are unemployed non-household recipients is estimated to be 1,335,000+871,000 (number of unemployed and lone parent recipients in 1991 from Table A2.04 in Department of Social Security (1992)×0.0175 (UMP from Table 11.1) as a proportion of 4,487,000 (total number of recipients in 1991 from Table A2.04 in *ibid.*).

The proportion of those who are non-household disabled recipients of income support is estimated to be 375,000 (number of disabled recipients in 1991 from Table A2.04 in *ibid.*)×0.1112 (PSK from Table 11.1) as a proportion of 4,487,000 (total number of recipients in 1991 from Table A2.04 in *ibid.*).

The adjustments applied to the remaining benefits are as follows (all from Table 11.1): family credit, 0.31% (CHD); community charge benefit, 2.3% (see notes to Table 11.2); housing benefit, 2.81% (TOT).

Notes

1 It is possible, in principle, to gross-up FES data according to several other criteria, such as the economic or tenure status of respondents. Chapter 4 discusses such an exercise. This has not been attempted in this validation, although we do discuss the extent to which the FES sample is representative in these dimensions.

2 Evans (1995) cautions that the match between the Census definition of the non-household population and those excluded from the FES sampling frame is not exact. We attempt to compensate for this by making adjustments to the non-household population count. See notes to Table 11.1.

3 For example, Evans notes that there are no rough sleepers identified in the 1991 Northern Ireland Census.

4 Overall, Evans (1995) finds that the effect of including the non-household population in aggregating national income in the UK is to reduce mean income of the population as a whole by between 0.1% and 0.7%. However, the distribution of income, as well as the average, is likely to be affected by this inclusion.

5 Redmond and Wilson (1995) show the relationship of POLIMOD original income outputs to the POLIMOD input variables described in the Appendix.

6 They found that unweighted and age weighted differences between the FES and the Blue Book ranged between 90.2% and 94.4%.

7 The method of excluding those whose pay is affected by absence and the method of adjusting the FES data to April 1991 for the purposes of comparison is the same as that described in Wilson (1995b).

8 The adjustment is that calculated by Atkinson, Smith and Sutherland (1986) from Table 3 in Atkinson (1984). The factor is the unexplained difference between SPI and Blue Book self-employment (assumed to be informal economy income) as a proportion of SPI net self-employment income in 1982/3. The Blue Book adjustment for evasion in 1980 represented some 14% of total income from self-employment (Central Statistical Office, 1985, p. 59).

9 See Atkinson and Micklewright (1983, pp. 39–41) for a detailed discussion of differences that applied for the period 1970–77. One difference which they observed in that period concerned the exclusion of tax deductible amounts, such as interest payments, from the FES estimate of self-employment income which were included in the Blue Book figures. The Blue Book self-employment figures for 1991 exclude tax deductible interest payments as do the FES figures.

10 The same adjustment factor is used for investment and self-employment income.

11 This is equal to a grossed-up total of about 20 million persons. This total is estimated by taking those interviewed in the 1991/92 tax year only, so that the figures relate to the same tax threshold, and grossing-up using family weights adjusted to compensate for the missing one quarter of respondents.

12 Government Actuary's Department (1991) pp. 23–4.

13 These are amounts paid by employers and reclaimed from insurance schemes (Central Statistical Office, 1985, p. 62).

14 Board of the Inland Revenue (1994) Table 3.5, 1991–92.

15 It is not surprising that the POLIMOD estimate of the total number of families with children who are eligible for child benefit is a good one, as the grossing-up weights used by POLIMOD are in part derived from statistics on the total number of families who are in receipt of child benefit.

16 Blue Book figures do not include expenditure on those resident overseas.

17 Calculated on the basis of the proportion of retirement pension recipients in the Great Britain *Social Security Statistics* (Department of Social Security, 1993c) who are resident overseas. See Appendix 11.2.

18 For example, if we assume identical weekly earnings, 10 people working 1/10th of a year would pay less combined tax than one person working all year.

19 Tax relief at source is not deducted from the Blue Book estimate of UK taxes on income (Central Statistical Office, 1985, p. 53). However Table 9.6 of the Blue Book shows how much these reliefs cost the government each year. The amount of income tax shown in Table 11.18 is net of these reliefs.

20 The Blue Book income tax estimates have an A reliability rating (90% probability that the true value of the figure lies within $\pm 3\%$ of the reported figure).

21 This has been discussed by Jones *et al.* (1991).

22 FES respondents are asked to recall their expenditure on motor vehicles, public transport season tickets, telephone and domestic fuel bills, property transactions, holidays and furniture, but not food, clothing or durables such as televisions or microwave ovens. It is worth pointing out that Smeaton and Hancock (1995), in an assessment of pensioners' expenditure in the period 1979 to 1991 using FES data, found that the use of recall data on expenditure (where it was available) made a significant difference to results.

23 Murray L. Greenberg, Consumers' Expenditure Section, Output and Expenditure Branch of the Central Statistical Office, in a letter to the authors.

12 Distributions

12.1 Introduction

Underlying the aggregate outputs from POLIMOD are distributions of elements of income and taxes which determine the overall distributional effect of changes to each. It is the assessment of these distributional impacts that is the main contribution that tax–benefit microsimulation models like POLIMOD make to policy analysis. This chapter sets out the comparison of several of the key income and tax distributions in POLIMOD with external surveys for 1991. These are the distributions of earnings, self-employment income, investment income, total taxable income, income tax, and means-tested benefits. It is not possible to validate the POLIMOD distribution of indirect taxes as there are no external data against which this can be done. Distributions of non-means-tested benefits are also not validated for want of comparable published data.

12.2 Earnings

The New Earnings Survey (NES) is based on a 1% random sample of employees in Great Britain carried out in April each year. It asks employers to supply information about wages, hours of work and other characteristics for selected employees. One of its main advantages is its large sample size. The number of employees in the 1991 survey was around 27 times the number of employees in the 1991 FES.[1]

Table 12.1 compares the distribution of gross earnings from full-time employment from POLIMOD with that from the New Earnings Survey for all employees, regardless of whether or not they received pay in the survey period. The POLIMOD measure is normal earnings which for 80% of respondents is the same as actual earnings the last time paid. The NES measure is actual earnings. The earnings intervals shown are the most detailed available from the published tables of the NES. Because the NES

Table 12.1. *Distribution of gross weekly earnings of full-time employees: NES versus POLIMOD, 1991*[a]

Earnings (£s)	NES (%)	POLIMOD (%)
Nil	1.1	0.8
1–100	3.6	4.3
101–110	1.7	1.9
111–120	2.2	2.4
121–130	2.7	3.0
131–140	3.1	3.1
141–150	3.4	3.8
151–160	3.6	3.8
161–170	3.9	3.8
171–180	4.0	3.6
181–190	3.9	3.9
191–200	3.7	3.9
201–210	3.7	3.5
211–230	7.0	7.1
231–270	12.6	11.9
271–300	7.6	7.8
301–330	6.5	6.4
331–360	6.0	5.8
361–390	4.3	4.1
391–420	3.2	3.1
421–480	4.4	4.5
481–540	2.5	2.4
541–600	1.5	1.2
601–700	1.5	1.6
701+	2.3	2.2
Total (%)	100	100

Notes:
[a] A number of adjustments are made to the POLIMOD figures to improve comparability with the NES. Subsidiary earnings are assumed to be part-time. Earnings are adjusted to April values using log linear interpolation of NES data on earnings by sex and manual/non-manual status. Employees in the armed forces are excluded, and Northern Ireland respondents are excluded. The definition of full-time is the same as that used in the NES.
Source: Department of Employment (1991) Part A, Table 19, all full-time males and females on adult and other rates, including those who received no pay for the survey pay period.

Table 12.2. *Distribution of taxable self-employment income: SPI (1991–1992) versus POLIMOD, (Q2–Q4 1991)*

Range of self-employment income (lower limit) (£s pa)	Per cent of those with taxable self-employment income			Per cent aggregate taxable self-employment income		
		POLIMOD			POLIMOD	
	SPI	income updated	income not updated	SPI	income updated	income not updated
negative	0.6	2.4	2.4	-0.3	-0.1	-0.1
0	7.5	7.5	8.6	0.3	0.3	0.4
1,000	12.3	9.6	12.4	2.2	1.3	2.1
3,000	13.4	9.1	9.1	4.7	2.5	3.0
5,000	17.2	11.8	14.3	9.3	5.1	7.3
7,500	11.7	9.8	14.4	9.0	5.9	10.6
10,000	17.1	21.4	16.5	18.3	17.9	16.5
15,000	7.7	9.7	9.2	11.6	11.7	13.4
20,000	6.5	10.0	6.8	13.9	16.8	13.8
30,000	3.9	5.3	3.6	13.1	14.0	11.2
50,000	2.2	3.4	2.5	17.8	24.7	21.8
Total number (000s)		3,860	3,010	3,010		
Total income (£s)				43,300	43,550	35,605

Source: Board of the Inland Revenue, 1994, Table 3.9.

does not cover all part-time employees, we do not attempt to make a similar comparison here for earnings from part-time employment.[2]

The distributions show remarkable similarity with a slightly less pronounced peak in the modal range of the POLIMOD distribution. There is also slightly greater concentration at lower earnings and slightly less concentration at upper earnings levels in the POLIMOD distribution. In Wilson (1995) we find that for sub-groups of earners, the correspondence of the two sources is not as close, but that the differences are not of a sufficient size or nature to cause concern about the representativeness of FES based earnings distributions. It is possible that the minor differences that are observed can be explained by the differences in the sampling methods, definitions, and timing of the two surveys. For example, tips are included in the earnings declared by employees to the FES but not in those reported by employers to the NES.

12.3 Income from self-employment

The Survey of Personal Incomes (SPI) is based on information on persons liable to UK income tax.[3] It provides data on the distribution of taxable self-employment income, which is taxable profit, less allowable losses and capital allowances. POLIMOD assumes that all of the direct self-employment income recorded in the FES is taxable and makes no attempt to attribute allowable losses and capital allowances.[4]

Table 12.2 compares the distributions of these measures: taxable self-employment income from the SPI and self-employment income from POLIMOD. The POLIMOD distributions are based on the subset of POLIMOD cases who face the tax regime that applied in 1991/92 (those interviewed in the second through to the fourth quarters of 1991), grossed-up to represent the whole population by adjusting the family weights.[5] POLIMOD output is based on self-employment income updated to the survey year. The distribution of this measure is shown in the 'income updated' column. It has a greater concentration of income earners and income at high levels of self-employment income than the SPI. While self-employment income is updated to 1991 in POLIMOD, no such adjustment applies to the SPI figures and this may explain some of the difference. In addition, the updating factors used are based on movement in average self-employment incomes. There may be differences in growth across the distribution that are not taken account of.

The distribution of POLIMOD taxable income from self-employment *without* updating of income is also shown for comparison on Table 12.2 ('income not updated'). There is still slight over-representation of those with high self-employment incomes and over-estimation of the self-

Table 12.3. *Distribution of taxable investment income by total taxable income: SPI (1991–1992) versus POLIMOD (Q2–Q4 1991)*

Range of total income (lower limit) (£s p.a.)	Per cent of those with taxable investment income		Per cent of total taxable investment income	
	SPI	POLIMOD	SPI	POLIMOD
3,295	11.6	15.0	4.5	7.3
5,000	31.2	30.2	17.3	20.2
10,000	24.1	24.0	15.5	14.7
15,000	15.0	15.3	11.8	13.7
20,000	11.6	10.5	15.5	13.6
30,000	4.7	4.0	12.7	14.6
50,000	1.8	1.1	22.8	15.9
Total number (000s)	23,700	20,190		
Total income (£m)			39,800	30,410

Source: Board of the Inland Revenue, 1994, Table 3.6.

employment incomes of those on high incomes. This may be the result of the fairly crude adjustment for under-reporting of self-employment income that is made in POLIMOD. Self-employment income is adjusted upwards by 19.5% in an effort to take account of undeclared self-employment income. The adjustment factor used may be too high for those at the top of the self-employment income distribution. It may also be the result of selection bias that arises from the way that self-employment income is filtered for use in POLIMOD – earnings are only counted if the respondent is currently in self-employment. It may also be that those who are both currently self-employed and able to report past self-employment income are disproportionately the more successful. There are timing differences between the two surveys that may also account for the differences between the distributions. The SPI only shows income assessable in 1991/92. In the main, this is profit arising in the 1990 calendar year (Board of the Inland Revenue, 1994, p. 32). Likewise, profit reported in POLIMOD tends to relate to a prior period. However, it is more likely that profits reported in the FES relate to a period prior to 1990 and that these may have been assessable as taxable income in a year prior to 1991/92. Only 40% of declared profits and losses in the 1991 FES relate to earnings for a 12-month period ending in 1990. The differences observed might reflect a drop in the self-employment incomes of those in the upper income range between the declaration period and the survey year.

12.4 Taxable investment income

The SPI provides data on the distribution of earners of taxable investment income and taxable investment income itself by total taxable income. These are compared with POLIMOD distributions of the same in Table 12.3.[6] The most pronounced differences are at the extremes of the total taxable income range shown. POLIMOD has greater and smaller concentrations of taxable investment income earners at low and high total income levels respectively. A greater proportion of total taxable investment income is received by those with low total income in POLIMOD. This may be due to the shortcomings of the SPI data. A large amount of investment income included in the table is estimated, and the potential margin of error is substantial (Board of the Inland Revenue, 1994, p. 32).

12.5 Total taxable income and income tax

Table 12.4 compares the distributions of total taxable income from the SPI and from POLIMOD for all individuals with taxable income above the tax threshold and for taxpayers only. As with the comparisons with SPI distributions above, the subset of POLIMOD cases who face the tax threshold that applies for the 1991/92 SPI data are grossed-up to represent the whole population. The distributions compare reasonably well, except for the under-representation of those with high taxable incomes in POLIMOD. The total numbers with taxable income compare extremely well.

The SPI and POLIMOD distributions of income tax liabilities shown in Table 12.5 are comparable. Both are distributions of liabilities calculated on the basis of taxable income. The slight under-representation in POLIMOD of those with high taxable income shown in Table 12.4 gives rise to substantial under-estimation of those with high income tax liabilities in Table 12.5. POLIMOD under-estimates the proportion of income tax payers paying £10,000 or more by a fifth and under-estimates the proportion of tax paid by them by almost one quarter. With the exception of this top income tax range, however, the proximity of the distributions is impressive.

12.6 Means-tested benefits

Table 12.6 shows the distribution of income support payments from the Department of Social Security's 1% sample of claimant records and from POLIMOD.

The estimates are comparable in that both are before deductions for repayment of Social Fund loans and before deductions for direct payments. They are also comparable in that the POLIMOD simulations are

Table 12.4. *Distribution of total taxable income before tax: SPI (1991–1992)* versus POLIMOD *(Q2–Q4 1991)*

Range of total income (lower limit) (£ p.a.)	% of all with taxable income above threshold		% of taxpayers with income above threshold	
	SPI	POLIMOD	SPI	POLIMOD
3,295	1.8	2.4	1.0	1.1
3,500	4.1	4.9	2.4	2.5
4,000	4.2	4.2	3.1	3.1
4,500	4.1	3.8	3.2	3.2
5,000	4.1	3.6	3.6	3.5
5,500	3.5	3.5	3.0	3.3
6,000	6.7	6.6	6.4	6.7
7,000	6.4	6.5	6.6	7.0
8,000	12.1	13.0	12.9	14.0
10,000	10.7	11.0	11.5	11.8
12,000	12.7	13.5	13.8	14.6
15,000	14.0	13.7	15.1	14.8
20,000	10.3	9.0	11.1	9.7
30,000	4.1	3.4	4.4	3.7
50,000	1.2	0.6	1.3	0.6
100,000	0.4	0.2	0.4	0.2
Total number	28,100	27,990	25,900	25,960

Source: Board of the Inland Revenue, 1994, Table 3.1.

based on those surveyed in the second and third quarters of 1991, the period for which the rates current in May 1991 applied,[7] grossed-up to the total population. However, no adjustment has been made to exclude the non-household population from the Department of Social Security distribution. This may explain part of the difference observed. The average payments of recipients in residential care and nursing homes, for example, were £124.30 per week and £202.30 per week respectively, compared with the overall average of £46.93 in May 1991 (see Appendix 11.4). That those in non-household living situations are missing from the FES sample may explain the absence of cases with payments over £70 per week among POLIMOD recipients aged 60 or over. The over-representation of those with small payments in POLIMOD is in part due to the take-up adjustment, as discussed in Chapter 11.

Table 12.7 compares distributions of family credit from POLIMOD and from the Department of Social Security's 5% sample of claimant records.

Table 12.5. *Total income tax liabilities, by range of total income tax: SPI (1991–1992) versus* POLIMOD *(Q2–Q4 1991)*

Range of total income (lower limit) (£s p.a.)	Per cent of taxpayers		Per cent of aggregate tax	
	SPI	POLIMOD	SPI	POLIMOD
1	4.0	3.1	0.1	0.1
100	14.6	12.8	1.8	1.7
500	15.7	16.5	4.8	5.4
1,000	14.9	15.7	7.6	8.4
1,500	13.0	13.5	9.3	10.2
2,000	9.4	9.5	8.6	9.2
2,500	6.8	8.1	7.6	9.6
3,000	9.1	9.5	12.8	14.2
4,000	4.5	4.6	8.1	8.8
5,000	5.4	4.7	14.7	13.8
10,000	2.6	2.1	24.7	18.8
Total payers (millions)	25.9	25.3		
Total tax (£ billion)			63.5	58.4

Source: Board of the Inland Revenue, 1994, Table 2.4.

POLIMOD over- and under-states the proportions of recipients who have low and high payments respectively. This is likely to be associated with the take-up assumptions made in POLIMOD.

Table 12.8 shows the distribution of housing benefit payments for local authority and other tenants simulated by POLIMOD compared with the distribution for the Department of Social Security sample. In both comparisons, there is slight over-estimation of the proportion with payments under £5 per week by POLIMOD. This is can be explained by the simple nature of the non-take-up adjustments made in POLIMOD. In the main, the distributions are reasonably close.

The distributions of community charge benefit payments are compared in Table 12.9. Unlike other means-tested benefits, the POLIMOD distribution under-states the proportion with low payments and over-states the proportion with high payments.

This may be associated with non-payment of community charge among the DSS sample which is not taken account of in the POLIMOD simulation. The difference is consistent with non-payment being associated with low income and, therefore, high community charge benefit entitlements.

Table 12.6. *Distribution of income support payments: DSS (May 1991)* versus *POLIMOD (Q2–Q3 1991)*

Range of income support (£s p.w.)	Per cent of all income support recipients		Per cent of recipients aged 60 or over	
	DSS	POLIMOD	DSS	POLIMOD
0.00–10.00	22.7	29.2	56.3	71.0
10.01–20.00	5.5	5.7	5.5	8.0
20.01–30.00	4.6	5.4	5.5	7.6
30.01–40.00	24.9	20.3	5.7	4.6
40.01–50.00	3.2	3.7	1.5	1.8
50.01–60.00	13.8	13.8	8.4	4.6
60.01–70.00	7.0	5.4	1.1	2.4
70.01–80.00	3.3	5.8	0.9	0.0
80.01–90.00	4.8	3.9	3.5	0.0
90.01–100.00	2.0	0.9	1.1	0.0
100.01+	8.4	5.8	10.4	0.0
Total (%)	100.0	100.0	100.0	100.0
Total number (000s)	4,487	3,260	1,575	1,080

Source: Department of Social Security, 1992, Table A2.06, based on a 1% sample of claimant records.

Table 12.7. *Distribution of family credit payments: DSS (Jan. 1992)* versus *POLIMOD (Q2–Q4 1991)*

Range of family credit (£s p.w.)	Per cent all family credit recipients	
	DSS	POLIMOD
0.00–9.99	13.5	21.4
10.00–19.99	16.9	24.7
20.00–29.99	16.6	17.5
30.00–39.99	14.3	10.0
40.00–49.99	15.2	11.6
50.00–59.99	11.2	7.0
60.00+	12.3	7.8
Total (%)	100.0	100.0
Total number (000s)	349	290

Source: Department of Social Security, 1992, Table A1.03, based on a 5% sample of claimant records as at 31 January 1992.

Table 12.8. *Distribution of housing benefit payments: DSS (May 1991) versus POLIMOD (Q2–Q3 1991)*

Range of housing benefit (£s p.a.)	Percentage of recipients who are local authority tenants		Percentage of recipients who are not local authority tenants	
	DSS	POLIMOD	DSS	POLIMOD
0.00–5.00	3.7	6.2	2.7	3.8
5.01–10.00	6.6	5.7	5.2	8.5
10.01–15.00	10.0	7.9	7.7	6.7
15.01–20.00	17.0	14.2	11.0	9.0
20.01–25.00	24.9	24.3	13.8	15.6
25.01–30.00	19.0	21.6	14.4	13.2
30.01–35.00	10.3	11.6	12.2	8.7
35.01+	8.4	8.4	33.3	34.5
Total (%)	100.0	100.0	100.0	100.0
Total number (000s)	2,937	2,636	1,084	948

Source: Department of Social Security, 1992, Tables A3.03 and A3.04, based on a 1% sample of income support claimant records and a 1% sample of non-income support housing benefit claimant records.

Table 12.9. *Distribution of community charge benefit payments: DSS (May 1991) versus POLIMOD (Q2–Q3 1991)*

Range of community charge benefit (£s p.w.)	All community charge benefit recipients (%)		Recipients also receiving income support (%)	
	DSS	POLIMOD	DSS	POLIMOD
0.00–1.00	8.0	3.4	2.3	2.0
1.01–3.00	32.0	21.8	25.0	10.9
3.01–5.00	46.4	51.9	58.2	61.5
5.01–7.00	9.1	11.8	9.3	10.1
7.01–9.00	3.9	8.4	4.4	10.9
9.01+	0.7	2.7	0.9	4.7
Total (%)	100.0	100.0	100.0	100.0
Total number (000s)	6,330	6,900	3,403	3,230

Source: Department of Social Security, 1992, Table A3.23, based on a 1% sample of claimant records.

12.7 Conclusions

Like the validation of POLIMOD's aggregate outputs, the validation of POLIMOD's distributions is hampered by our limited ability to isolate the contribution of the non-household population to each comparison, and by the fact that some external data are not directly comparable. It is also limited by a lack of external distributional data against which to validate POLIMOD distributions of expenditure, indirect taxes and non-means-tested benefits. (Our main findings are summarised in the conclusion to Chapter 9.)

Notes

1 The NES is discussed in Appendix 11.1 to Chapter 11.
2 A comparison that attempts to match the censoring of the NES sample by excluding a proportion of the FES sample is in Wilson (1995b).
3 The SPI is discussed in Appendix 11.1 to Chapter 11.
4 This amount is after the deduction of tax deductible expenses but before the deduction of money drawn for respondents' own use. This is the POLIMOD input variable *SEINC*. See the Appendix to this book for its derivation. That part of self-employment income which is assumed not to be taxable is the value of self-supply goods (*SEINCNT*) and the assumed amount of non-declared self-employment income.

5 By the ratio of the total family weighted FES population in 1991 to the subset interviewed after the first quarter of 1991.
6 To match the definition of SPI taxable investment income (Board of the Inland Revenue, 1994, p. 32), taxable investment income from POLIMOD is calculated as the sum of the input variables *INV1A* (interest from building society accounts), *INV1B* (interest from high street bank savings accounts), *INV2* (investment income taxed at the marginal rate in the year of interview), *PPEN* (amount of private pension received), *COV* (amount of covenant income received) and *MAINT* (amount of maintenance payments received). See the Appendix to this book.
7 Income support, housing benefit and community charge benefit rates changed in April and in October 1991.

Appendix: the POLIMOD database

A.1 Introduction

This Appendix describes how 1991 Family Expenditure Survey (FES) microdata are transformed into the four datasets that provide the input database for POLIMOD. These are datasets defined at the level of the household, family unit and individual. Variables used by POLIMOD are defined in terms of the raw and derived FES datasets on MIDAS, the national computer service run by the University of Manchester. The structure of FES data is outlined in section A.2 and a guide to how this is adapted in the POLIMOD database is provided. The derivation of household level variables is described in section A.3. Variables in the family-level dataset are described in section A.4, and individual level variables are outlined in section A.5. The data on household expenditures are described in section A.6. Finally, section A.7 describes how the data from 1991 are updated to later years.

A.2 The structure of FES data

The FES is primarily a survey of households. In the survey, a household is defined as 'one person living alone or a group of people living at the same address having meals prepared together and with common housekeeping . . . Members of a household are not necessarily related by blood or marriage' (Central Statistical Office, 1992, p. 78). This definition of the household is also used by POLIMOD.

Households are divided into family units, also known as benefit units. In both the FES and POLIMOD, a family unit can consist of an adult, his/her partner of the opposite sex, whether legally married or not, and any children for whom they are responsible. Therefore, within a family unit, there is nearly always at least one adult, and never more than two. If there are two adults, it is because they are living in a marriage-like situation. In the FES, a person's position in a benefit unit is identified by the variable $A009$ (1=head, 2=partner, 3=dependent child). If a benefit unit head is temporarily absent from the home when the household is sampled but his partner is present (*A006*=2), then no one is coded as head of the benefit unit. In POLIMOD, in these cases, the partner is recoded as head of the family unit. The FES defines the male partner in the case of a couple to be the head of the family unit. For the first family in the household, this person is also defined as the head of household. Although POLIMOD adopts this convention for convenience, it has no implications for the way in which tax liability or benefit entitlements are simulated, except where the gender and marital status of the individual are explicitly an issue.

Children in the household are added to the family unit whose head (or partner) is responsible for them. In POLIMOD, children are defined as persons in respect of whom child benefit was payable in 1991: all persons aged under 16, and all persons aged under 19 who are in full-time non-advanced education. In the FES, foster children are classified as heads of their own benefit units and are not counted as 'children'. In POLIMOD, foster child cases are recoded as children attached to a responsible adult's benefit unit.[1]

Some FES data are collected from the head of household in respect of the entire household, and other data are collected from each individual adult member. Data on tenure and housing costs are only collected from the household head. These data are therefore only available at the level of the household, and POLIMOD stores them at this level in a file with one record for each household, of which there are 7,056 in the 1991 FES dataset. Other data which are common for all members of a household are also in this file: the region in which they live, the quarter of the year in which they were interviewed and the estimated value of their dwelling. The derivation of household level variables is explained in section A.3.

Some data in the FES are collected at the level of the benefit unit. These mostly concern family composition, means-tested and contingency benefits. POLIMOD stores these data in a separate file with one record for each family unit. The derivation of variables in each family unit record is explained in section A.4. After recoding, there are 8,724 records in the family level POLIMOD file.

Data are also stored for each person within a household and family. These data include personal characteristics such as the person's sex, age, marital status and economic status, which household and family they belong to, and detailed information on the amounts of income they receive from various sources, for example, earnings, National Insurance benefits and income from savings and investments. Again, these data are stored in a separate file with one record for each individual (of whom there are 17,089 in the 1991 FES and in the POLIMOD person-level file). Section A.5 contains a detailed account of the derivation of these variables from the FES.

Expenditure data in the FES are collected in two ways – firstly from a diary of expenditure that each member of a respondent household aged 16 and over completes over a two-week period (FES variables derived from diaries are known as 'D' codes), and secondly from the interview with the head of household, where she or he is asked about the purchase of large items, consumer durables and services, such as insurance, that are consumed over a long period ('B' codes). Expenditure on food, clothing and other 'day-to-day' items is only recorded in the diaries. Weekly amounts are then imputed for all items of expenditure.

There are about 400 individual expenditure variables in the FES, but for POLIMOD these are aggregated into about 50 expenditure groups that allow us to model all the recent regimes of VAT, excise duties and the *ad valorem* tax on insurance premiums. Table A.4 in section A.7 lists the expenditure aggregates in the POLIMOD database.

Not all variables used as microdata input in POLIMOD are derived directly from the FES. Some variables relating to local taxation are not included in publicly available FES data for reasons of maintaining respondent anonymity, and are imputed separately by the Department of Social Security (DSS) on a regional average basis. These variables are referred to as 'DSS-defined': they are imputed for each FES respondent, family unit or household by the DSS in such a way as to reflect approximately the circumstances of FES respondents without compromising their anonymity.

A.3 The derivation of household-level variables from the 1991 FES

This section describes the derivation of household variables from the FES originals. In what follows we present POLIMOD variables in lower case italics, and FES variables in upper case italics. Each FES variable used in the derivation of a POLIMOD variable is described in the relevant subsection.

H.1 *hsid household identifier*
hsid=*CASENO*−110000
CASENO Household identifier

H.2 *nfams number of families in household*
nfams=number of occurrences within household of (individual level variable)
A009=1
A009 Position in benefit unit

H.3 *npers number of persons in household*
npers=Number of individual records where *CASENO* remains the same

H.4 *region region of UK in which household resides*
region=*A098*
A098 Region in UK

H.5 *lacode   local authority group code*
lacode=LACODE, a variable derived by DSS. Each code represents about six or seven local authorities within one of the eleven regions of England, Wales and Scotland. Local authorities were grouped according to the level of community charge in 1991/2, and DSS supplied a file with an *LACODE* for each *CASENO* in the 1991 FES.

In order to guarantee respondent anonymity, users of the FES are not allowed data on the exact local authority area in which FES respondents live. Therefore, *LACODE* is the best (i.e., the most local) option available for POLIMOD to use in calculating liability to local taxation

H.6 *quarter   quarter of 1991 in which FES interview took place*
quarter=A099
A099 Quarter of interview

H.7 *tenure   household tenure*
tenure=A121
A121 Householder's tenure

H.8 *ctband   council tax banding allocated to dwelling*
ctband is imputed separately for each household on the basis of *purprice* (see H.12 below). The method of imputation is described in Chapter 7

H.9 *hbrec   household reported receiving housing benefit in FES*
IF *B040+B230>0* THEN *hbrec*=1; OTHERWISE *hbrec*=0
B040 Rate rebate deducted from last rates/rent: amount deducted
B230 Rent rebate: amount received

H.10 *rent   rent paid by household*
Only tenant households will have a positive value for *rent*. In Northern Ireland, if rates or water rates are included in the rent, then these are subtracted from the rent figure given in the FES
(if household is owner occupied or rent free)
IF *A121>4* THEN *rent=0*
(if tenant household: rent paid)
IF *A121<=4* THEN *rent=B010+B020+B230*
  (if rates/water rates included in rent, Northern Ireland only)
  IF *A173=1* THEN *rent=rent+B040−P211*
    (if water rates included in rent, Northern Ireland only)
    IF *B050=0* THEN *rent=rent−(P566+P567+P573)*
A121 Householder's tenure
A173 Are rates included in rent
B010 Rent/rates: last net payment
B020 Rent/rates including non-separable service element: net
B040 Rate rebate deducted from last rates/rent: amount deducted
B050 Water charges: last net payment
B230 Rent rebate: amount received
P211 Calculated domestic rates
P566 Calculated domestic water rates

P567 Calculated sewerage rates
P573 Calculated environmental rates

H.11   *grent   ground rent paid by household*
(if the home is owned outright or with mortgage)
IF $(A121=5, 6 \text{ or } 7)$ THEN *grent*$=B060$
A121 Householder's tenure
B060 Other regular housing payments

H.12   *purprice   estimated value of dwelling*
purprice is imputed in the 1991 FES using data from the 1988 Building Society
Mortgages Survey (BSMS), where the contributions of dwelling characteristics to
the value of the dwelling are estimated in the BSMS, which includes data on the
purchase price of dwellings, and applied to the FES, which does not. This method
is more fully explained in Chapter 7

H.13   *rval   rateable value of dwelling*
rval$=B070$
B070 Rateable value for part of dwelling occupied

H.14   *rates   domestic rates paid by household (Northern Ireland only)*
This variable will only have a positive value for Northern Ireland respondents.
rates$=B030+B040$
(if domestic rates and water rates are both paid, we need to separate them)
(calculation of *water* shown at H.15 below)
IF $((P211 \neq P579) \text{ AND } (P579 > 0))$ THEN *rates*$=rates-water$
B030 Domestic rates: last net payment
B040 Rate rebate deducted from last rates/rent: amount deducted
P211 Calculated domestic rates
P579 Calculated domestic/environmental/sewerage rates less rebates

H.15   *water   water rates paid by household*
Firstly, for England and Wales:
IF $(A098 < 11)$ THEN . . .
    water$=B050$
    IF $B050=0$ THEN *water*$=P566+P567+P573$
Then for Scotland:
(in Scotland, water charges are levied as part of community charges. *CCWATER* is
derived by DSS for each LA group in Scotland. Water charges for Scottish FES
respondents are therefore always imputed rather than reported amounts)
IF $(A098=11)$ THEN *water*$=CCWATER$
Then for Northern Ireland:
IF $(A098=12)$ THEN . . .
    water$=B050$
    IF $B050=0$ THEN *water*$=P566+P567+P573$
    (if calculated domestic rates are not equal to domestic rates plus water rates
    then water rates are equal to domestic rates plus water rates less domestic
    rates)
    IF $((P211 \neq P579) \text{ AND } (P579 > 0))$ THEN *water*$=P579-P211$

A098 Region in UK
B050 Water charges: last net payment
P211 Calculated domestic rates
P566 Calculated domestic water rates
P567 Calculated sewerage rates
P573 Calculated environmental rates
P579 Calculated domestic/environmental/sewerage rates less rebates

H.16 *grossmi   gross mortgage paid by household*

The calculation of *grossmi* is divided into two parts:

(a) calculate current weekly mortgage interest (after the deduction of mortgage interest relief at source, MIRAS), *mi*, given that for some households only the net mortgage interest payment, including the repayment of capital, is reported.

(b) estimate gross weekly mortgage interest before deduction of MIRAS. This involves calculating the amount of MIRAS that has been deducted, and adding it to current mortgage interest as calculated at (a)

(a) The calculation of weekly mortgage interest, mi

In the 1991 FES there are 3,005 households who report paying mortgage interest (including 13 households who report rental purchase agreements). Of these, we do not have any record of mortgage interest paid for nine households. These are assumed to be mis-coded owner occupiers who have already paid off their mortgages and they are recoded accordingly. Therefore:

IF $(B130 + B150 + B200 = 0)$ AND $(tenure = 5)$ THEN $tenure = 7$

For the purposes of calculating *mi*, the remaining 2,996 households are placed in three categories:

1 If *B130* (interest on interest-only mortgage) is positive, then this is taken to be current mortgage interest after the deduction of MIRAS. This is the case for 2,086 households. (Thirteen households in this group also report paying mortgage interest and principal, suggesting that they have more than one type of mortgage. In such a case, the second mortgage is ignored. However, it is worth noting that the data do not allow us to determine whether a household is paying two mortgages of the same type, as they are added together into the one variable) IF $B130 > 0$ THEN $mi = B130$
The average amount of interest-only mortgage reported is £49.14.

2 If *B130* equals zero and *B200* (mortgage interest/principal, last payment) is positive, and *B150* (mortgage interest/principal: interest paid) is positive and refers to a recent period (i.e., for the 1991 FES, after July 1989) then mortgage interest after deduction of MIRAS equals *B150*:
IF $B130 = 0$ AND $B150 > 0$ AND $A158$ IS AFTER 0789 THEN $mi = B150$
In this group there are 379 households, and the average amount of interest reported is £41.84

3 If *B130* equals zero and *B150* equals zero then the proportion of total mortgage payment (*B200*) which is interest is estimated from the proportion that applies in (2) above, where both *B200* and *B150* are known. This is calibrated by the age of

the mortgage (*A133*) for these cases. For example, for mortgages that are less than 5 years old (*A133*<5) *B150/B200*=0.8833. Where *A133* is not known then *B150/B200* for all 379 households in (2) is taken as the proportion
IF *B130*=0 AND *B150*=0 AND *A158* IS BEFORE 0889 THEN ...
  IF *A133*<5 THEN *mi*=0.8833×*B200*
  IF *A133*>=5 AND *A133*<11 THEN *mi*=0.8301×*B200*
  IF *A133*>=11 THEN *mi*=0.7162×*B200*
  IF *A135*=1 OR 3 THEN ... (*A133* is not known)
    mi=0.8090×*B200*

(b) The calculation of mortgage interest relief at source (MIRAS), miras
There are 2,763 households (out of a total of 2,996 with mortgages) who report mortgage interest as net of tax (*A163*=1: 2,639 households), or who don't know if their mortgage interest is net of tax (*A163*=3: 124 households). We therefore estimate MIRAS for these households and add it to their mortgage interest, *mi*, to get gross mortgage interest before tax relief, *grossmi*. The latter group is included on the basis that it is the norm to have MIRAS deducted at source. The basic method is to calculate the total size of the mortgage by dividing the mortgage interest payment by the mortgage interest rate. The exact method of calculating *miras* varies according to which category the household belongs at (a) above.

1 With interest-only mortgages, the mortgage interest rate, *intrate*, used is the quarterly average,[2] and the tax rate, *taxrate*, is 0.25
2 With repayment mortgages where the interest element is known, *intrate* is taken as the midpoint of the year for which interest repayments are given. If that midpoint is before April 1988, then *taxrate*=0.27; otherwise it is 0.25
3 With repayment mortgages where the interest element is imputed, *intrate* is taken as the mean mortgage interest rate at (2) above, and *taxrate*=0.25
IF *mi*>0 THEN ...
  annual_mi=*mi*×52 (annualised weekly mortgage interest)
  mortgage=*annual_mi/(intrate/100)* (calculation of mortgage amount)
  (MIRAS only applies to the first £30,000 of a mortgage in 1991)
  IF *mortgage*<30000 THEN *annual_miras*=*intrate*×*mortgage*×*taxrate*
  IF *mortgage*>=30000 THEN *annual_miras*=*intrate*×30000×*taxrate*
  miras=*annual_miras/*52 (impute weekly amount for MIRAS)
  grossmi=*mi*+*miras* (weekly gross mortgage interest)
A133 Mortgage: years has run
A158 Mortgage interest: starting date
A163 Tax relief deducted from mortgage? (yes/no)
B130 Mortgage interest only: last payment
B150 Mortgage interest/principal: interest paid
B200 Mortgage interest/principal: last payment

H.17 *hwt household weight*
This variable is derived from the family-level POLIMOD variable *fuwt* (see **F.9**), using a method that produces consistent results at both the household and family unit levels of analysis (see Gomulka, 1994).

A.4 The derivation of family-level variables from the FES

This section describes the derivation of family-level POLIMOD variables from the FES originals. As with Section A.3, FES variables are in upper case italics, and are described at the end of each subsection, and POLIMOD variables are in lower case italics.

F.1   *hsid   household identifier*
hsid=*CASENO*−110000
CASENO   Household identifier

F.2   *famid   benefit unit, or family unit identifier*
IF *A002*=0 AND *A009*=1 THEN *famid*=1
IF NEXT *A009*=1 IN HOUSEHOLD THEN *famid*=2, etc.
A002   Relationship to head of household
A009   Position in benefit unit

F.3   *npers   number of persons in family*
npers=number of individual records where *CASENO* and *famid* remain the same
CASENO   Household identifier

F.4   *isact   income support receipt reported in FES data*
IF *A229*=1 THEN *isrec*=1
A229   Income support: receiving at present

F.5   *isweeks   number of weeks family reports being in receipt of income support in FES data*
IF *A229*=1 THEN *isweeks*=*A228*
A228   Income support: number of weeks received
A229   Income support: receiving at present

F.6   *fcact   family credit receipt reported in FES data*
IF *A257*=1 THEN *fcact*=1
A257   Family credit: receiving at present

F.7   *ccbrec   community charge benefit receipt reported in DSS supplied data*
DSS-defined variable; see Section A.2

F.8   *cctrans   amount of transitional relief for community charge reported in DSS supplied data*
DSS-defined variable; see Section A.2

F.9   *fuwt   family unit weight for grossing up sample to be representative of UK population*
DSS defines two sets of population estimates for different types of family which they use for grossing-up 1991 FES to be representative of the UK as a whole, one set for Great Britain and one for Northern Ireland. These estimates, and their associated weights, are listed in Table A.1. The weights, which gross-up according to family type, have been used to calculate household weights. In cases where there is

Table A.1. *Grossing-up weights for family units used in POLIMOD with the 1991 FES*

	Great Britain			Northern Ireland		
Category	Column 1 Population estimate (000 benefit units)[a]	Column 2 POLIMOD sample count	Column 3 Grossing factor col.1/col.2	Column 4 Population estimate (000 benefit units)[a]	Column 5 POLIMOD sample count	Column 6 Grossing factor col.4/col.5
Couple, 0 children	6,134	1,762	3.4813	120	25	4.7961
Couple, 1 child	2,167	669	3.2392	61	21	2.8857
Couple, 2 children	2,332	768	3.0365	67	19	3.5102
Couple, 3+ children	936	325	2.8800	60	9	6.6363
Pensioner couple aged 65–74	1,754	536	3.2724			
Pensioner couple aged 75	837	245	3.4163			
Pensioner couple aged 65+				52	13	4.0035
Single male aged 0–29	3,554	844	4.2109			
Single male aged 30–54	1,533	483	3.1739			
Single male aged 55–64	426	139	3.0647			
Single male age <65				143	32	4.4801
Single female aged 0–19	724	226	3.2035			
Single female aged 20–39	1,663	483	3.4431			
Single female aged 40–59	907	305	2.9738			
Single female aged <60				92	27	3.4069
Single male with children	115	24	4.7917			
Single female with children	1,176	343	3.4286			
Single parent				32	10	3.1527
Single male aged 65+	879	317	2.7729	26	7	3.6725
Single female aged 60–74	1,692	560	3.4202			
Single female aged 75+	1,758	514	3.4202			
Single female aged 60+				94	18	5.2890
Total benefit units	28,587	8,543		745	181	

Source:[a] DSS.

more than one family unit per household, the household weights combine family unit weights in such a way that the resulting household weight is within the range of family unit weights. The aggregate results achieved at the family level of analysis and at the household level of analysis are therefore identical (see Gomulka, 1994).

Owing to the recoding of family units and the inclusion of households containing absent spouses and partners, the weights used in POLIMOD are slightly different from the weights used by DSS in their grossing up of FES in their 'Households Below Average Income' series (Department of Social Security, 1995).

A.5 The derivation of individual-level variables from the 1991 FES

The POLIMOD individual-level file contains 58 variables for each observation. Most of these variables are derived from the FES, and some are imputed from DSS files. As before, FES variables are in upper case italics, and are described at the end of each subsection, and POLIMOD variables are in lower case italics.

I.1 *hsid   household identifier*
hsid=CASENO
CASENO   Household identifier

I.2 *famid   family unit identifier*
IF *A002*=0 AND *A009*=1 THEN *famid*=1
IF NEXT *A009*=1 IN HOUSEHOLD THEN *famid*=2, etc.
A002 Respondent's relationship to head of household
A009 Respondent's position in benefit unit

I.3 *persid   person identifier in household*
persid=PERSNO
PERSNO   Respondent's person number in household

I.4 *age   age of respondent*
age=A005
A005 Respondent's age

I.5 *a201   employment status*
a201=A200
A200 Respondent's employment status

I.6 *married   legal marital status indicator*
IF *A006*=1 OR 2 THEN *married*=1
OTHERWISE *married*=0
A006 Respondent's marital status

I.7 *male   sex indicator*
IF *A004*=2 THEN *male*=0
IF *A004*=1 THEN *male*=1
A004 Respondent's sex

I.8 fted current educational status
IF *A007*=1, 2, 3, 4, 5, 6 OR 7 THEN *fted*=1
IF *A007*=8 or 9 THEN *fted*=2
OTHERWISE *fted*=0
A007 Current full-time education of respondent

I.9 head head of family unit indicator
IF *A009*=1 THEN *head*=1
OTHERWISE *head*=0
A009 Respondent's position in benefit unit

I.10 dep dependent child in family indicator
IF *A009*=3 THEN *dep*=1
OTHERWISE *dep*=0
A009 Respondent's position in benefit unit

I.11 cocar number of company cars provided for respondent
(heads of family units)
IF *A285*=1 OR 3 THEN *cocar*=1
(spouses of heads, where company is provided by head's employer. In this case, *A285* is attached to the spouse's record, but its value must be transferred to head's record)
IF *A285*=2 THEN *cocar*=*cocar*+1 (where *cocar* is attached to head rather than spouse)
A285 Company car provided by respondent's or spouse's employer

I.12 seg socio-economic group
seg=*A215*
A215 Socio-economic group – main occupation

I.13 hrs employee's usual hours plus overtime
(if respondent is currently an employee)
IF (*A200*=1) THEN *hrs*=*A220*+*A244*
A200 Economic status
A220 Respondent's usual weekly hours (excluding breaks and overtime)
A244 Respondent's hours paid overtime usually worked

I.14 shrs self-employed, usual hours, defined as maximum of range
In the FES, hours worked by self-employed respondents are reported in categories, less than 24, 25–30 and over 30 hours. For POLIMOD, it is assumed that any respondent who reports earnings of less than £15 and who reports working for less than 24 hours a week, actually works for less than 16 hours. This has some implications for eligibility to family credit and income support
(if respondent is currently self-employed)
  IF (*A200*=2) THEN . . .
  IF ((*A203*=1) AND (*seinc*<15.00)) THEN *shrs*=15
  IF ((*A203*=1) AND (*seinc*>=15.00)) THEN *shrs*=23
  IF (*A203*=2) THEN *shrs*=30
  IF (*A203*=3) THEN *shrs*=40

A200 Economic status

A203 Self-employed respondent – hours usually worked

seinc self-employment earnings (see I.25)

I.15 *sspwks   number of weeks respondent has been receiving statutory sick pay*
IF *A279*=1 THEN *sspwks=A278*

A279 Statutory sick pay: receiving at present

A278 Statutory sick pay: number of weeks received

I.16 *NIC_stat   National Insurance Contributions regime*
The derivation of *NIC_stat* is fully explained in Chapter 6. Briefly, for each respondent where *gwage*>0 (see **I.19** below), three possible NI contributions are calculated using the regimes in existence during 1991, the non-contracted out rate, the contracted out rate and the married women's reduced rate. Actual weekly reported contributions (*B306*) are compared with the amounts calculated for each contribution regime, and the NIC regime allocated to the respondent is essentially the one with the closest calculated amount to *B306*, within the following parameters:

(a) To be eligible for married women's reduced rate contributions (value 3), respondents must be female, aged 30 or over in 1991 and be married or widowed, i.e.,
A004=2 AND *A005*>=30 AND *A006*=1, 2 OR 5

(b) If the difference between all calculated NICs and *B306* is greater than 10 pence or 5%, then, if the respondent is paying superannuation contributions, s/he is allocated to 'contracted out' (value 2); otherwise s/he is allocated to 'non-contracted out' (value 1)

A004 Respondent's sex

A005 Respondent's age

A006 Respondent's marital status

B306 National Insurance contributions: amount deducted from pay

I.17 *ccexempt   respondent exempt from community charge indicator*
DSS-defined variable; see Section A.2

I.18 *ccreduce   respondent entitled to 80% reduction in community charge indicator*
DSS-defined variable; see Section A.2

I.19 *gwage   current gross wage (last pay period) including subsidiary wages*
The earnings calculation used in POLIMOD is as follows:
(calculate gross earnings)
IF (*A250*=1) THEN . . .
  IF (*B315*>0) THEN *gwage=B315*
  OTHERWISE *gwage=P003*
(calculate subsidiary earnings)
IF (*A255*=1) THEN *subwage=P014*
(calculate gross earnings)
gwage=(gwage+subwage)

A250 Last pay for respondent's main job was last week or last month
A255 Subsidiary job covered by last pay
B315 Usual gross pay: employee
P003 Gross wage, salary last time paid (main job)
P014 Gross wage, salary last week/month (subsidiary employment)

I.20 super amount of occupational pension contributions
super = B318
B318 Deductions from pay for superannuation: amount

I.21 lv value of luncheon vouchers
lv = B316
B316 Luncheon vouchers: cash value in last week

I.22 gwagent amount of earnings not taxed
This variable is always set to zero as there are no 'in-kind' benefits recorded in 1991 FES

I.23 lap1 life assurance premiums: pre 1984
In 1991 life assurance premiums purchased before 1984 (*B196*) had 12.5% tax relief
$lap1 = B196/(1-0.125)$
B196 Life assurance before April 1984: amount of premium

I.24 lap2 life assurance premiums: post 1984
lap2 = B197 (Life assurance premiums purchased after 1984)
B197 Life assurance after April 1984: amount of premium

I.25 seinc self-employment income, updated to date of interview, no correction for under-reporting
Self-employed FES respondents are asked about net profits in the last 12 months for which they have information, or less if the business is newly established (*A226*). Half of self-employed respondents in 1991 declared profits/losses for 12 months ending in that year, 40% declared for 12 months ending in 1990 and most of the remainder declared for 1989. On this basis, self-employment earnings data in the FES refer to a different period than most other data on incomes and expenditures. The variable *seindex* adjusts self-employment earnings to allow for this.

Earnings of the self-employed in the FES are adjusted by *seindex* to June 1991, on the basis of the change in average earnings of the self-employed between midway through the year to which profits/losses relate and April 1991. Table A.2 shows estimated earnings from self-employment and numbers of self-employed between 1983 and 1991. Monthly estimates of average earnings from self-employment are calculated from the data in Table A.2 using the following loglinear interpolation method:

$seindex = e_{91} / [e_{y-1} + (e_y - e_{y-1})^{m/12}]$

where e_{91} is average annual earnings from self employment in June 1991 (see Table A.2), e_y is average annual earnings of the self-employed in the year for which year-ending profits/losses are reported, m is the 'year ending' month for reported profits and losses, *A226*, with July, the mid-point = 1. Therefore, for a respondent who reported profits for the year ending October 1989,

Table A.2. *Estimated earnings and numbers of self-employed, 1983–1991*

Year (July)	Gross earnings from self employment[a] (£ million)	Estimated numbers of self-employed[b] (000)	Average annual earnings of self-employed (£)
1983	24,750	2,221	11,144
1984	27,909	2,315	11,097
1985	30,404	2,610	11,649
1986	35,104	2,627	13,363
1987	40,122	2,860	14,029
1988	47,612	2,986	15,945
1989	54,453	3,253	16,739
1990	59,971	3,298	18,184
1991	57,507	3,143	18,297

Sources: [a] Blue Book, 1992, Table 4.4.
      [b] *Employment Gazette*, Table 1.1.

$$seindex = 18,297 / [(16,739 + (18,184 - 16,739)^{4/12}]$$
$$= 18,297 / 16,390.31$$
$$= 1.1163$$

(if self employment period reported)
IF $A226 > 0$ THEN ...

(if respondent currently self-employed or unemployed)
IF $A200 >= 2$ AND $<= 4$ THEN ...

Calculate *seindex* (see above)
IF $B326 > 0$ THEN $seinc = B326$
IF $B328 > 0$ THEN $subjob = B328$
IF $B307 \geq 0$ THEN $loss = B307$
IF $loss > 0$ AND $B326 = 0$ THEN $seinc = loss \times -1$ (making *loss* a minus figure)
$seinc = (seinc + subjob) \times seindex$ (multiply *seinc* by *seindex* to uprate to mid-1991 levels)

A200 Employment status
A226 Self-employment period (for accounting purposes) month and year
B307 Self-employed: amount of net loss
B326 Self-employed: amount of net profit
B328 Subsidiary job self-employed: amount of net profit

I.26   *seincnt   value of self-supply goods (assumed untaxed)*
seincnt = B327
B327 Self-supply goods: value from 'D' books

I.27   *invla   interest from building society accounts*
(if respondent interviewed in first quarter)
IF $(A099 = 1)$ THEN $invla = B402/(1 - 0.22) + B401$
(composite rate tax = 22% up to 31 March 1991)

OTHERWISE $inv1a = B402/(1-0.25) + B401$
(composite rate tax replaced by standard rate income tax from April 1991)
A099 Quarter of 1991 in which respondent interviewed
B401 High street bank: before tax interest received
B402 High street bank: after tax interest received

I.28 inv1b interest from high street bank savings accounts
(if respondent was interviewed in first quarter)
IF $(A099=1)$ THEN $inv1b = (B374 + B400)/(1-0.22) + B399$
(composite rate tax=22% up to 31 March 1991)
OTHERWISE $inv1b = (B374 + B400)/(1-0.25) + B399$
(composite rate tax replaced by standard rate income tax from April 1991).
A099 Quarter of 1991 in which respondent interviewed
B374 Other bank/soc savings: interest received
B399 Building society: before tax interest received
B400 Building society: after tax interest received

I.29 inv2 investment income taxed at marginal rate in year of interview
(interest received from National Savings is more then £70: only interest of over £70 per annum from National Savings non-investment accounts is taxable. All income from National Savings investment accounts is taxable)
IF $B373 > 70$ THEN $inv2 = (B378 + B409)/(1-0.25) + B373 - 70/52 + B360 + B333 + B384$
OTHERWISE $inv2 = (B378 + B409)/(1-0.25) + B360 + B333 + B384$
B378 Stocks, shares, dividends, after tax
B409 Gilt-edged stock and war loan: interest
B373 National Savings ordinary account: interest received
B360 Rent from property: amount received
B333 National Savings investment account: interest received
B384 Other unearned income: amount received

I.30 inv3 investment income not taxed in year of interview
(interest received from National Savings is more then £70)
IF $B373 > 70$ THEN $inv3 = 70/52 + B398$
OTHERWISE $inv3 = B373 + B398$
B373 National Savings ordinary account: interest received
B398 TESSA: interest received

I.31 open amount of current occupational pension received
$open = B348 + B349$
B348 Public/private pension: last net payment
B349 Public/private pension: tax deducted from last payment

I.32 stgrant amount of student grant received
$stgrant = B392 - B361$
IF $B392 - B361 < 0$ THEN $stgrant = 0$
B361 Education grant: total value less cash received
B392 Education grant: total value

I.33   *stloan*   *amount of student loan received*
stloan=B364
B364 Student top-up loan

I.34   *ppen*   *amount of private pension received*
ppen=ANUAMT
(if last payment was after tax)
IF *ANUTAXBA=2* THEN *ppen=ANUAMT+ANUTAXAM*
ANUTAXAM   Annuity/personal pension tax: amount
ANUAMT   Annuity/personal pension: amount
ANUTAXBA   Annuity/personal pension pre or post tax?

I.35   *cov*   *amount of covenant income received*
cov=TRSAMT
(if trust/covenant payment was after tax)
IF *TRSTAXBA=2* THEN *cov=cov+TRSTAXAM*
TRSTAXAM   Trust/covenant payments tax: amount
TRSAMT   Trust/covenant payments: amount
TRSTAXBA   Trust/covenant payment pre or post tax?

I.36   *oyt*   *amount of other taxable income received*
oyt=B381+B396
(if presently receiving regular allowance from non-spouse outside household)
IF *ALLPRES=1* THEN ...
    (if respondent is receiving allowance from organisation, EC training allowance
    or non local authority foster allowance)
    IF *ALLTYPE=2* OR 5 OR 6 THEN *oyt=oyt+B352*
ALLPRES   Regular allowance from non-spouse: receiving at present
ALLTYPE   Regular allowance from non-spouse: type received
          2 regular allowance from organisation
          5 allowance for foster child from non-local authority source
          6 EC training allowance
B352 Regular allowance, non-spouse: amount received
B381 Income from odd-jobs: amount
B396 Children's income: amount received

I.37   *oynt*   *amount of other untaxed income received*
oynt=B385
(if respondent receiving private benefits at present)
IF *A231=1* THEN *oynt=oynt+B366*
A231 Respondent receiving private benefits at present?
B366 Private benefits: last amount received
B385 Allowances from absent spouse: amount

I.38   *babysit*   *income from babysitting and child-minding*
babysit=B383
B383 Mailorder agent/babysitter: amount received

I.39 *foster   income from fostering allowances*
(if respondent is presently receiving regular allowance from non-spouse outside household)
IF *ALLPRES*=1 THEN . . .
  (if respondent is receiving fostering allowance from local authority)
  IF *ALLTYPE*=4 THEN . . .
    (if respondent was interviewed before September 1991)
    IF *A099*<=3 THEN *foster=foster+B352*−£7.25 for each foster child in the family unit
    (if respondent was interviewed after September 1991)
    IF *A099*=4 THEN *foster=foster+B352*−£7.50 for each foster child in the family unit
ALLPRES   Regular allowance from non-spouse: receiving at present
ALLTYPE   Regular allowance from non-spouse: type received
                 4 foster allowance from local authority
A099 Quarter
B352 Regular allowance, non-spouse: amount received

I.40 *maint   amount of maintenance payments received*
(if receiving regular allowance from non-spouse outside household)
IF *ALLPRES*=1 THEN . . .
  (if receiving maintenance)
  IF *ALLTYPE*=3 THEN *maint=B352*
ALLPRES   Regular allowance from non-spouse: receiving at present
ALLTYPE   Regular allowance from non-spouse: type received
                 3 maintenance/separation allowance
B352 Regular allowance, non-spouse: amount received

I.41 *relly   amount of income from relatives received*
(if receiving regular allowance from non-spouse outside household)
IF *ALLPRES*=1 THEN . . .
  (if receiving regular allowance from friend or relative)
  IF *ALLTYPE*=1 THEN *relly=B352*
ALLPRES   Regular allowance from non-spouse: receiving at present
ALLTYPE   Regular allowance from non-spouse: type received
                 1 regular allowance from friend/relative
B352 Regular allowance, non-spouse: amount received

I.42 *ub   amount of unemployment benefit received*
IF *A223*=1 THEN *ub=B362*
A223 Unemployment benefit: receiving at present
B362 Unemployment benefit: last amount received

I.43 *sick   amount of sickness benefit received*
IF *A225*=1 THEN *sick=B363*
A225 NI sickness benefit: receiving at present
B363 NI sickness benefit: last amount received

I.44   *ivb   amount of invalidity benefit received*
IF *A259*=1 THEN *ivb*=*B369*
A259 Contributory invalidity pension: receiving at present
B369 Invalidity pension: last amount received

I.45   *mat   amount of maternity allowance received*
IF *A240*=1 THEN *mat*=*B341*
A240 Maternity allowance: receiving at present
B341 Maternity allowance: amount received

I.46   *wid   amount of widow's benefits received*
IF *B339*>0 THEN *wid*=*B339*
B339 NI widow's benefit: amount of last payment

I.47   *pen   current NI retirement pension, plus graduated pension and SERPS*
IF *B338*>0 THEN *pen*=*B338*
B338 NI retirement pension: last amount received

I.48   *sda   amount of severe disablement allowance received*
IF *B418*>0 THEN *sda*=*B418*
B418 Severe disability allowance amount received

I.49   *ica   amount of invalid care allowance received*
IF *A295*=1 THEN *ica*=*B343*
A295 Invalid care allowance: receiving now
B343 Invalid care allowance amount received

I.50   *indis   amount of industrial disablement pension received*
IF *A238*=1 THEN *indis*=*B325*
A238 Industrial injury disablement pension: receiving at present
B325 Industrial injury disablement pension: last amount received

I.51   *oben   amount of other benefits received*
IF *A233*=1 THEN *oben*=*B367*
A233 Other state benefits: receiving at present
B367 Other state benefits: last amount received

I.52   *train   amount of training allowance received*
IF *A273*=1 THEN *train*=*B382*
A273 Government training scheme: receiving benefit at present
B382 Government training scheme: allowance received

I.53   *ssp   amount of statutory sick pay received*
IF *A279*=1 THEN *ssp*=*B388*
A279 Statutory sick pay: receiving at present
B388 Statutory sick pay: imputed gross amount

I.54   *smp   amount of statutory maternity pay received*
IF *SMPBENPR*=1 THEN *smp*=*B342*
SMPBENPR Statutory maternity pay: receiving at present
B342 Statutory maternity pay: amount received

I.55 *attal   amount of attendance allowance received*
attal=B421
B421 Attendance allowance: last amount received

I.56 *mobal   amount of mobility allowance received*
mobal=B417
B417 Mobility allowance: last amount received

I.57 *war   amount of war pension received*
war=B340
B340 War disability pension: last amount received

I.58 *ccq1   community charge, quarter 1 of 1991*
DSS-defined variable; see Section A.2

I.59 *ccq24   community charge, quarters 2 to 4 of 1991*
DSS-defined variable; see Section A.2

A.6 The derivation of expenditure variables from the 1991 FES

The expenditure variables used in POLIMOD are listed in Table A.5 in the next section. All variables are at the level of the household. Details of the composition of the aggregates are given in Redmond (1995).

A.7 Updating the POLIMOD database

This section describes the method of updating FES income and expenditure data used by POLIMOD from the survey year (a calendar year: 1991) to the policy year of interest (a fiscal year: 1996/7 is used as an example). Three different methods are used:

1 For most items of income and expenditure, a single updating factor is applied regardless of the month of interview. The factor is equal to the movement between the midpoint of the survey year (1 July) and the midpoint of the modelled year (1 October). Two major assumptions underlie the use of a single updating factor: the first is that levels of income and expenditure do not change significantly between the start and the end of the survey year. The average annual rate of inflation during 1991 was 5.9%. The second assumption is that the characteristics of the sample interviewed in the last quarter of the survey year are not significantly different from the characteristics of those interviewed in the first quarter.
2 Different updating factors are applied according to the quarter in which the household was interviewed in the survey year. This is the method used to take account of upratings for non-means-tested benefits

where receipt is taken from the survey data themselves and is not simulated, and also to fine-tune the uprating of earnings.

3 With employee earnings data, different updating factors are applied according to position in the 1991 FES earnings distribution. If the distribution of employee earnings becomes more unequal between the survey year and the policy year, then the updating method used will reflect this.

Data from the latest available official statistics are used to calculate changes in household and individual income and expenditure since the survey year. Estimated or forecast changes in incomes and expenditures between the latest available official statistics and the midpoint of the policy year of interest are based on average predictions of the Panel of Independent Forecasters (POIF; HM Treasury, 1995a) where possible, or on projections based on the rate of the change in the latest year for which data are available, or on known information, such as the expected amount by which benefits will increase in the policy year. Table A.3 summarises the methods by which different elements of income and expenditure are updated. The detailed treatment of each element of income and expenditure is discussed in the remainder of this section in the order listed in Table A.3.

Many of the data we use to update POLIMOD variables are only published on an annual basis. In particular, all data from the Blue Book (Central Statistical Office, 1995c) and POIF forecasts are annual. However, we are interested in updating POLIMOD to the midpoint of a financial year – October 1996 in the case of the the analyses in this book. Therefore, we need to impute monthly changes in indices to estimate, for example, the increase in inflation between January and October 1996. There are several methods of doing this, and it is difficult to choose objectively among them. We use the relatively straightforward method of log-linear interpolation, which assumes that the imputed percentage change in the index remains constant throughout the period, and that the product of imputed monthly percentage changes is exactly equal to the reported annual change. Imputed monthly change can be expressed as:

$$m = (i_t / i_{t-1})^{(1/12)}$$

where m is the imputed constant change between years $t-1$ and t, and i is the index for years $t-1$ and t.

Employee earnings

Employee earnings are the single most important source of income for households both in the FES sample and in the UK population. For

Table A.3. *Summary of methods used to update POLIMOD variables*

Item to be updated	Adjustment in 1991	Adjustment from 1991	Forecast
Employee earnings	From qtr of interview to April 1991	Disaggregated New Earnings Survey Data and average growth in earnings from *Economic Trends*	POIF forecast on growth in earnings
Income from self-employment	From end of accounting month/year to June 1991	Aggregate data from *UK National Accounts* and *Employment Gazette*	Assume rate of growth in the last year continues
Income from investments		Aggregate data from *UK National Accounts*	POIF forecast on prices and interest rates
Income from occupational pensions		Average growth in earnings from *Economic Trends*	POIF forecast on growth in earnings
Income from other sources		Growth in all items retail prices index	POIF forecast on prices
Student grants and loans		Actual change in maximum grant	All items RPI in year to September 1995
Non-means tested benefits		Actual change in benefits	All items RPI in year to September 1995
Household rent, rates and water changes		Change in rent RPI, all items RPI and water and other payments RPI respectively	POIF forecast on prices
Gross mortgage interest		Change in mortgage interest payments RPI	POIF forecast on interest rates
All items of expenditure		Changes in sub-group of RPI which most closely corresponds to the expenditure item	POIF forecast on prices

this reason, and because data from the New Earnings Survey (NES) are published every year within six months of sampling (see Department of Employment, 1991; Central Statistical Office, 1995b), we update all employee earnings (full-time and part-time) according to changes in the *distribution* of earnings in the NES, rather than simply according to changes in *mean* earnings. The NES is carried out in April each year and provides a rich and reliable source of information on the movement of earnings for employees who pay income tax under the PAYE scheme. In terms of POLIMOD updating, it is important to note that updating according to a distribution such as that from the NES is the exception, and is not carried out on any other item of income or expenditure.

As an updating tool for POLIMOD, the NES has some weaknesses. These are explored more in Wilson (1995b), but are summarised here. Firstly, the populations of the FES and the NES are different – the NES excludes employees whose earnings are below the income tax threshold, and published tables refer to full-time employees only. Therefore, it is possible that the updating factors we use in POLIMOD may not adequately reflect changes in the earnings of the very low paid, or part-time workers. The earnings of part-time workers are adjusted to their full-time equivalents ($40 \times$(earnings/hours worked)) so that uprating factors may be calculated. Secondly, while FES respondents are continuously sampled throughout the year, all NES respondents are sampled in April. Therefore, as is shown below, the FES sample has to be adjusted to April of the survey year before updating factors derived from NES can be applied.

The updating factor has three components:

$Q_{GWAGE}{}^q$ Adjustment factor to convert earnings for each individual in the survey to an as-at-April value according to the quarter in which the interview was conducted, derived from the Average Earnings Index by dividing the index for April by the average index for the relevant quarter (ending March, June, September or December, q=1 to 4).
Source: *Economic Trends*, October 1993, Table 25, average earnings index (Great Britain), whole economy.

$N_{GWAGE}{}^{y,sex}$ Adjustment factors to update from April of the survey year to April of the most recent NES year disaggregated by 5 percentiles of earnings (y=1 to 20) and by sex. These factors represent growth in the upper limit of each 5 percentile group for men and women separately from the distribution of NES gross weekly earnings (including overtime pay) for full-time employees excluding those whose pay for the survey pay-period was affected by absence.

Sources: (1) Department of Employment, 1991, Part A, p. A23.1, all males, all females; (2) Central Statistical Office, 1995b, Part A, p. A23.1, Table 23, all males, all females.

The upper limit of each 5 percentile group in each year is derived using linear interpolation.

P_{GWAGE} Actual and forecast earnings movement from April of the most recent NES to October of the modelled year.

Sources: (1) for updating from April 1995 to July 1995: *Economic Trends*, October 1995, Table 4.1, average earnings index, whole economy. (2) for updating from July 1995 to October 1996: HM Treasury, 1995a, Table average Panel of Independent Forecasters (POIF) forecast of average earnings growth 1995 and 1996.

$$U_{GWAGE}^{q,y,sex} = Q_{GWAGE}^{q} \times N_{GWAGE}^{y,sex} \times P_{GWAGE}$$

Example: updating 1991 data to 1996/7 for a woman in bottom 5% of the earnings distribution (after adjusting for part-time status) interviewed in first quarter of 1991:

Q_{GWAGE}
Average Earnings Index in April 1991 is 127.5 (1988=100)
Average Earnings Index in Q1 1991 is 126.0 (1988=100)
$Q_{GWAGE}^{1} = 127.5/126.0 = 1.0119$

N_{GWAGE}
Upper bound of lowest 5% of female earners April 1991 = £107.31
Upper bound of lowest 5% of female earners April 1995 = £123.64
$N_{GWAGE}^{1,female} = 123.64/107.31 = 1.1522$

P_{GWAGE}
Average Earnings Index April 1995 (date of last available NES) = 126.4
Average Earnings Index in July 1995 (provisional, last available) = 126.5
$126.5/126.4 = 1.0008$
Average POIF forecast earnings growth for 1995 = 3.50%
Average POIF forecast earnings growth for 1996 = 4.27%
$1.0350^{(5/12)} \times 1.0427^{(9/12)}$
$= 1.0144 \times 1.0319$
$= 1.0468$
$P_{GWAGE} = 1.0008 \times 1.0468 = 1.0476$

$U_{GWAGE}^{1,1,female} = 1.0119 \times 1.1522 \times 1.0476 = \mathbf{1.2214}$

Income from self-employment

In contrast to employee incomes, all income from self-employment is updated according to a single factor derived from aggregate statistics. This is because no adequate recent survey sample on incomes of the self-employed that we could use to update FES-reported incomes exists. The effect of using a single updating factor may be to over-estimate increases among self-employed people with low incomes, and under-estimate increases for those with high incomes. For example, Jenkins (1995) suggests that in the first half of the 1980s, changes in self-employment income appear to have had a very large influence on the growth in overall income inequality during that period.

A further problem with updating incomes of the self-employed lies in the way in which they are reported in the FES. While employee earnings refer to 'last week or last month', incomes from self-employment refer to 'the last 12 months for which you have information': this can mean a period which ended more than two years before the respondent was sampled, and adjustment must therefore be made for this time-lag, so that all self-employment incomes are adjusted to halfway through the survey year (July in the case of the 1991 FES). This adjustment is fully discussed in Section A.5 above, and the description of updating that follows assumes that this adjustment has already been made.

A_{SEINC} Actual change in average income from self-employment to the latest available date. Average income from self-employment is calculated as total income from self-employment from the National Accounts divided by the number of self-employed persons in each year, imputed from quarterly figures in the *Employment Gazette*.

Sources: (1) Central Statistical Office, 1995c, *UK National Accounts: The Blue Book,* Table 4.4, Income from self-employment after providing for depreciation and stock appreciation. (2) *Employment Gazette*, Table 1.1, self-employed persons – UK – unadjusted; average of quarterly figures (October 1995 issue for figures relating to 1992, 1993 and 1994; June 1995 issue for figures relating to 1991).

P_{SEINC} Projected change in self-employment income from latest available actual to October of the policy year assuming that the projected rate of growth is equal to the the historical rate of growth. (There are no forecasts of income from self-employment.)

U_{SEINC} $= A_{SEINC} \times P_{SEINC}$

Example: updating 1991 data to 1996/97
Blue Book; *Employment Gazette*

	Calendar year				Change
	1991	1992	1993	1994	1991–94
Income from self-employed (£m)	530,772	53,830	56,673	59,585	
Number of self-employed (000s)	3,368	3,232	3,193	3,305	
Average income (£ pa)	15,758	16,655	17,749	18,029	1.1441

$A_{SEINC} = 1.1441$
$P_{SEINC} = 1.1441^{(27/36)} = 1.1062$
$U_{SEINC} = 1.1441 \times 1.1062 = \mathbf{1.2656}$

Income from investments

Incomes from investment in the FES are the respondents' estimate of total income generated or received in this way in the 12 months before interview. In updating income from investments, POLIMOD assumes that this income was being received *at the time of interview*. Furthermore, no allowance is made for when the interview took place (one might expect income from investments to be different in December and January), or for the type of investment that is involved. Because the value of any investment can go down as well as up, not only is the uprating of incomes from investments an error-laden process, but in addition, it is difficult even to predict the direction of that error. For this reason, the approach taken to updating incomes from investment in POLIMOD is a straightforward and transparent one. All incomes from investments (including interest from building society accounts (*INV1A*), interest from high street bank savings accounts (*INV1B*), investment income subject to tax in the year of interview (*INV2*) and investment income not taxed in the year of interview (*INV3*)) are updated according to the same factor. This factor is calculated as follows:

A_{INV} Actual growth in income from rent, dividends and interest to the most recently available figures.
Source: Central Statistical Office, 1995c, *UK National Accounts: The Blue Book*, Table 3.1, Personal sector: current income and expenditure; income before tax, rent, dividends and interest.

P_{INV} Projected growth in income from rent, dividends and interest from the most recently available figures. This is derived by applying actual and forecast interest rate growth for that part that is interest and actual and forecast RPI growth for the remainder.

Sources: (1) HM Treasury, 1995a, average of Panel of Independent Forecasters, Table B1, forecast of interest rates; forecast of change in Retail Prices Index. (2) *Monthly Digest of Statistics*, Table 17.5, Selected retail banks' base rate (March 1995: average of 1994 rates; November 1995: latest rate). (3) Central Statistical Office, 1995c, *UK National Accounts: The Blue Book*, Table 3.8, Sector allocation of dividends and interest. (4) *Employment Gazette*, October 1995, Table 6.1, Retail Price index, all items.

$$U_{INV} = A_{INV} \times P_{INV}$$

Example: updating 1991 data to 1996/97
Blue Book:

	Calendar year				Change	
	1991	1992	1993	1994	1991–94	1993–94
Rents, dividends and net interest (£m)	56,813	64,783	67,226	72,338	1.2733	1.0760

$A_{INV} = 1.2733$

P_{INV1}
Change in actual RPI in the 12 months to July 1995 is 3.5%.
Increase in actual RPI July to September 1995 (150.6/149.1) is 1.01%.
Average POIF forecasts of RPI growth: 3.4% in the year ending in quarter 4 1995; 2.46% in the year ending quarter 4 1996.
Actual and forecast change in RPI July 1994 to October 1996:

$$P_{INV1} = 1.035 \times 1.0101 \times 1.034^{(4/12)} \times 1.0246^{(9/12)}$$
$$= 1.035 \times 1.0101 \times 1.0112 \times 1.0184 = 1.0766$$

P_{INV2}
Selected retail banks' interest rate average for 1994 is 5.48%.
(rate in January: 5.5%; February–August: 5.25%; September–November: 5.75%; December: 6.25%)
Selected retail banks' interest rate average as at October 1995 is 5.75%.
Average POIF forecast base rate: 6.69% in quarter 4 1995; 6.4% in quarter 4 1996.
Actual and forecast change in interest rates July 1994 to October 1996:

$$P_{INV2} = (1.0675/1.0548) \times (1.064/1.0669)$$
$$= 1.0126 \times 0.9973 = 0.999$$

Of income from rents, dividends and net interest, 58.9% is from rent, and 8.2% is from tax credits on company dividends in 1994 (see Central

Statistical Office, 1995c, Table 3.8). We assume that income from these two sources (67.1% of all income from investments) will increase in line with the increase in prices between July 1994 and October 1996 (P_{INV1}). The remaining 32.9% of income from rents, dividends and net interest in 1994 comes from investments in shares, unit trusts and building societies, etc. We assume that this proportion of income from investments increases in line with changes in interest rates (P_{INV2}).

$P_{INV1} = 1.0766 \times 0.671 = 0.7515$
$P_{INV2} = 0.9999 \times 0.329 = 0.3290$
$P_{INV} = 0.7515 + 0.3290 = 1.0805$
$U_{INV} = 1.2733 \times 1.0805 = \mathbf{1.3758}$

Income from occupational pensions

Income from occupational pensions is updated by actual and forecast change in mean earnings for men and women combined.

A_{OPEN} Actual growth in the Average Earnings Index to the most recently available figures.

Sources: (1) *Economic Trends*, October 1993, Table 25, average earnings index (Great Britain), whole economy. (2) *Economic Trends*, October 1995, Table 4.1, average earnings index, whole economy, seasonally adjusted figures.

P_{OPEN} Forecast growth in average earnings for men and women combined from latest actual figures onwards from POIF forecasts.

Source: HM Treasury, 1995a, Table B4: average of Panel of Independent Forecasters forecast of average earnings growth.

U_{OPEN} $= A_{OPEN} \times P_{OPEN}$

Example: updating 1991 data to 1996/97

A_{OPEN}
Average Earnings Index 1991 = 107.0
Average Earnings Index July 1995 (provisional) = 126.5
$A_{OPEN} = 126.5/107.0 = 1.1822$
P_{OPEN}
Average POIF forecast earnings growth for 1995 = 3.50%
Average POIF forecast earnings growth for 1996 = 4.27%
$1.0350^{(5/12)} \times 1.0427^{(9/12)}$
$= 1.0144 \times 1.0319$
$= 1.0468$
$U_{OPEN} = 1.1822 \times 1.0468 = \mathbf{1.2375}$

Income from other sources

Other taxable income (*OYT*), income from babysitting (*BABYSIT*), fostering allowances (*FOSTER*), maintenance (*MAINT*) and allowances from
relatives *RELLY* are updated according to actual and forecast movement
in retail prices.

A_{OY} Actual growth in the RPI (all items) up to latest available figures.
Source: *Employment Gazette*, October 1995, Table 6.4: Retail prices:
general index of retail prices, United Kingdom, all items.

P_{OY} Forecast growth in RPI from latest actual figures onwards from
POIF forecasts.
Source: HM Treasury, 1995a, Table B1: average Panel of
Independent Forecasters forecast of change in RPI.

$U_{OY} = A_{OY} \times P_{OY}$

Example: updating 1991 data to 1996/97
Employment Gazette, Table 6.4:

	(Jan. 1987=100)		Change
	Ave. 1991	Sept. 1995	1991–Sept. 95
RPI	133.5	150.6	1.1281

$A_{OY} = 1.1281$
P_{OY}
Average POIF forecast of change in RPI is 3.40% for the year ending
quarter 4 1995, and 2.46% for the year ending quarter 4 1996.
$P_{OY} = 1.034^{(3/12)} \times 1.0246^{(9/12)}$
$= 1.0084 \times 1.0184 = 1.0270$
$U_{OY} = 1.1281 \times 1.0270 = \mathbf{1.1586}$

Student grants and student loans

Student grants were frozen between 1990/91 and 1993/94, were cut by 10%
in 1994/5, by 5.2% in 1995/6, and by 9.2% in 1996/7. For example, a
student living in the parental home received a grant of £1,795 in the acade-
mic years 1990/91, 1991/92, 1992/93 and 1993/94. In 1994/95, this was
reduced to £1,615, and further reduced to £1,530 and £1,400 respectively
in 1995/96 and 1996/97.
Source: Matthewman, 1993, p. 377; Matthewman 1995, p. 447; Matthewman, 1996, p. 479.

$U_{STGRANT} = 0.9 \times 0.948 \times 0.908 = \textbf{0.7747}$

Student loans are uprated by the same factor as other income, that is, recorded and forecast growth in the all-items Retail Prices Index (see above).

$U_{STLOAN} = U_{OY}$

Income from private pensions and covenants

The updating factors applied to these types of income are the same as that applied to investment income (see above).

$U_{PPEN} = U_{INV}$
$U_{COV} = U_{INV}$

Non-means-tested benefits

Most non-means-tested benefits are not currently simulated in POLIMOD, and amounts reported by respondents are uprated from the survey year to the policy year. This is done separately for the flat-rate elements of benefits, and for the earnings-related elements of benefits.

(a) Flat-rate benefits

Firstly, all flat-rate benefits, and flat-rate elements of earnings-related benefits, are updated from the survey year to the modelled year according to ratios of the standard rates (SRs) known or expected to apply in October of the policy year to the standard rates prevailing at the time of survey. These differ depending on whether the respondent was interviewed before or after the benefit uprating in the survey year. The benefits received by respondents interviewed in Quarter 1 (January to March) are assumed to be paid at 1990/1 rates. Benefits received by respondents interviewed in Quarters 2 to 4 (April to December) are assumed to be paid at 1991/2 rates. Sources: Rowland, 1990 and 1991.

$U_{BEN} = SR_{BEN}^{MODELYR} / SR_{BEN}^{SURVEYYR}$

The standard rates used in order to construct the uprating factors are given in Table A.4.

To estimate the expected standard benefit rates for the modelled policy year (if these are not available) we assume that the standard uprating applies: benefit rates for the year prior to the policy year are uprated according to the growth in retail prices in the year to September of the year before the policy year. Therefore, to uprate benefits to 1996/7 rates, the uprating factor is equal to the growth in retail prices in the year to September 1995 (see *Employment Gazette*, November 1995, Table 6.1).

Table A.4. *The standard rates used for updating non-means-tested benefits in POLIMOD*

Parameter	Benefit name	Standard rate of benefit used for updating	Standard rates			Updating factors	
			1990/1	1991/2	1996/7	1st qtr	qtrs 2–4
PEN	NI pension	Class A claimant rate	£46.90	£52.00	£61.15	1.3038	1.1760
UB	Unemployment benefit	Claimant rate	£37.35	£41.40	£48.25	1.2918	1.1655
SICK	Sickness benefit	Up to 1994/5, under pensionable age rate 1995/6 onwards: short-term incapacity benefit	£35.70	£39.60	£46.15	1.2927	1.1654
MAT	Maternity allowance	Claimant rate	£35.70	£40.60	£47.35	1.3263	1.1663
IVB	Invalidity benefit	Up to 1994/95: invalidity pension claimant rate 1995/96 onwards: long-term incapacity benefit	£46.90	£52.00	£61.15	1.3038	1.1760
SSP	Statutory sick pay	Average of higher rate and lower rate	£45.88	£48.00	£54.55	1.1890	1.1365
SMP	Statutory maternity pay	Lower rate	£39.25	£44.50	£54.55	1.3898	1.2258
WID	Widow's pension	Widow's pension rate	£46.90	£52.00	£61.15	1.3038	1.1760
SDA	Severe disablement allowance	Claimant rate, no age-related additions	£28.20	£31.25	£36.95	1.3103	1.1824
ICA	Invalid care allowance	Claimant rate	£28.20	£31.25	£36.60	1.2979	1.1712
INDIS	Industrial disablement pension	Disablement benefit: 100% disablement, higher rate	£76.60	£84.90	£99.00	1.2924	1.1661
OBEN	Other benefits	Updating factor for PEN applies				1.3038	1.1760
TRAIN	Training allowance	Unemployment benefit +£10	£47.35	£51.40	£58.25	1.2302	1.1333
ATTAL	Attendance allowance	Higher rate	£37.55	£41.65	£48.50	1.2916	1.1645
MOBAL	Mobility allowance	Up to 1991/92: higher rate allowance; 1992/93 onwards: Disability living allowance, higher rate mobility component	£26.25	£29.10	£33.90	1.2914	1.1649
WAR	War pension	100% rate for war pension	£76.60	£84.90	£105.00	1.3708	1.2367

Uprating for individual benefits is rounded to the nearest 5 pence. Where there are changes to benefit levels other than the usual uprating these are added. For example in 1994/5, this was done for benefits with a flat rate adjustment for VAT on domestic fuel.

Example: updating 1991 data to 1996/97
Table A.4 shows the uprating factors calculated for non-means-tested benefit income reported in the first and second to fourth quarters of the 1991 survey year.

(b) Earnings-related elements of benefits

Three non-means-tested benefits have earnings-related (that is, based on past earnings and contributions records) as well as flat-rate elements. These are retirement pension (*PEN*), widow's pension (*WID*) and invalidity pension/long-term incapacity benefit (*IVB*). FES data do not record how much of these benefits comprise the earnings-related element, so POLIMOD assumes that all amounts in receipt in the survey year in excess of the flat-rate retirement, widow's and invalidity pensions are earnings-related. These earnings-related amounts are updated in the same way as occupational pensions are updated. Therefore, we are assuming that earnings-related pensions received from the SERPS increase in line with average earnings.

A_{ERP} Actual growth in the Average Earnings Index to the most recently available figures.
(1) *Economic Trends*, October 1993, Table 25, average earnings index (Great Britain), whole economy.
(2) *Economic Trends*, October 1995, Table 4.1, average earnings index, whole economy, seasonally adjusted figures.
P_{ERP} Forecast growth in average earnings for men and women combined from latest actual figures onwards from POIF forecasts.
Source: HM Treasury, 1995a, average Panel of Independent Forecasters forecast of average earnings growth.
$U_{ERP} = A_{ERP} \times P_{ERP}$
(for example, see page 277 – occupational pensions)

Household rent

All rent reported in the FES, that is, private and local authority rent, is uprated by the growth in rent Retail Prices Index up to the latest available figure and by forecast all items RPI to 1 October of the modelled year. It is worth noting that is possible with POLIMOD to apply differential growth rates to rent according to tenure type. However, by default, the same uprating factor is applied to all rent.

A_{RENT} Actual growth in the rent RPI up to latest available figures.
Source: *Employment Gazette*, March 1991 to March 1992 and October 1995, Table 6.2 Retail prices: detailed figures for various groups, sub-groups and sections, Section: Housing, Sub-group: Rent.

P_{RENT} Forecast growth in all items RPI from latest actual figures onwards from Panel of Independent Forecasters forecasts.
Source: IIM Treasury, 1995a, average Panel of Independent Forecasters forecast of RPI.

U_{RENT} $= A_{RENT} \times P_{RENT}$

Example: updating 1991 data to 1996/97
Employment Gazette, Table 6.2.:

	(Jan. 1987=100)		Change
	Ave. 1991	Aug. 1995	1991–Aug. 95
Rent RPI	152.9	202.9	1.3270

$A_{RENT} = 1.3270$
P_{RENT}
Average of POIF forecast of change in RPI over year previous is 3.40% for quarter 4 1995, and 2.46% for quarter 4 1996.
$P_{RENT} = 1.034^{(4/12)} \times 1.0246^{(9/12)}$
$\quad\quad = 1.0112 \times 1.0184 = 1.0298$
$U_{RENT} = 1.3270 \times 1.0298 = \textbf{1.3665}$

Water charges

Water expenses are uprated by the growth in water and other payments RPI up to the latest available figure and by forecast all items RPI onwards to 1 October of the modelled year.

A_{WATER} Actual growth in the water and other payments RPI up to latest available figures.
Source: *Employment Gazette*, March 1991 to March 1992 and October 1995, Table 6.2 Retail prices: detailed figures for various groups, sub-groups and sections, Section: Housing, Sub-group: Water and other payments.

P_{WATER} Forecast growth in all items RPI from latest actual figures onwards from POIF forecasts.
Source: HM Treasury, 1995a, average Panel of Independent Forecasters forecast of RPI.

U_{WATER} $= A_{WATER} \times P_{WATER}$

Example: Updating 1991 data to 1996/97
Employment Gazette, Table 6.2:

| | (Jan. 1987=100) | | Change |
	Ave. 1991	Aug. 1995	1991–Aug. 95
Water and other payments RPI	167.65	234.8	1.4005

$A_{WATER} = 1.4005$
P_{WATER}
Average POIF forecast of change in RPI over year previous is 3.4% for quarter 4 1995, 2.46% for quarter 4 1996
$P_{WATER} = 1.034^{(4/12)} \times 1.0246^{(9/12)}$
$\qquad = 1.0112 \times 1.0184 = 1.0298$
$U_{WATER} = 1.4005 \times 1.0298 = \mathbf{1.4422}$

Gross mortgage interest

Gross mortgage interest is updated by the growth in mortgage interest payments RPI up to the latest available figure and by forecast interest rate movement to the midpoint of the policy year.

$A_{GROSSMI}$ Actual growth in the mortgage interest payments RPI up to latest available figures.
Source: *Employment Gazette*, March 1991 to March 1992 and October 1995, Table 6.2, Retail prices: detailed figures for various groups, sub-groups and sections, Section: Housing, Sub-group: Mortgage interest payments.

$P_{GROSSMI}$ Forecast growth in interest rates from latest RPI figures onwards from POIF forecasts.
Source: HM Treasury, 1995a, average Panel of Independent Forecasters forecast of interest rates.

$U_{GROSSMI}$ $= A_{GROSSMI} \times P_{GROSSMI}$

Example: updating the 1991 data to 1996/97
Employment Gazette, Table 6.2:

	(Jan. 1987=100)		Change
	Ave. 1991	Aug. 1995	1991–Aug. 95
Mortgage interest payments RPI	200.4	180.6	0.9012

$A_{GROSSMI} = 0.9012$

$P_{GROSSMI}$

Average POIF forecast base rate is 6.69% in quarter 4 1995; 6.40% in quarter 4 1996.

$P_{GROSSMI} = 1.0669/1.064 = 1.0027$

$U_{GROSSMI} = 0.9012 \times 1.0027 = \mathbf{0.9036}$

Domestic rates

While households rates have been replaced by other forms of local taxation in most parts of the UK, they are still the principal form of local taxation in Northern Ireland. A retail prices index for domestic rates is no longer produced, so the updating factor used for other income applies.

$\mathbf{U_{RATES} = U_{OY}}$

Expenditure

Expenditure data aggregated for use in POLIMOD is updated according to the movement in an appropriate sub-group of the RPI and according to the overall movement in consumer expenditure.

A_{EXP} Actual growth in the RPI sub-group which most closely corresponds with the expenditure item.
Source: *Employment Gazette*, March 1991 to March 1992 and October 1995, Table 6.2 Retail prices: detailed figures for various groups, sub-groups and sections.

P_{EXP} Forecast growth in all items RPI from latest actual figures onwards from POIF forecasts.
Source: HM Treasury, 1995a, average Panel of Independent Forecasters forecast of RPI.

C_{EXP} Overall growth in consumer expenditure, actual and forecast.
Sources: (actual) *Economic Trends*, October 1995, Table 2.4, consumer expenditure at 1990 prices; (forecast) HM Treasury, 1995a,

average Panel of Independent Forecasters forecast of consumer expenditure.

$$U_{EXP} = A_{EXP} \times P_{EXP} \times C_{EXP}$$

Example: updating 1991 data to 1996/97

P_{EXP}

Average POIF forecast of change in RPI is 3.4% for the year ending quarter 4 1995, and 2.46% for the year ending quarter 4 1996.

$P_{EXP} = 1.034^{(3/12)} \times 1.0246^{(9/12)}$

$\qquad = 1.0084 \times 1.0184 = 1.0270$

C_{EXP}

Per capita consumer expenditure in 1991 = £5,896

Per capita consumer expenditure in the 2nd quarter of 1994 = £1,564

Average POIF forecast of consumer expenditure growth is 1.92% for 1995, 2.42% for 1996.

$C_{EXP} = 1,564/(5,896/4) \times 1.0192^{6/12} \times 1.0242^{9/12} = 1.0907$

A_{EXP} and U_{EXP} for each item are shown in Table A.5.

Table A.5. *POLIMOD expenditure variables and uprating factors*

	POLIMOD variable	RPI subgroup applied	RPI (Jan. 1987=100)			
			1991 average	September 1995	A_{EXP}	U_{EXP}
E1.	Housing expenditure	Housing	160.8	169.1	1.0516	1.1780
E2.	Motoring expenditure	Motoring expenditure	129.9	153.0	1.1778	1.3193
E3.	Household services	Household services	129.5	140.9	1.0880	1.2187
E4.	Food (VATable)	Catering	139.1	170.4	1.2250	1.3722
E5.	Leisure goods and services	Leisure goods	117.7	121.8	1.0348	1.1592
E6.	Clothing and footwear	Clothing and footwear	118.5	122.6	1.0346	1.1589
E7.	Household goods	Household goods	122.6	134.9	1.1003	1.2325
E8.	Personal goods and services	Personal goods and services	133.4	160.0	1.1994	1.3435
E9.	Other household expenditure (VATable)	All items excluding housing	128.3	146.7	1.1434	1.2808
E10.	Motoring fuels other than petrol and diesel	Petrol and oil	128.3	156.1	1.2167	1.3629
E11.	Misc. items which do not attract VAT	All items excl. mortgage interest	130.3	149.2	1.1450	1.2826
E12.	Licences and other misc. taxes	Household services	129.5	140.9	1.0880	1.2187
E13.	Food (zero rated)	Food	125.6	139.1	1.1075	1.2406
E14	Water and sewerage	Water and other payments	167.7	234.8	1.4001	1.5683
E15.	Books and newspapers	Books and newspapers	142.0	167.8	1.1817	1.3237
E16.	Domestic fuel and power	Fuel and light	125.1	134.7	1.0767	1.2061
E17.	Transport	Fares and other travel costs	135.5	160.0	1.1808	1.3227
E18.	Caravans and houseboats	Purchase of motor vehicles	123.1	134.9	1.0959	1.2276
E19.	Drugs and medicines	Chemists' goods	137.7	166.1	1.2062	1.3511
E20.	Charitable gifts	All items	133.5	150.6	1.1281	1.2636
E21.	Children's clothes	Children's outerwear	118.3	119.8	1.0127	1.1344
E22.	Insurance (not life insurance)	Dwelling insurance and ground rent	189.4	197.2	1.0412	1.1663
E23.	Life insurance	Fees and subscriptions	134.8	158.3	1.1743	1.3154
E24.	Postal services	Postage	12.7	146.3	1.1280	1.2635

Code	Description	Category				
E25.	Finance	Personal services	153.0	201.8	1.3190	1.4774
E26.	Education	Leisure services	138.8	170.1	1.2255	1.3728
E27.	Health	Personal services	153.0	201.8	1.3190	1.4774
E28.	Burial and cremation	Household services	129.5	140.9	1.0880	1.2187
E29.	Trade unions and professional	Fees and subscriptions	134.8	158.3	1.1743	1.3154
E30.	Holidays in the UK and Ireland	Fares and other travel costs	135.5	160.0	1.1808	1.3227
E31.	Foreign holidays	Fares and other travel costs	135.5	160.0	1.1808	1.3227
E32.	Air travel	Fares and other travel costs	135.5	160.0	1.1808	1.3227
E33.	Alcoholic drink (off sales): beer, stout, ale, shandy	Beer: off sales	131.1	178.1	1.3585	1.5217
E34.	Alcoholic drink (off sales): cider, perry	Beer: off sales	131.1	178.1	1.3585	1.5217
E35.	Alcoholic drink (off sales): fortified wine	Wines and spirits: off sales	130.7	146.7	1.1224	1.2573
E36.	Alcoholic drink (off sales): non-fortified wine	Wines and spirits: off sales	130.7	146.7	1.1224	1.2573
E37.	Alcoholic drink (off sales): spirits, liqueurs	Wines and spirits: off sales	130.7	146.7	1.1224	1.2573
E38.	Alcoholic drink (on sales): beer, stout, ale, shandy	Beer: on sales	144.0	173.6	1.2056	1.3504
E39.	Alcoholic drink (on sales): cider, perry	Beer: on sales	144.0	173.6	1.2056	1.3504
E40.	Alcoholic drink (on sales): fortified wine	Wines and spirits: on sales	139.2	169.8	1.2198	1.3663
E41.	Alcoholic drink (on sales): non-fortified wine	Wines and spirits: on sales	139.2	169.8	1.2198	1.3663
E42.	Alcoholic drink (on sales): spirits, liqueurs	Wines and spirits: on sales	139.2	169.8	1.2198	1.3663
E43.	Petrol	Petrol and oil	128.3	156.1	1.2167	1.3629
E44.	Diesel oil	Petrol and oil	128.3	156.1	1.2167	1.3629
E45.	Pipe tobacco	Tobacco	126.2	180.1	1.4271	1.5985
E46.	Cigars and snuff	Tobacco	126.2	180.1	1.4271	1.5985
E47.	Cigarettes	Cigarettes	130.5	181.5	1.3908	1.5579
E48.	Betting on football pools	Entertainment and other recreation	153.1	206.5	1.3488	1.5108
E49.	Other betting	Entertainment and other recreation	153.1	206.5	1.3488	1.5108
E50.	Number of motor cars in household[a]	No index: qty cars only	1	1		

Note: [a] This is not an expenditure variable, but since excise duties are charged on the possession of motor cars rather than their purchase, it is treated alongside other expenditure variables.

Notes

1 In addition, a close examination of FES data showed that some children were allocated to the wrong benefit unit in a household, typically to that of a grandparent rather than that of a parent. These cases (5 in all in 1991) are edited for POLIMOD.
2 *Source: Financial Statistics*, June 1992, Table 13.12 – *Average mortgage rates.*

Bibliography

Ashworth, K. and Walker, R., 1994. 'Measuring claimant populations: time, fractals and social security', in N. Buck, J. Gershuny, D. Rose and J. Scott (eds), *Changing Households: The British Household Panel Survey 1990–1992*, ESRC Centre on Micro-Social Change, University of Essex

Atkinson, A. B., 1969. *Poverty in Britain and the Reform of Social Security*, DAE Occasional Paper No. 18, Cambridge: Cambridge University Press

　1984. 'The Costs of the Social Dividend and Tax Credit Schemes', ESRC Programme on Taxation, Incentives and the Distribution of Income, Discussion Paper No. 63, London School of Economics

Atkinson, A. B., Gomulka, J. and Sutherland, H., 1988. 'Grossing-up FES data for tax-benefit models', in A. B. Atkinson and H. Sutherland (eds), *Tax–Benefit Models*, STICERD Occasional Paper No. 10, London: London School of Economics

Atkinson, A. B. and Micklewright, J., 1983. 'On the reliability of income data in the Family Expenditure Survey 1970–1977', *Journal of the Royal Statistical Society, Series A*, Vol. 146, 33–61

Atkinson, A. B., Smith, J. M. and Sutherland, H., 1986. 'FES Data on the Self-employed and Tax–Benefit Models', ESRC Programme on Taxation, Incentives and the Distribution of Income, Research Note 11, London School of Economics

Atkinson, A. B. and Sutherland, H., 1983. 'Hypothetical Families in the DHSS Tax/Benefit Model and Families in the Family Expenditure Survey 1980', ESRC Programme on Taxation, Incentives and the Distribution of Income, Research Note 1, London School of Economics

Board of the Inland Revenue, various dates. *Survey of Personal Incomes*, annually to 1985, London: HMSO

　1979. *Inland Revenue Statistics 1979*, London: HMSO

　1989. *Inland Revenue Statistics 1989*, London: HMSO

　1993. *Inland Revenue Statistics 1993*, London: Inland Revenue Statistics and Economics Office

　1994. *Inland Revenue Statistics 1994*, London: Inland Revenue Statistics and Economics Office

Booth, N., 1991. *National Insurance Contributions 1991–2*, Croydon: Tolley Publishing Company

Bulding Society Mortgages Survey (BSMS) 1988. Great Britain Department of the Environment *5% Sample Survey of Building Society Mortgages, 1974–1991* [computer file], Colchester: ESRC Data Archive, 1992

Central Statistical Office, 1985. *United Kingdom National Accounts: Sources and Methods*, Third Edition, London: HMSO

   1992. *Family Spending: A Report on the 1991 Family Expenditure Survey*, London: HMSO

   1993a. 'Effects of taxes and benefits on household income, 1991, *Economic Trends* 475, May, 92–127

   1993b. *United Kingdom National Accounts 1993: The Blue Book*, London: HMSO

   1994. *United Kingdom National Accounts 1994: The Blue Book*, London: HMSO

   1995a. *Annual Abstract of Statistics 1995*, London: HMSO

   1995b. *New Earnings Survey 1995*, London: HMSO

   1995c. *United Kingdom National Accounts 1995: The Blue Book*, London: HMSO

   1996a. *Family Spending: A Report on the 1995/6 Family Expenditure Survey*, London: HMSO

   1996b. *United Kingdom National Accounts 1996: The Blue Book*, London: HMSO

Chartered Institute of Public Finance and Accountancy (CIPFA) Statistical Information Service, various years. *Rating Demands and Precepts* (annually to 1989), *Community Charge Demands and Precepts* (annually 1990 to 1992), *Council Tax Demands and Precepts* (annually 1993 to present), Croydon: CIPFA

   1979. *Finance and General Statistics 1978–9*, Croydon: CIPFA

   1990a. *Finance and General Statistics 1989–90*, Croydon: CIPFA

   1990b. *Rate Collection Statistics 1989–90 Actuals*, Croydon: CIPFA

CIPFA Scottish Branch, 1992. *Rating Review Estimates of Income and Expenditure, 1992–3 Summary Volume*, Edinburgh: CIPFA

Coulter, F., Cowell, F. and Jenkins, S., 1992. 'Equivalence scale relativities and the extent of inequality and poverty', *Economic Journal* 102, 1067–82

Davies, J. and Rajah, N., 1992. 'A Hedonic Price Index for Housing', unpublished paper, Institute for Fiscal Studies, London

Department of Employment, 1979. *Family Expenditure Survey 1978*, London: HMSO

   1991. *New Earnings Survey 1991*, London: HMSO

   1994. *Employment Gazette*, December, London: HMSO

Department of Social Security, 1992. *Social Security Statistics, 1992*, London: HMSO

   1993a. *The Growth of Social Security*, London: HMSO

   1993b. *Households Below Average Income: A Statistical Analysis 1979–1990/1*, London: HMSO

1993c. *Social Security Statistics, 1993*, London: HMSO

1994a. *Income Related Benefits: Estimates of Take-up in 1990 and 1991*, London: Analytical Services Division, Department of Social Security

1994b. *Social Security Statistics, 1994*, London: HMSO

1994c. *Social Security Departmental Report, The Government's Expenditure Plans, 1994–95 to 1996–97*, Cm2513, London: HMSO

1995. *Households Below Average Income: A Statistical Analysis 1979–1992/3*, London: HMSO

1996a. *Social Security Statistics, 1996*, London: HMSO

1996b. *The Abstract of Statistics for Social Security Benefits and Contributions and Indices of Prices and Earnings, 1996 Edition*, Newcastle-upon-Tyne: Department of Social Security, Analytical Services Division

undated. 'The psm in the British Department of Social Security', unpublished paper, Department of Social Security, Analytical Services Division, Newcastle-upon-Tyne

Eardley, T. and Corden, A., 1994. 'Earnings from Self-Employment: The Problem of Measurement and the Effect on the Income Distribution in the UK', paper prepared for the 23rd General Conference of the International Association for Research on Income and Wealth, New Brunswick, Canada, August 1994

Employment Gazette, monthly to October 1995, London: HMSO

ESRC Data Archive, 1992. *Family Expenditure Survey 1991 User Guide*, Colchester: University of Essex

Evans, M., 1995. 'Out for the Count: The Incomes of the Non-household Population and the Effect of their Exclusion from National Income Profiles', Welfare State Programme Discussion Paper WSP/111, STICERD, London School of Economics

Evans, M., Piachaud, D. and Sutherland, H., 1994. 'Designed for the Poor – Poorer by Design? The Effects of the 1986 Social Security Act on Family Incomes', Welfare State Programme Discussion Paper 105, London School of Economics

Evans, M. and Sutherland, H., 1992. 'Social Security Benefits in the Family Expenditure Survey: An Accurate Basis for Modelling?', paper presented to the Welfare Policy and Analysis Seminar at the London School of Economics, 9 December 1992

Family Expenditure Survey (FES) 1991. *Family Spending, A Report on the Family Expenditure Survey*, London: Central Statistical Office

Foster, K., 1994. 'Census Check on FES Non-response', presentation given to the ESRC Data Archive FES user's workshop, London, 14 November 1994

Giles, C. and Johnson, P., 1994. *Taxes Down, Taxes Up: The Effects of a Decade of Tax Changes*, Institute for Fiscal Studies Commentary No. 41, London: Institute for Fiscal Studies

Giles, C. and McCrae, J., 1995. 'The IFS Microsimulation Tax and Benefit Model', IFS Working Paper No. 95/19, Institute for Fiscal Studies, London

Giles, C. and Webb, S., undated. 'Model Comparisons Study', unpublished paper, Institute for Fiscal Studies, London

Gomulka, J., 1992. 'Grossing up revisited', in R. Hancock and H. Sutherland (eds), *Microsimulation Models for Public Policy Analysis: New Frontiers*, STICERD Occasional Paper No. 17, London: London School of Economics
1994. 'Grossing up: A Note on Calculating Household Weights from Family Composition Totals', Microsimulation Unit Research Note MU/RN/4, Department of Applied Economics, University of Cambridge

Goodman, A. and Webb, S., 1995. *The Distribution of UK Household Expenditure, 1979–92*, IFS Commentary No. 49, London: Institute for Fiscal Studies

Government Actuary's Department, 1991. *Occupational Pension Schemes 1991: Ninth Survey by the Government's Actuary, 1994*, London: HMSO

Halifax Price Index, quarterly, Halifax: Halifax plc

Hancock, R. and Sutherland, H. (eds), 1992. *Microsimulation Models for Public Policy Analysis: New Frontiers*, STICERD Occasional Paper 17, London: London School of Economics

Hansard, various dates. *Parliamentary Debates (Hansard) House of Commons Official Report*, London: HMSO

HM Customs and Excise, 1996. *Annual Report 1995/6*, London: HMSO

HM Treasury, 1994a. *Tax Ready Reckoner and Tax Reliefs*, July, London: HM Treasury
1994b. *Forecasts for the UK Economy, August 1994*, London: HM Treasury
1995a. *Forecasts for the UK Economy, November 1995*, London: HM Treasury
1995b. *Tax Ready Reckoner and Tax Reliefs*, July, London: HM Treasury

Hills, J., 1991. 'Hedonic Price Indices for Housing Derived from the 1988 5 Per Cent Survey of Building Society Mortgages', Welfare State Programme Research Note 21, London School of Economics

Hope, S., 1988. 'Model validation', in A. B. Atkinson and H. Sutherland (eds), *Tax-Benefit Models*, STICERD Occasional Paper 10, London: London School of Economics

Jenkins, S., 1995. 'Accounting for inequality trends: decomposition analyses for the UK, 1971–86', *Economica* 62, 29–63

Johnson, P. and Webb, S., 1992. 'Explaining the growth in UK income inequality: 1979–1988', *Economic Journal* 103, 429–35

Jones, J., Stark, G. and Webb, S., 1991. 'Modelling Benefit Expenditures Using the FES', Working Paper No. W91/13, Institute for Fiscal Studies, London

Keenay, G., 1995. 'Personal Income Tax Modelling in the UK Inland Revenue', Microsimulation Unit Discussion Paper MU9502, Department of Applied Economics, University of Cambridge

Kemsley, W. F. F., Redpath, R. U. and Holmes, M., 1980. *Family Expenditure Survey Handbook*, London: Office of Population Censuses and Surveys, Social Survey Division

Kent, C., 1994. 'DIM – Imputation of Rates', unpublished paper, 6 December 1994, Analytical Services Division, Department of Social Security

Lakhani, B. and Read, J., 1990. *National Welfare Benefits Handbook*, Twentieth Edition, 1990/91, London: Child Poverty Action Group

Lambert, S., Percival, R., Schofield, D. and Paul, S., 1994. 'An Introduction to

Stinmod: A Static Microsimulation Model', Stinmod Technical Paper No. 1, National Centre for Social and Economic Modelling, Faculty of Management, University of Canberra

McClements, L., 1977. 'Equivalence scales for children', *Journal of Public Economics* 8, 191–210

Matthewman, J., 1990. *Social Security and State Benefits 1990–91*, London: Tolley's Publishing Company

1991. *Social Security and State Benefits 1991–92*, London: Tolley's Publishing Company

1993. *Social Security and State Benefits 1993–4*, London: Tolley's Publishing Company.

1994. *Social Security and State Benefits 1994–95*, London: Tolley's Publishing Company

1995. *Social Security and State Benefits 1995–96*, London: Tolley's Publishing Company

1996. *Social Security and State Benefits 1996–97*, London: Tolley's Publishing Company

Mercader-Prats, M., 1995. 'Identifying Low Standards of Living: Evidence from Spain', paper presented at XIth World Congress of the International Economic Association, Tunis, December 1995

Northern Ireland Office, 1993. *Expenditure Plans and Priorities, Northern Ireland: The Government's Expenditure Plans 1993–94 to 1995–96*, CM2213, London: HMSO

Office for National Statistics, 1996. *Labour Market Trends December*, London: HMSO

Office of Population Censuses and Surveys, 1992. *Labour Force Survey 1990 and 1991*, London: HMSO

1993a. *1991 Census Report for Great Britain (Part 1, Volume 2 of 3*, London: HMSO

1993b. *1991 Census: Communal Establishments, Great Britain, Volumes 1 and 2*, London: HMSO

1993c. *1991 Census Report for Great Britain, Part 1, Volume 1 of 3*, London: HMSO

1993d. *1991 Census: Sex, Age and Marital Status Great Britain*, London: HMSO

Pudney, S. and Sutherland, H., 1994. 'How reliable are microsimulation results? An analysis of the role of sampling error in a UK tax–benefit model', *Journal of Public Economics* 53, 327–65

1996. 'Statistical reliability in microsimulation models with econometrically-estimated behavioural responses', in A. Harding (ed.), *Microsimulation and Public Policy*, Amsterdam: Elsevier

Redmond, G., 1995. 'POLIMOD: The Calculation of VAT and Excise Duties on Household Expenditure', Microsimulation Unit Research Note MU/RN/11, Department of Applied Economics, University of Cambridge

1996. 'Simulating Local Taxation in POLIMOD', Microsimulation Unit Research

Note MU/RN/12, Department of Applied Economics, University of Cambridge

Redmond, G., and Sutherland, H., 1995. 'How Has Tax and Social Security Policy Changed since 1978? A Distributional Analysis', Microsimulation Unit Discussion Paper MU9508, Department of Applied Economics, University of Cambridge

Redmond, G. and Wilson, M., 1995. 'Validating POLIMOD Output', Microsimulation Unit Research Note MU/RN/14, Department of Applied Economics, University of Cambridge

Redpath, R. U., 1986. 'Family expenditure survey: a second study of differential non-response comparing census characteristics of FES respondents and non-respondents', *Statistical News* 72, February

Ridge, M. and Smith, S., 1991. *Local Taxation: The Options and the Arguments*, IFS Report Series No. 38, London: Institute for Fiscal Studies

Rowland, M., 1990. *Rights Guide to Non-means-tested Benefits*, Thirteenth Edition, 1990/91, London: Child Poverty Action Group

1991. *National Welfare Benefits Handbook*, Twenty-first Edition, 1991/92, London: Child Poverty Action Group

Rowland, M. and Webster, L., 1991. *Rights Guide to Non-means-tested Benefits*, Fourteenth Edition, 1991/92, London: Child Poverty Action Group

Smeaton, D. and Hancock, R., 1995. *Pensioners' Expenditure: An Assessment of Changes in Living Standards, 1979–1991*, London: Age Concern Institute of Gerontology, King's College

Sutherland, H., 1994. 'The Commission on Social Justice's Proposals for Child Benefit: A Comment', Microsimulation Unit Research Note MU/RN/8, Department of Applied Economics, University of Cambridge

1996. 'Households, Individuals and the Re-distribution of Income', Microsimulation Unit Discussion Paper MU9601, Department of Applied Economics, University of Cambridge

Ward, M., 1993. *Council Tax Handbook*, First Edition, 1993/1994, London: Child Poverty Action Group

Williams, J., Hutton, S. and Ditch, J., 1993. 'Evaluation of Policy Option Models', Working Paper JRF 1091, Social Policy Research Unit, University of York

Wilson, M., 1995a. 'Non-means-tested Social Security Benefits and the Family Expenditure Survey: Disaggregating the 1991 Data', Microsimulation Unit Research Note MU/RN/7, Department of Applied Economics, University of Cambridge

1995b. 'Earnings Distributions from the Family Expenditure Survey and the New Earnings Survey Compared', Microsimulation Unit Discussion Paper MU9505, Department of Applied Economics, University of Cambridge

Index